CW01143854

A Step or Two of Faith

Nigel Paget

Copyright © 2021 Nigel Paget

Revised edition April 2022

ISBN 978-1-915292-02-5

Printed in Great Britain by
Biddles Books Limited, King's Lynn, Norfolk

Foreword

Often, "reports" are sent from the mission field describing great "results", conversions, changed lives, growing churches, etc. which is wonderful! But they don't always "tell it as it is". A truly "prayer-raising" report is one that initiates not only praise, but also one that moves people to pray about the hard times, too: ill health, spiritual opposition, moments of despair and/or loneliness, while surrounded by thousands of people without hope, ie. -real situations that those in mission often have to face.

This book is like a giant prayer-letter, full of great things to praise God for, of course - but also it tells of some of the frustrating, time-consuming, darker sides of mission life. These can include: travelling long distances with break-downs in communications, connections and vehicles; language difficulties, endless paper-work, politics, tough decisions to be made; loneliness, separation from loved ones or family; sacrifices to be faced; resistance, rejection – and coping with the health issues that always seem to crop up at critical moments.

It's so refreshing (and encouraging!) to read Nigel and Jane's account of how the Lord led them to a moment in time when they decided to dive into uncharted waters and follow the Lord's plan for their lives. They do what the Lord states clearly in His word, the Bible. He says "THIS is the way; walk in it" (Is. 30:21)

As we read their account we see constantly that, as they walk with the Lord, He walks with them. He opens doors, He organises contacts, He multiplies limited resources, He protects and provides in times of great need; He gives them love, close fellowship, healing, protection, provision, courage – and a sure and certain trust in His plans.

Throughout the Pagets' story, in every phase of their ministry we find that, as they walk with the Lord, His promises are true for them as individuals, and as a couple. We see fulfilled in them that wonderful passage in Ecclesiastes 4:9-12. As Nigel and Jane walk together- with the Lord- they are part of "….a triple braided cord that is not easily broken"

"Doing mission" of any kind is a challenge, but the Lord calls us all to it in some measure. He called Nigel and Jane to take their knowledge, experience and expertise to needy people in far-away places. But it wasn't just health for people's bodies they aimed for! They offered spiritual food, healing – and wholeness of the soul through Jesus too.

All this as they constantly shared, with empty and lost people, the most treasures experience and knowledge they have. That is, of personally knowing the Father's love and grace, of enjoying Jesus' love and the new life He gives through His sacrifice for us- and of receiving the Holy Spirit's love and power, by His gifts to us- to use in His service and for ministry.

No one can do effective mission without the Lord, but with Him, wonderful things happen- as Nigel and Jane describe here in "A Step or Two of Faith". This book is stimulating, exciting, informative, challenging- a joy and a blessing to read!

GLORIA DEAN, *Missionary in Chile 1971 to 1995, with SAMS -South American Mission and SEAN - Study by Extension for All Nations, then, from the UK, continued with the latter's world-wide ministry in TEE (Theological Education by Extension) 1995-2010.*

These pages are full of fascination. Here are two people who know God and walk with Him. Nigel and Jane tell a story that is at the same time both ordinary and remarkable. Brought together from diverse backgrounds, their tale testifies to the grace of God at work in them and through them. This finds expression across the globe in energetic, practical acts of compassion combined with words of gospel hope. Any who know them will recognise their love and generosity of spirit which oozes out of every page. Read on and you will find yourself alternately moved, rivetted, and led to reflect on how you will invest the one life you have been given. Soli Deo Gloria.

Reverend Kevin Newman, *Senior Pastor, ChristChurch Banstead*

I am sure that this book is going to be a blessing and encouragement to many Christians but also a real challenge. Nigel and Jane have been stepping out on a journey of faith as God has lead them over the last years and they have seen God wonderfully honour their faith, trust, courage, obedience and sacrifice in amazing provisions and answers to prayer, at times, in miraculous ways. He has taken them to places that they had never dreamed they would go to; but God wanted them there to make them a blessing to the poor, practically through their dentistry but also spiritually as they have shared God's living and transforming word. Following Jesus isn't always easy, but it can be an adventure of faith like no other! I believe Nigel and Jane have shown us in their story what God can do with a couple 'taking a step or two of faith' in total dedication to him. May God's anointing rest upon this book to His glory. Matt. 10:39 'Whoever finds his life will lose it and whoever loses his life, for my sake, will find it'.

Peter Bisset *C.D.A., N.D.A., C.D.F.M., C.R.K. (Lond) Missionary in Nepal 1971-1999*

Matthew ch 10 v 39: *'Whoever finds his life will lose it and whoever loses his life, for my sake, will find it'*.

Everybody loves a good story. Whether the narrative is fast moving or full of descriptive detail, it is the unpredictable which electrifies the reader into turning another page. Such is Nigel Paget's book - a really good read!

Packed with fascinating adventures which will absorb the reader, you sometimes must pinch yourself to realise it is not fiction but the unvarnished truth. Nigel and Jane are two very different people from opposite sides of the world, who fell in love and embarked on a journey that they could never have dreamed about.

This book is an honest, amusing and often self-deprecating account of how a couple of dentists had the courage to sell their practice in the UK. Why? They had an inner conviction that they must use what God gave them to serve people who had nothing, and at their own expense - the desperately poor, physically and emotionally wounded, suffering and abused. Some walked barefoot for days or weeks to seek help, often in severe pain.

Nigel and Jane did not just treat their rotten teeth, facial infections and tumours, but told them the gospel story of God's love through Jesus' sacrifice, inviting them to receive His forgiveness and love.

Words like 'self-sacrifice', 'devoted passion' and 'humble service' come to mind as we see Nigel and Jane work hard for days on end with great skill and little sleep in sweltering conditions; yet filled with love and joy. The pages are peppered with impossible problems and difficulties, but as they prayed, God provided for them - answering countless prayers, arranging miraculously timed meetings and transport, protecting them from danger, and enabling them to hold their own serious health concerns lightly. He is the real hero of these enthralling stories.

It has been a privilege to know Nigel and Jane. Their action-packed book brings alive some highlights from God's personalised training programme as he shaped them into effective, and big-hearted, disciples of Jesus Christ. Their unique story is sculptured by another book, the Bible. They read it every day, learning how to follow their Master and become like Him, and praying for guidance, courage and strength.

Their book is not finished. Even after Jesus calls them home to heaven, many transformed lives from around the globe will still praise God for what He did through two humble and willing servants who loved each other and loved them; because Nigel and Jane dared to receive God's truth and love … and share it, very practically.

Dr Paul Adams

Prologue

"Computers are infallible, it's humans that are at fault," so the saying goes.

My efforts at tracking down fifteen years of logs, records and photos, spread about on a selection of laptops, desktops and mobile phones, has been a challenge.

Being a bit slow on the uptake, I have only now come to realise that, when you transfer a file of information from one computer to another, not all of it transfers. In fact, great chunks can simply evaporate.

Piecing together our various mission trips, which involved journeying to remote parts of the world, assembling our life story and placing them into something that is readable, informative and enjoyable, has taken longer than I thought. Much longer.

How our lives pan out, decisions made, directions taken, highs and lows, can only be seen in hindsight.

As you read about each excursion we took, look on it as a slow reveal. A little like the children's game of pass the parcel, where layers of colourful wrapping paper are removed to show a new covering and, finally, to expose the prize at the end.

Every time we returned to *Mercy Ships*, we witnessed and heard about different things, we saw unique places and people.

Exceptional events happened on each venture.

Likewise with Burma, the Philippines, Mongolia and Lawas, in Sarawak.

My hope is for you, the reader, to gradually build up a picture of what happens when you build trust, experience and relationships in the service of Jesus.

Note that our first few trips were coloured with awe, amazement, fear and trepidation. But, after a year or two, our ventures to these really remote areas, became almost "Normal".

I'd like to say this sense of normality occurred because our Faith, (I spell "Faith" with a capital because our Faith is crucial to how we live), reliance and confidence in God had strengthened. But this happened only because we had leant on God and found him dependable and trustworthy.

Before we get on to the journeys, you'll hear our own story.

Why tell our story?

I hope you will see God working throughout our lives. The thing to note, as with all of us on our walk with God, is that, as we progress through our life, we become more aware of our God and learn to depend and rely on him more and more. Our confidence increases.

So that now, as I write these words, aged sixty-six, my personal understanding and Faith continue to grow.

Our tale is probably nothing to make the headlines, but I trust it will build a picture of two people who encounter Jesus along their pathway of life, and the amazing things that happen as a result.

My hope, in recording it, is to inspire you, the reader, to also build the desire and longing to do things to promote the Gospel of Jesus.

I am thankful for the world's first international lockdown.

Being confined to our home in the UK for a year has forced us to tidy every cupboard, and to fix up the garden. It has created space and time to piece together the past fifteen years of our lives and to put pen to paper.

In the book you'll find plenty of photos and also some simple videos. These are accessed via QR codes that link you to *YouTube*. With an *iPhone*, you just point it at the QR code in photo setting and the link comes up. In android setting, you may need a QR code-reading app. Just dip in to get a taste of our journeys.

Thanks must go to my wife Jane, who has been very patient and understanding with her rather distracted, and often grumpy husband, stuck in front of his computer for four to five hours at a time, typing then retyping, editing then re-editing this story. Often listening to my ramblings about Burma or Africa and quietly slipping cups of tea across my keyboard. Always encouraging.

Thanks to my son James who urged me to re-write uninteresting segments and raise the bar on quality and friend Paul Adams who always encourages anything that promotes the Gospel.

Great thanks also to Lane Butt, Philip Marsden and Gloria Dean who have helped with the proof reading and editing.

Maps of Countries and Places Visited

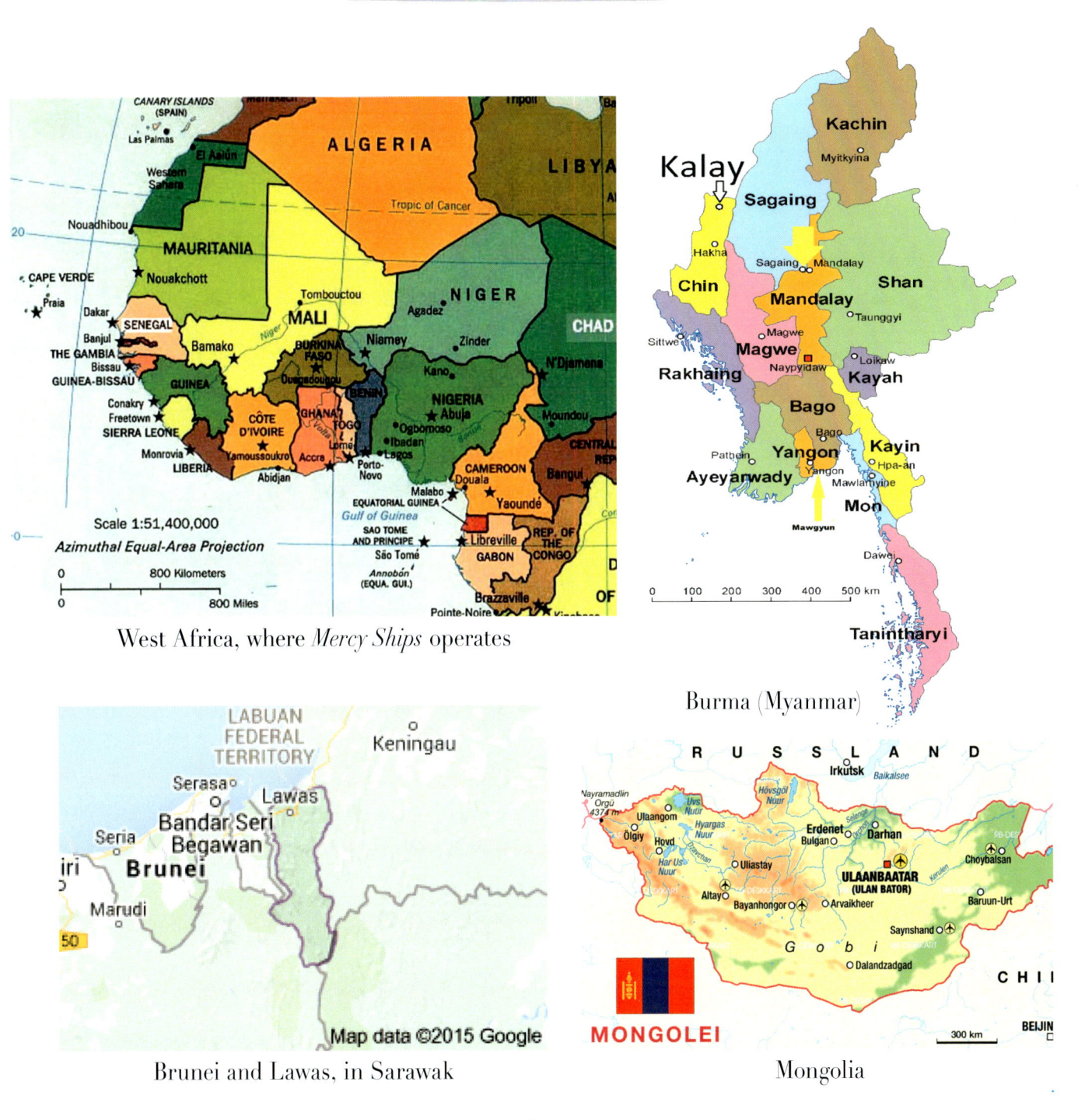

West Africa, where *Mercy Ships* operates

Burma (Myanmar)

Brunei and Lawas, in Sarawak

Mongolia

Contents

Chapter 1	Liberia 2006	1
Chapter 2	1954 Our childhoods	5
Chapter 3	14-18 years old (1968-1972)	20
Chapter 4	University years (1973-1979)	31
Chapter 5	Gift of Tongues (1974)	36
Chapter 6	Years 1979-1989, Just Married	39
Chapter 7	Years 1990-2000, Family Life	48
Chapter 8	Cornwall	51
Chapter 9	Years 2000-2010	54
Chapter 10	Liberia 2006 Continued	57
Chapter 11	First Return to UK (2006)	67
Chapter 12	Liberia 2008	71
Chapter 13	First Visit to Burma	81
Chapter 14	Benin 2009	86
Chapter 15	Burma 2010	92
Chapter 16	Return from Burma 2010	102
Chapter 17	Togo	105
Chapter 18	Burma 2011	113

Chapter 19	China and Mongolia 2011	120
Chapter 20	Burma 2012	132
Chapter 21	Guinea 2012	142
Chapter 22	Burma 2013	154
Chapter 23	Manila 2013	163
Chapter 24	Burma 6th Visit	170
Chapter 25	Pointe Noire, Congo 2014	182
Chapter 26	Mawgyum, Burma 2015	192
Chapter 27	Kalay, Burma 2015	201
Chapter 28	Tondo, Manila 2015	211
Chapter 29	Kalay, Burma 2016	218
Chapter 30	Brunei and Lawas 2017	226
Chapter 31	Burma 2017	232
Chapter 32	Lawas. Sharing Jesus Conference 2018	235
Chapter 33	Burma. Last Trip to Pakokku 2019	241
Chapter 34	Years 2010-2020	247
Chapter 35	Lawas. Dental Outreach 2019	252
Chapter 36	Final Thoughts	258

Chapter 1

With a heavy thud, the *Astraeus* Boeing 737 from Gatwick hit the Freetown runway. The impact was so strong, I briefly felt that the undercarriage might have given way.

I had been told by a retired pilot friend that a propeller plane lands as gently as a bird, but a jet plane has to be powered all the way down.

Either the pilot had clearly taken this maxim very much to heart, or his altimeter was set a few feet lower than the actual height of the tarmac. Perhaps both, since I'm sure that we dented the runway on landing. However, we continued to decelerate and were safely on the ground. Which brought to mind the other important flying maxim, that any landing you can walk away from is a success.

A cheer and some clapping broke out amongst the passengers. It was a wonderful relief after the oppressive quiet that had set in during the last fifty minutes of our flight that had been frankly, highly traumatic. Joy, to be on the ground, instantly replaced tense and worried expressions. Joy instantly replacing tense and worried expressions.

When the plane came to a halt, the cockpit door immediately opened, revealing the solid frame of our pilot. He stood out amongst the colourfully-dressed passengers in his white, crisp shirt, with captain's epaulettes adorning his shoulders and his pilot's hat sitting rakishly, a little back on his head. A broad grin spread across his face as he greeted the well-heeled front-row passengers. Gentle applause began as he shook a few hands. This increased and spread, like a breaking wave, as he advanced down the gangway; the clapping steadily escalated, people were standing up to congratulate and cheer him. By the time he reached us, hands were being shaken and high fives and fist bumps exchanged. He progressed slowly along the length of the aircraft, laughing openly and exchanging banter here and there, his back gently being slapped from time to time by grateful men and women.

Jane and I had never witnessed anything like it before. This was a first, and we hadn't even got to our destination yet. We still had another connecting flight to Monrovia, the capital of Liberia. It felt a long way from Wallington.

What had we let ourselves in for?

As we taxied out again to our take-off position for the short hop to Liberia, I was fascinated and a bit disquieted to see bits of old aircraft wings, wheels and engine dotted about the airfield, some with lines of bullet holes. Obviously, some not-so-successful landings had occurred over the years.

Perhaps it was fortunate that the airport, situated outside Monrovia, was less visible in the dark. Two small rooms and one lightbulb barely lit the arrivals hall. It was pretty basic, to say the least. We were herded into the cramped, hot and humid space to get our paperwork checked.

Monrovia's commercial airport had been destroyed in the civil war so here, at the old military airport, we emerged into an excited, night-time arrivals area, with swarms of locals trying to earn a dollar or two by grabbing our bags and heading off with the call, "Taxi! Taxi!"

UN officials and troops shouted through megaphones, issuing unintelligible instructions. Cars, bikes, motorcycles and wheelbarrows, people were everywhere. Fortunately, we were met by some crew from the MV *Anastasis* (the Greek word for 'Resurrection') with their *Mercy Ships* Land Rover.

It was dark and 29°C outside; there were no street lights, or headlights from oncoming cars.

The ride was decidedly bumpy. It seemed we found every pot-hole. We progressed cautiously for ninety minutes, heading for the ship; passing odd groups of locals along the route, squatting and lying beside flaming cooking-pots. Flickering glimpses of humanity revealed in a dark, moonless night.

UN checkpoints kept obstructing our way. Their barriers were set across the road, and large, barbed-wire-covered concrete blocks were positioned at the roadsides to prevent any avoidance manoeuvres. Nigerian troops, each with a large "UN" in white on his blue helmet, would wave us to a stop. We immediately had to wind our windows down to allow the soldiers to see our faces, whereupon they'd point their rifles at us, with torches duct-taped to the barrels.

Pretty unnerving the first few times.

Our quickly-learnt response was to show them our *Mercy Ships* passes and all chorus, "Mercy Ships."

It seemed to work like magic and allow us to continue on our journey.

Leaving the outskirts, we started to enter the city itself; the hot, dark, unlit streets of Monrovia were filled with humanity. People were everywhere - sitting,

Chapter 1

standing, curious to see our vehicle and crowding around it. We were literally driving through a sea of bodies.

By 10.45pm we reached the *Anastasis*, which was heartening well-lit and humming with activity. It felt like an oasis of safety and organisation. This area was protected by a garrison of British Army Gurkhas, to provide added security.

But the international ship's complement were warm and welcoming, despite the masses of forms to fill in, induction talks, medical and fire-safety checks.

What were we doing there?

Liberia had experienced a fourteen-year civil war, in which 250,000 died. The healthcare system and infrastructure, which have never been comprehensive, were totally destroyed.

The country was in tatters. Unemployment was running at 90% of the 3.4 million population. Life expectancy was low - 37 for males and 40 for females. 15,000 United Nations soldiers watched over an uneasy peace, and we two dentists were on our way to serve in the capital, Monrovia, for three weeks.

We were to see and treat child-soldiers who had survived the war, but who were totally traumatised.

We had never been to anywhere in Africa before so, when we had filled in our application forms to serve with the *Mercy Ships* organisation, we had little idea of what to expect.

Originally it was destination Benin, but that was changed three weeks before our departure. We'd had all the necessary vaccinations, Hepatitis A, B and C, yellow fever, rabies, polio, cholera, typhoid and tetanus boosters. We had obtained all the references, plus the General Dental Council and Medical Protection certificates required to get a legal permit to work in Liberia.

We had also renewed our wills.

Why had we embarked on this seemingly crazy trip?

What had prompted us to leave the comfort of our civilised, South London home, where we had run a family general dental practice for 25 years?

Were we madder than the trip itself?

A lot of people thought so.

Both our families, mine scattered around England and Jane's scattered around the world, were aghast at our intended venture into a war-torn, impoverished part of the world.

"Why are you travelling to such a dangerous place?"

"What do you mean, you won't be paid?"

"We can get you a job in Brunei, if you cannot find work in the UK."

"How are you funding this? Whaat?! You have to actually pay to stay on the Hospital Ship? That's not right!"

"What about your own Wallington patients? How will they manage?"

And many more comments were thrown our way.

But it was to be life-changing for the two of us; an adventure we never regretted going on. It was the start to many trips we were to make over the coming years.

Chapter 2

My Early Years

I was born in November 1954, in St Helier Hospital, Carshalton, Surrey.

My earliest memory was helping my father in the family garden. He had got me, aged three, to trundle heavy clumps of forget-me-nots round to the back of our house using my wooden wheelbarrow. But, to my tearful disappointment, it collapsed and broke when overloaded.

My father was a traditional "old school" family doctor, starting up his practice in an old, rambling house on the corner of Shirley Road, Wallington. He had completed his National Service in the Navy and got the Wallington job, chosen out of sixty other applicants.

Our life, as a family, revolved around his responsibilities as a 24/7 doctor. We always had to stay near the phone in case there was an emergency, so we spent a lot of our early years in and around the house.

I was child number three, with two elder sisters, Nicola and Helen, and one younger sister, Sarah.

Dad's surgery was actually situated in our home. Patients would be at our front door by 7.45am, Monday to Saturdays, and they returned for the evening surgery at 5pm. They would wander and shuffle along our entrance hall, through the corner of our living room, and they would wait in our dining room, seated on all four sides on a variety of chairs. Our dining table sat in the middle, piled high with magazines.

My mother, a trained Barts nurse, would act as receptionist, secretary and assistant for my dad, as well as being Mum to the four of us. To help, we usually had a selection of Dutch au pair girls to lend a hand and to improve their English. To this mix we accumulated a saluki dog, Jabal, a cat, Shar, a tortoise, Fred and various guinea pigs and a hamster.

Childhood was, therefore, varied and chaotic in many ways. My father was, on reflection sixty-odd years later, a very dedicated, excellent doctor, delivering babies, doing home visits, sorting out all the patient emergencies himself, day or night, treating young and old, sick, injured and mentally-challenged with equal energy and humour.

We, therefore, grew up in this shared environment, people always in our home, with their needs and wants.

The patients loved this arrangement.

We, most evenings, ended up huddled together doing our homework round the kitchen table in the small room adjacent to the tiny galley kitchen, this being only big enough for two to stand in. The breakfast room, as it was known, was warm, as it had a nice, coke-fired boiler which provided the hot water. We did not have central heating, just a few gas fires. It was really the only place that afforded any privacy downstairs.

My mum would spend her time preparing food in the kitchen, answering the phone and rushing back and forth to find patient notes or to dress a leg ulcer. In the early evenings, as we sat round doing our homework, Dad would occasionally poke his head round the breakfast-room door and would crook his finger at one of us children. If chosen, we would be taken into the surgery, where some small, rather frightened child would be sitting.

"Now watch," he'd say to the trembling infant, "there's nothing to it," he'd state, grabbing our arm and pushing up the sleeve of our jumper.

At that point, he'd grab his syringe and stick the needle into our arm and then out again.

"See? I told you so," Dad would exclaim, "nothing to worry about. OK, your turn now."

At which point, the real patient would usually acquiesce and be willing to be injected too.

This technique would be used for tablet-taking, plaster removal, medicine-swallowing and other random issues. Sarah was the best at tablet-taking, Nicola with difficult teenagers, Helen plasters and bandages, and I was the injection pro.

Our old house had a resident collection of mice whose existence to us, who had never known anything else, seemed quite normal. If spotted, a mouse would be gently herded into a corner and a glass or jamjar would be plonked on top. His or her tail, which usually stretched outside the rim, would be painted with purple gentian violet and then the mouse released outside our house. The idea was to monitor if any released mice ever got back inside.

It was a fairly slick, well-practised routine, which we carried out without much comment or fuss.

One evening, as we sat round the table, there was a gentle knock at the door and a patient was standing there, white as a sheet. "Could you please come into the waiting room?" she requested. "We have a bit of a problem."

Chapter 2

We entered the room to find all the patients standing on the chairs. This they continued to do as we four children crawled about on the floor, jamjars in hand, going after the darting mouse.

Because Dad was always in demand and busy we, as a family, had to do the rest. I peeled potatoes, ran errands, and cleaned and laid the coal fire each day. Helen hoovered and Nicola helped with the twin tub and wringer on wash days. Sarah was the keen runner, fetching and carrying. Saturdays were usually garden days, where we were expected to help tidy, trim and cut, where instructed. Because so many people came to our house, our parents felt it was important that they could look out on a nice, well-stocked garden. As a result, they became very keen gardeners over the years.

We would set off to our various schools in different directions, on the bus or by bike, or simply walking.

In the early days we had one car, which was for Dad to use with his job. Whatever model we had, they were all temperamental and poor starters. Many a time, our morning toast was accompanied by 4 spark plugs under the grill, and one of us would be detailed off to place a hot water bottle over the distributer to dry off any damp.

Shopping in town was one mile down the road, a penny ride away by bus, so things were delivered; funnily enough, just as they are today. The milkman would call every morning, the grocer would drop by on Tuesday, Wednesday was the baker, Thursday the butcher, and Friday was the fishmonger. They'd stop their van outside, grab a large basket under their arm and walk round to the back door, which opened straight into our tiny kitchen. There they'd present their wares to Mum, who'd haggle a price and get what she'd need. Once a month, a grubby lorry would shudder to a smoky halt outside in Shirley Road and two grimy men, wearing coal-encrusted donkey jackets with reinforced shoulder-pads, would carry sacks of coke and empty them in our coal shed.

My school was boys only, and the teachers were mostly ex-army or self-taught. Only the headmaster, Mr Dodd, had a teaching degree. All I can really recall was an environment of fear. If we, as individuals, failed to pass a test, recite a poem, or entered poor homework, it was always assumed this had been done deliberately and so punishments were duly applied. With little educational back-up at home, due to parental busyness, this resulted in all of us children struggling with our schooling. I'm afraid my studies floundered.

The end-of-term reports were always a total dread. Dad, being an ex-Cambridge and Barts man, could not understand why I was doing so poorly. I began to throw myself into other activities, that provided a better sense of self-worth. Building a huge treehouse in the garden, exploring the surrounding area on my bike with friends. Tobogganing when we had lots of snow in those early years. Building model planes, huge papier mâché mountains and castles. I'd quite often get into trouble as a result of being a bit of a "free-range" child.

One person we did have at my primary school was an inspirational choirmaster called Mr Herdman. In hindsight, he really was the golden nugget in our school. We learnt to sing and were taken to perform in churches and cathedrals, we made a record for Benjamin Brittan, I sang at Westminster Abbey, Covent Garden and St Paul's Cathedral, and spent one summer actually living in the cloisters of Westminster Abbey, doing the services there. It seemed great to us, because we often had time away from school. It was a shame that, at no point, did I hear or understand the Gospel, or realise what all the singing was for.

On occasional Sundays my grandparents would arrive, like royalty, in an old Armstrong Siddeley car with running-boards and huge, bulbous headlights. We would all be washed and pressed and presented. They would lunch with us and take a tour of the garden. Grandpa wore a glass monocle, plus cigarette in a long black holder, and usually sported a beige jacket. He was a retired dentist. Two memorable things about him come to mind: his Harley Street practice was hit by a bomb in the war, completely destroying it, and one of his patients had been the Sultan of Brunei. (My grandmother was still alive when Jane and I were courting, and she was thrilled to hear we had met at the Royal Dental Hospital, where she, too, had met her husband. She showed Jane a hand-crafted, solid-silver boat given to my grandfather by the Sultan. The silversmith who made it lived just around the corner from Jane's home in Brunci!)

When I was about 7 years old, we started to attend St Michael and All Angels Church in Wallington. It was fairly high Anglican, with all the robes, choir, incense, etc. I can remember going, but cannot remember understanding much. Certainly, the Gospel story was never really explained to me.

A few signature events stick in my memory:

The arrival of our first T.V. set was one. It had a 12 inch screen, set in a fine walnut cabinet. The device took about two and a half minutes to warm up. We used to peer into the back of the vented casing to watch the valves glowing orange, just to check something was happening. Slowly the black and white screen would begin to glow, revealing the B.B.C. test card which, in our excitement we used to enjoy watching.

Chapter 2

Transmission form the BBC was only a few hours each day, at first, but I can remember our house filling up with neighbour's who would come round to watch important events such as a Royal Marriage.

One Saturday afternoon we were all clustered round the T.V. and over a period of half an hour the sky outside got darker and darker, so murky in fact that it looked like night.

There was a tremendous Flash accompanied with a loud Bang. The whole family, dog and cat included, jumped up in alarm. Our house had been struck by lightening, setting the chimney on fire. The fire brigade was called. Great excitement.

When I was about twelve years old, a friend John and I learnt practical Chemistry. We discovered if you mixed weedkiller and sugar together (readily available from shops in those days) packed it into a tight container, such as an old brass door knob and lit it with a fuse of some sort, it would explode with a very satisfying BANG! Leaving a two foot crater in the ground.

Various fuse refinements were made over the months and it was decided that the filament from a 6 volt bulb worked best. Later on I made a very nice steel canon, turned using the school lathe at school.

It would happily fire a steel ball bearing through a five inch thick piece of wood.

Another time Ian, Michael and I, Sons of the dentist, the vet and the doctor respectively, all living next to each other, were employed to clear and tidy the Hackforth's garden. A largish affair just over the road from where we lived.

We spent the morning cutting and clearing and by midday had assembled a huge mountain of branches, cuttings and wood.

In those days skips were not used and there was no council tip, so bonfires were the normal disposal method.

As everything was pretty damp, it was felt some paraffin was needed to get a good bonfire started. We checked all the containers in the old musty garage but only a jerry can of petrol could be found.

We knew it was inflammable and probably better than paraffin.

The contents were poured over the eight foot high pile of garden waste and a trail was flowed away from the bonfire along the grass. To act as a fuse.

It took a bit of time to locate some matches which were eventually found inside the Hackforth's house.(they were out at the time)

There was some concern that the petrol might have evaporated.

We needn't have worried.

Ian put a match to the grass fuse, there was a whooomph, a flash and the biggest Bang I have ever witnessed.

The contents of the bonfire were lifted fifty foot up into the air and then they descended. Many fragments were in flames.

We were thrown off our feet by the blast.

A very impressive, doughnut shaped cloud of smoke hung in the air, like some ancient smoke signal. Ian was hopping around the garden doing some sort of American Indian war dance. The frayed tassels on his jeans had caught fire. So we had to quickly put the sparking fragments out with a bucket of water.

The Fire brigade arrived, neighbours came round.

Another lesson was learnt.

It's only through God's grace that I still have ten fingers and two eyes.

By the time I had reached thirteen, it was decided that I should attend a boarding school. I suspect I was getting a bit unruly, and it was felt that a bit of organisation and discipline would do me good. So, 1968 found me heading off for Cheltenham College.

Jane's Early Recollections in Her Own Words

I WAS BORN IN NOVEMBER 1954, in Brunei, four days before Nigel, but 6994 miles away from the UK.

Brunei is a tiny country, placed in the northern tip of Borneo. It is right on the Equator.

My earliest memories would be looking over the shoulder of my Cantonese amah whilst I was strapped to her back as she went about her daily chores. There was the wonderful smell of cooking as she prepared food for the family. The sizzling of the large wok, the finely chopped ginger and garlic thrown in at the last minute before the finely diced meat was added; then came the loud frying of the vegetables. It bombarded my senses, with the aromatic smells and the noisy scraping of the spoon on wok. Watching the clouds of steam in the kitchen as she used another large pan to steam savoury egg custards with seasoned herbs. The agitation of freshly-cooked rice, to stop the grains from being too sticky, was interspersed with singing of Cantonese nursery rhymes. Sometimes, when I close my eyes, I can hear her singing and reciting these poems.

My mother taught English at the local Chinese school, which had about a thousand children, aged from six to seventeen years old. Most of them were from immigrant families who had

Chapter 2

escaped the communist regime in China. They had never heard English spoken before.

Papa worked in the newly-registered Hong Kong and Shanghai Banking Corporation, learning and working in the English banking system.

Malay is the national language of my country. We learnt it alongside the English and Chinese languages, depending on which school we attended.

I was the sixth child to be born to my parents. Mummy was thirty-five and Papa was forty then.

I have four older brothers and one older sister. It was a busy time for my parents. They were at maximum stretch, post-war, trying to rebuild their lives after three years of Japanese occupation. Papa had been in a concentration camp, from where he managed to escape, by the Grace of God. They had lost everything they possessed.

Seven years after I was born, my parents had my sister Wendy, who had Down's syndrome. Wendy was such a blessing to our chaotic family. Her life is another book.

Come Sunday, St Andrews, where our Anglican church services were held, was the highlight of the week. It and one other Catholic church, St Georges, were the only two churches allowed in Bandar Seri Begawan.

Our ancestors came from China. I am the fifth generation of Chinese Christians from a village near Ningbo in China, where Hudson Taylor worked. My great-grandmother lived to well over a hundred. She came as a young bride from a Christian family to marry my great-grandfather, who was also from a Christian family who settled in Sarawak, East Malaysia. This was during the Manchu dynasty in China. She had bound feet and wore cloth shoes specially made for her. She loved the Lord with all her heart.

This lovely lady went on to have sixteen children.

Both my grandmothers were her daughters and they, too, loved the Lord with all their hearts.

More than half the church members were related to us. The pews were taken by our families. Soon, inter-marrying took place between other families and, over time, we were related to most people in the church, either by marriage or by blood.

There were lots of us. We sang in the choir and served in the church. We never quite learned the art of making friends. We were cousins. Problems were usually resolved by Poh Poh, my maternal grandmother, who always got to hear any grievances, and we were made to apologise to each other in front of her.

Almost every other month there would be a family get-together. Each family would bring a signature dish to share. It would take place wherever my grandmother was staying. She would stay with different children during the year. There were steaming pots of rice, curries, stuffed tofus, peppers, etc., roasted chicken, duck, satays and noodles. Grace was said and the lunch would begin. After that, the children would rush off to play, the adults would sit and chat, the piano would be played and the singing would start. Hymns and popular songs would be belted out.

Our family home was half concrete and half timber. It was built part-way up a hill, surrounded by local fruit trees like mangoes, jackfruit, terap, rambutan, coconut and bananas. We also had a small pineapple grove planted up the hill directly behind the house. These bromeliads love well-drained soil.

The kitchen section was built into the hillside, while the sitting room and bedrooms were built as a separate building on a flat piece of land in front of it. The section connecting these two buildings was our dining room. It had a huge roof extending almost two metres each side, to stop the lashing monsoon rains from coming in. The sides were covered with wooden slats. It was a very happy place. As children, we could dangle our legs out between the slats and swing them about, pretending that we were in a treehouse. Mummy had planted bright red poinsettias below, and the smell of the jasmine was intoxicating after the rains.

Next to the kitchen was the maid's room cum ironing room, and there was the storeroom next to that.

Having been through the Japanese occupation, my parents were always ready for the next invasion. There were shelves full of tinned sardines, corned beef, pilchards in tomato sauce, baked beans, peas, sweetcorn, mixed fruit, milk, etc., not to mention sacks of rice and packets of noodles. It was like a grocery shop. On the other side of the kitchen were the bathroom and wc.

The sitting room had eight windows. Perched up high, we had a good view of treetops and rooftops, looking across the town of Bandar Seri Begawan. The shiny wooden floor was fabulous for sliding on with socks and a touch of talcum powder. Then, to the side, there was a narrow corridor leading to five bedrooms and a narrow office for Papa. Downstairs had four bedrooms, sitting room, plus kitchen and bathroom. This was later converted into a self-contained flat for my Uncle Kitt, his wife and my grandmother to stay.

Chapter 2

It was a busy household. When our faithful amah finally left when I was seven, she was replaced by two maids - a washer-lady, who came and did the laundry, and a full-time maid, who cleaned the house and prepared the meals for us. A man called Salleh would wash the cars, and there was a gardener, who had a constant battle to keep the jungle in check. We had two resident dogs and six cats. Later on, Mummy reared budgerigars and a talkative mynah bird. They would lure the wild birds close to our house.

The ceiling was a busy motorway of chi-chaks, or house lizards, who kept the flies and mosquito population down to a dull roar. The cats and dogs were very territorial and kept the snakes at bay. They provided an early warning system, if the odd snake had accidentally strayed into the house, usually in the pursuit of a mouse or rat. The cats would start hissing at it, and the dogs would surround and bark at the rearing and slithering creature. Meanwhile, we would get ready our sulphur flares to burn and waft in the snake's direction so as to shoo it out of the house. Failing that, out would come the wooden bendy-snake stick, which we used to kill the poisonous triangular-headed cobras.

The suspended dining room gave us a fabulous vantage point for visiting jungle animals that wandered into our garden. We sometimes had a full-sized pangolin, or armoured anteater, wander in in search of termites. If our dogs spotted him, we would have to rescue this rolled-up ball of armoured scales and carry him back to the jungle.

My eldest brother, Arthur, is twelve years older than me, and he went off to boarding school, so I did not see a lot of him. My sister Connie is eleven older than me. She was very sophisticated with dancing lessons and numerous suitors. She had a busy social life. I always admired her amazing wardrobe of dresses with can-cans and matching accessories. When she had her first pay cheque she took me to have some dresses made. What I really wanted was to grow up fast so I could wear her dresses. Alas, they went out of fashion by the time I could wear them.

Connie came to London in 1963 to train as a nurse and later on as a midwife.

She is very dear to me, amazingly, living only 400 yards from our home. She's the best big sister that anyone could wish for. I am so pleased God made it possible for her to be near to me here in Wallington. As I grow older, I learn to love her more, we go to a Bible study together and share cups of tea.

The second and third brothers (William and Fred) liked their music, so Papa bought them electric guitars and drums. Initially, they practised downstairs and gathered a lot of young people to the house. The house thrummed with music from The Beatles, The Shadows, Elvis and Neil Diamond, to mention but a few. We all grew up singing hymns, plantation songs by Stephen Foster and, of course, The Beatles' music.

Meanwhile, the brother just older than me, Noel, had a gang of friends who were interested in cowboys and Indians. They would charge round the garden and inside the house, with the dogs joining in. The maids would scream at them to stop bringing the dogs into the house with all the mud on their feet. The cats would fly out of their way.

Our home was always full of people, full of our extended family. It was always hot and humid, 365 days a year; the only changes we had were wet or dry months, and which fruits were in season.

I started school at St Andrews, an Anglican Mission School. It was behind our church and, in the early days, it was built on stilts to avoid the flash floods that occurred in the monsoon season. The roof was made of atap leaves. These were large fronds from special palm trees that grow by the riverside. It was always fascinating to watch the rain water rush off the roof and run down the fronds to form a solid curtain of water just outside our classroom windows, which had no glass.

The roof was later replaced with corrugated galvanised sheeting, which looked all shiny and new but would resonate when it rained, and the noise would drown out the teacher's voice. Much to our glee.

They struggled to teach whenever there was a thunderstorm, or the usual heavy rain.

We loved rainy days.

The teachers fought back by coming prepared with printed sheets of arithmetic or grammar, which they would hand out as soon as it started to rain.

Just as suddenly, the rain would cease, the clatter on the roof disappeared and we would sit and watch the rainwater evaporate in the strong, Brunei sunshine. The leaves would glisten and there would be a mystical, steamy atmosphere stretching across to the nearby jungle.

We would all troop off to school together, passing the odd house and rice fields along the way. The little ones, like me, would soon fall behind since it was a great time to catch grasshoppers or fill up my empty matchbox with fighting ants, which I'd coax out of their hole with a blade of grass.

The fighting ants were great for challenges we'd set each other at break time. These little insects would fight each other. Friends would bring their own champion ants, and we'd all huddle round and watch the gladiatorial combat. Someone

Chapter 2

would be proclaimed champion for the day.

On the path to school, there was a favourite chameleon which would sit in the hibiscus tree and try to blend in. Other times, he'd sit amongst some bamboo bushes. It was a great form of hide and seek.

During the rubber seed season, there would be a great popping everywhere as the seed pods exploded, sending the rubber seeds far and wide. They could sound like a gunshot and there would be a great clatter of seeds hitting our tin roofs. For us, this was the time to collect the beautiful, shiny, brown seeds, about the size of a hazel nut. Rather like conkers in the UK.

We would stuff our pockets and take them to school for competitions. One seed was placed on top of the other and you'd bash them hard with your fist. The winner was the owner of the seed that did not break.

As you can imagine, there would be all sorts of treatments and doctoring to try and harden the rubber seed. My brother Noel had a perfect seed that was the school champion for three years running. He was the envy of all of us.

One day, years later, I found his precious rubber seed sitting on his desk at home.

Unattended.

Well, I was flabbergasted. It turned out to be a stone, which had the exact shape and colour of a real rubber seed!

I used to go past a very sweet Hainanese lady. She had four children of her own, who were older than me.

I'd call out, "Morning Ah Toh," on my way to school.

I became very friendly with her, and she'd invite me in to her simple home and give me a bowl of her special Hainanese chicken rice. It was delicious.

She ran a laundry service for the area, so there were always white sheets and shirts drying everywhere.

One day I was feeling quite unwell; my amah had returned to China and the new maids were not sympathetic to any ailments. Mummy and Papa had gone off to work so, setting off for school, I soon dropped behind my siblings.

By the time I reached Ah Toh's house, I was struggling to walk. She was pegging up some white shirts on a line. She took me into her house and made me lie on a bench and gave me some warm herbal tea. It was not long before I'd dropped off to sleep.

I woke up to the sound of her thumping her heavy, metal iron, filled with hot coals. She was working her way through a huge pile of shirts. There was a wonderful smell of freshly-laundered clothing. In between her ironing, she fed me a bowl of her special chicken rice. Her cooker was coal- and wood-fired, with an enormous wok sitting on the grating with flames licking its sides. The smell was wonderful. She was cooking skins of mandarin oranges, which were then hung up to dry. From where I lay, I could see rows and rows of pickled mustard greens, fermented red tofu and salted eggs, all preserved in tall glass jars, plus loads of garlic, ginger and onions hanging about in clusters everywhere.

I lay there watching her hang up the ironed shirts on to metal hangers and then wrapping them with brown paper. The sheets she beautifully ironed, carefully folded and sealed with nylon strips, to be placed into large, flat-bottomed baskets. She would then carefully write out a label for each item in Mandarin.

When my school finished, and my brothers and sisters walked past her home, I would sneak out and fall in behind them. They were usually too busy chatting to notice my sudden appearance. Ah Toh showed me such kindness, and she taught me how to write labels in Mandarin. That was my lesson for the day.

Sometimes after church on Sunday we were allowed to go with our uncle Henry in his jeep to Muara. This was a large estuarine area, before the Brunei port had been built. Uncle Henry was building jetties for people to alight from boats in the natural harbour.

We would go swimming and I would be totally fascinated by the sea grasses to be found in the shallower areas near the mangrove forest.

Clinging on by their tails to these grasses were tiny sea horses, about two to three inches in height. They were green, yellow or even red and like my friendly chameleon, I'd see on the way to school, they matched their colour to the sea grass.

One day I'd taken a large jam jar from home and managed to collect three of those beautiful creatures still clinging to pieces of sea grass. I put them carefully into my jar and took them back to proudly show my mum.

When I returned home Mummy was horrified.

"They won't survive away from the sea Jane" She told me "You'll have to put them back straight away"

We had to get in the car and rush back to Maura and put them back in the place I had found them. It was a two hour return journey.

I was sad to see them go.

Nowadays, because of all the port activity and oil pollution, the water is not

Chapter 2

clear enough for the sea horses to live in Maura.

Just along the same beach I also found a lot of mud skippers. They were three to four inches long, fish like in appearance but with large eyes on the top of their heads. Their front fins were very strong and they were able to climb out of the sea water on to mud flats or mangrove roots. They would sit there, puffing out their cheeks and they'd skip forwards.

After the sea horse episode I resisted the temptation to take them home. I would watch them for hours as they gulped air through their mouths. So different from any other fish I'd seen

Up to then I thought fish could only exist under water .

The mangrove swamp was a special place for me. There would be bats hanging upside down on the branches eating any juicy fruit they could find. Red juices would run down their faces, along their ears and would drip into the water below.

Brunei offered education up to O-level, but pure sciences, i.e., Biology, Physics and Chemistry, were not really available at A-level.

The years passed quickly by so, when I was fifteen years old, my papa took the huge decision to send me off to the UK to attend a girls' boarding school, recommended to him by his work colleague at the Hong Kong Bank.

It was going to prove to be a traumatic experience.

Nigel's family, 1962

Jane's family, 1961

Nicola, Helen, Sarah and Nigel, plus Jabal the saluki dog, 1963

Jane aged ten

Cornwall, 1963

Jane's Twenty-first Birthday (page 33)

Chapter 2

Christmas 1965

Jane kneeling, at right of centre, with some of her family and relatives. Christmas 1965

Mud skippers

Brunei Sea horse

Nigel, Nicola Helen and Jabal 1958

Nigel digging irrigation trenches on the Hosford farm 1972 (see page 24)

19

Chapter 3

Nigel 14-18 years

I arrived at Cheltenham College in September 1968.

It had 460 boys, arranged and housed in eight separate houses and compounds with names like Leconfield, Cristow, Hazlewood and Thirlstone.

My house was Boyne House.

The school was situated at the western edge of the town, only ten minutes' walk from the Spa town centre. It had playing fields, for the seasonal rugby, hockey and cricket, plus a running track and swimming pool. The buildings were mainly faced in Cotswold limestone, set around a quadrangle and a high-vaulted chapel.

My fellow newbies had come from all over the country. Mark Eynon, Miles Peckham, Guy Wheatcroft, Jock Grant, Jim Hosford, myself and six others, were quartered in the upper dormitory where, for the first year, we learnt how to fit into school life, how to be self-reliant and to be responsible for all that we did and didn't do.

My first report from my housemaster went like this:

"Paget has settled in well for his first term. In fact, I'd say he's settled in too well."

I loved the routine, the camaraderie, the exercise and banter.

After three weeks, our group of twelve was getting a bit lively, and it was deemed we had too much energy. So, every morning at 6am, we had to set off on the quarter-mile trip to the school running track, do eight laps, and then return for a shower and change before breakfast at 7.15.

All this seemed to achieve was to get us fitter.

Breakfast, lunch and supper were provided for the whole school, sitting together in the old, high-vaulted assembly hall. We all walked along the streets back and forth from our houses to the refectory, sitting on benches alongside tables for eleven, in eight long lines, house by house.

Chapter 3

You started your time at the lowest table and, over the five years, you worked your way to the top table, whereafter, if you were made a prefect, you'd return to sit at the head of one of your house tables to keep order and dish out the food. Fairly and without bias.

Meal times lasted fifteen minutes. You learnt, early on, not to shut your eyes for the "Benedictus Benedicat" grace, otherwise the sausage on your plate might have disappeared when you opened them.

If you arrived late for breakfast or supper, you'd find the large wooden doors shut, to be opened only after grace had been said. Your name would be taken, Tardy Book given, and you would have the Friday-morning joy of running eight times round the running track at 6am.

Life was disciplined, organised and full. Compared to my rather chaotic life at home, it was great.

At weekends we would either have matches against other houses or schools, or were expected to support on the touchline. We could then walk into town and look about, grab a snack and chat. Sundays was chapel in the morning, and then we would often go and explore the surrounding countryside on our bikes.

Leckhampton Hill was the nearest high point to our school, so we would push, lift and carry our bikes to the top and career down the other side, with many a mishap along the way.

Boyne House accommodated sixty boys, aged thirteen to eighteen. You progressed from the Upper Dorm to the Middle Dorm and then entered Long Dorm, which had thirty beds, with wooden partitions between each one. This afforded some privacy, but the Long Dorm was pretty basic - just wooden floorboards, as was the rest of the house.

Homework, or prep as it was called, took place in the sweat-room when you first started, with small desks, progressing to the senior room and then to Shacks passage, which had twenty study rooms. These you shared at first, two to a shack until, for the sixth form, you had a study to yourself. You could decorate them as you wanted, and every possible type of music would be played, from record players, to radio, to tape decks, guitars to violins. But not during prep hours.

We had to do house cleaning straight after breakfast and then it was lessons for the day.

There was a kitchen to cook snacks and make drinks, a common room with a very worn quarter-size snooker table and full-size table-tennis table. There would be running knockout competitions for these two throughout the term. We had a yard area for ball games, and a croquet lawn, where tempers often became frayed.

The school had had an historic link with the British Army's Officer College, Sandhurst over the years, so there was a sizable CCF (Combined Cadet Force), with a full-time Colour Sergeant, a parade square, assault course and two army trucks.

Every Wednesday we'd don our army gear, get yelled at for dirty kit, and would be marched up and down the square. We were all pretty hopeless and there was a lot of laughter at each other's misfortune. The assault course was a challenge when you started at thirteen but, as we grew, it became more a quest to beat the record time.

We had a proper armoury, with two hundred .303 Lee-Enfield bolt-action rifles. These were handed out for drill lessons and, once or twice a term, we were taken to a firing range to actually learn how to use them. In the CCF block we also had an indoor .22 rifle range, where we would learn to shoot. Those showing a bit of aptitude were given more time. So it was that some of us would travel up to the Army shooting range at Bisley to shoot live .303 rounds at 100-, 500- and 1000-yd targets. We would take it in turns to man the targets where, after each shot, you'd haul the 10-ft target down on its sliding rollers, slap a bright orange sticker over the hole where the bullet had struck and then raise the thing back up. This allowed the person firing to see where he had hit so he could adjust his sights.

Other great adventures were constructing rope bridges over fast-flowing rivers, rock climbing and abseiling.

But their most favourite exercise was to drop us off miles from anywhere, with only an Ordnance Survey map and tell us to locate, say, four way points on the map and then find our way home.

This was called orienteering. Many an afternoon, often, it seemed, in continuous drizzle, would find us in groups of twos or fours wandering, wet, tired and disconsolate, around the Forest of Dean or the Wye Valley.

After two years general CCF, I progressed into the RAF section and learnt to fly Chipmunk trainers at Filton Airfield, Bristol. But, due to my hay fever, I was not allowed to join the full Flying Scholarship course.

Once a year, a senior Army official would arrive to inspect our company. Usually a Brigadier or Colonel. He would walk up and down our paraded ranks, chatting to the Naval and RAF sections. Then, whilst he had a cup of tea, we'd be loaded into our army trucks and positioned for a pre-prepared exercise.

My most memorable event was when we were spread all around this large, tufted, cattle field with full camouflage paint, and grass and straw in our hats and uniforms. We were each given one blank .303 round to fire when our number was called. This was to reveal our hidden position.

After we had been lying still for thirty minutes our Colonel arrived, and stood on a raised platform to try and spot our concealed positions. After a few minutes of us being examined, a rather fruity voice called out,

"OK, Number One, fire your weapon."

A loud report and a puff of smoke emitted from some concealed spot.

"OK, Number Two, fire your weapon."

And so on, until it came to Number Eight, who fired his gun with a loud bang. We all watched, in fascination at first, and then with growing horror, as a great big cow staggered and collapsed to the ground. Dead.

Number Eight had thought it might be a bit of fun to place a pencil up the barrel of his rifle and point it at the animal, which happened to be just in front of his concealed position.

We all learnt a lesson that day. Blanks in the wrong hands….

At the age of fifteen, the normal practice was for everyone to be confirmed in their faith. This seemed a pretty streamlined affair. We all attended a series of talks on the Christian Faith and, at the end of the three talks, the ninety of us were booked into our chapel for the confirmation service.

It was overseen by the local Bishop, with invitations to parents and families to attend.

Only three of us took the decision not to go through with it.

I was one of them.

I did not understand the Gospel - it had never been explained to me. I did not know who and why Jesus came. I wasn't sure God existed. We had no "one-to-one conversations" and none of my questions was being answered.

There was just an air of assumption that, because everyone else did it at your age, so should you.

It was not to be until 1989 that I got confirmed by the Bishop of Croydon, and 2019 that I was baptised by my own choice. But that is for later.

The years flew by. I took part in rowing eights and sculls, as I found my hay fever was not too troublesome on the water. We learnt to canoe on the white-water parts of the River Wye, set in a deep gorge.

The school had some great workshops, with lathes, welding and brazing gear, and an electronic workshop above.

Mr Rust, the master in charge, used to allow my friend Jim Hosford and I access to the workshops at weekends, so we'd learn to strip down car engines, get motorcycles working and construct things like a hovercraft. I made a small cannon that would fire steel ball bearings, using weedkiller and sugar as the explosive.

In the holidays, I'd get invited to help on his father's farm near Milton Abbas, in Dorset. We'd milk cows, lay water pipes, help with straw carting, drive motorbikes all over the fields and lanes and, during our last year, Jim and I did contract wheat-and-barley harvesting, driving an old, second-hand Class Matador combine harvester. We'd be up at dawn and finish at dusk.

I nearly went into farming.

Jim and I keep in touch. Forty-eight years on he has became an inventor, designing and building unblockable water-pumps. His company is called *Rotorflush*.

It was whilst down on the farm, in the summer of 1973, that I received my A-level results. They were one grade short of getting into Barts to do medicine.

In hindsight, it was almost certainly due to the new, experimental Physics with Maths course. The top O-level Physics set was placed into this newfangled A-level curriculum that no one quite understood. Hundreds of mathematical proofs to learn, differential calculus, and very little physics proper. It was deemed a disaster, and was dropped a year or two later.

This was coupled with the fact that I had to take four to five Piriton a day during the summer exams in June, to suppress my hay fever. (I was to discover later that antihistamines suppressed memory, too.)

Anyway, that's my excuse.

Life does not always go as we expect; we have to continuously plan, pray and adjust.

The quicker you can adjust, the better your life will be.

I find it amazing to think that, whilst I was going through this part of my life, God was there, watching and waiting. He does that with every human being on this planet. Just like the painting on the ceiling of the Vatican chapel, His finger is only millimetres away from our own. All we have to do is recognise who God is, and why He sent His son, Jesus. John Ch 3 v 16.

So I had a year to fill before starting my dental course. A series of jobs filled the space; Guest International was an electronics company supplying components all over the world, followed by Field Aircraft Ltd, situated in the old Croydon Airport. They took in RAF turboprop engines after 10,000 hours of use and totally refurbished them. My job was to ferry the parts, using a huge, noisy, three-tiered metal trolley, all over the factory floor.

If you were a minute late clocking in, you lost an hour's wage.

With my nomadic job, I was able to follow the whole process from engine strip-down to cleaning, examination and reassembly. Finally, the reassembled turboprop engines were tested up at Park Royal, in a huge, concrete structure resembling a set from a James Bond movie.

That was fascinating.

I next worked as an assistant to the civil engineers on the M23/M25 being built in the Merstham area, holding the theodolite poles, driving a Land Rover up hill and down dale where the construction was going on.

Glad to say it is still there today, although it has now become a not-so-smart motorway.

Finally, I did a few months of landscape gardening in and around Dorking, learning how to do crazy paving, drystone walls, rustic rose pergolas, etc.

So, by September 1974, I had saved some funds and was all set to start my dental degree.

Looking back from today, in 2021, dropping my A-levels changed the total direction of my life.

I'm convinced, for the better.

For it was at Barts I was to meet my future wife.

Jane aged 15-18

AT AGE FOURTEEN, I APPLIED and was accepted at Sultan Omar Ali Saifuddin College in Brunei. I was very sad to leave my St Andrews school. It was a Christian Mission school and I had been there since the age of four. But I did not have a choice. I had set my mind on studying pure sciences, and there was only one school that had that facility - the school owned by the Sultan of Brunei. With a heavy heart, I left my friends and went to SOAS college. There were only five girls in my class, with forty-five boys. It was a boys' school that took girls in the fourth and fifth forms.

One evening, Papa told me that a man had come from Singapore and he was going to give a Christian message at Pehin Lim Cheng Choo's house.

It was a Friday evening, and Cliff Richard's *Summer Holiday* was due for its first showing at our local cinema. All my friends were going to see it, but Papa was adamant that I should accompany my elder sister to the meeting.

It was a large hall, and there were almost one hundred and fifty of us seated in this room. We were early, so I chose a seat right at the back corner of the room so that, if I fell asleep through boredom, no one would notice. Sis and I sat down, and the room filled up quickly.

An Indian gentleman stood up in the front and introduced himself as Dr Joseph. He was a cardiologist from Singapore who had come for the week to do some operations at the local hospital. Billy Graham was doing a crusade in Singapore, and commissioned him to take the Word of God to Brunei as he himself was not allowed to enter Brunei. Brunei did not welcome Christian evangelists. I had been to Sunday school and attended all sorts of services at church. Being the rebellious teenager, I thought I knew it all. I thought that this was going to be a waste of time.

Dr Joseph started by saying that, when God made man, He wanted a special relationship with him. He created a space in man's heart for himself. All over the world, in every nation and tribe, each of us was aware of a greater being who had created the world, and there was some sort of order in the universe. So we tended to put something into that space, from idols to people, to totem poles. We were also aware that we had wronged God and wanted to win favours with him. Hence there were all sorts of sacrifices brought to the altars.

Yet the God of the Old Testament was the same as the God of the New Testament. He was the creator of all things. He did not want anything from us; or did He?

In the Old Testament, we look at Abraham. God tested Abraham by asking him to sacrifice his son, Isaac, but The Lord had already prepared a sacrificial ram for Abraham. He did not want him to sacrifice his son Isaac.

In the New Testament we were, once again, made aware of our sins and, this time, God had prepared His own son, Jesus, as the sacrificial lamb to die in our place for us. Yet all He asked is for us to believe that He would send his only son into the world like a lamb who was pure and holy, without blemish. Everything in the world is tainted with sin.

Unbeknown to anyone, I had to pass seven altars on my way to school. There were always sacrificial items on these altars. My Indian friends would have the half-elephant and half-man god, and they would burn incense and place fruit and flowers on their altar. My Chinese ancestral worshipping friends would place joss sticks, oranges and the occasional cooked chicken, etc. My Buddhist friends would have joss sticks, lotus blooms and fruit on their altars. I would ask myself, "Why does my God not want anything from me?"

Dr Joseph went on to explain that God is the creator of all things visible and invisible. Heaven is His throne and the

Earth His footstool. What could I give Him that was not made by Him?

I felt hot tears coursing down my cheeks; I could not stop sobbing. It was as if a dam had broken in my heart. "This is my God." He had made the Heavens and the Earth. It suddenly dawned on me that all He wanted was my obedience to believe that Jesus is His son. The perfect sacrifice for all our sins. I felt so loved and humbled. Totally overwhelmed that God loved me so much to give His own son that I may be forgiven.

During the past few months, I had noticed that some of my Sunday school friends had changed for the better.

They had a peace and joy that I coveted.

When they prayed, it was as if they knew Jesus personally and God became their father. I wanted it too, but I did not know how to be born again. It all sounded too difficult and impossible. So, when Dr Joseph called all those who wanted Jesus as their saviour to come forward, I was the first one in the room to stand up. My seat was on fire. We went forward and he prayed for us.

My new life had started. The old had gone for ever. Looking back, it was my watershed moment, and my life took a different direction.

At the end of August 1970, it was decided to send me to boarding school in England. I was going to start my A-levels at Queenswood School, Hertfordshire.

It would take me three days to get there.

My five older siblings were already in the UK, doing various courses.

I flew from Brunei to Singapore with my cousin Janice, who was going to do a State Registered Nurse (SRN) nursing course. We travelled in a Fokker Friendship plane. It took us about three hours. We stayed overnight at a hotel and, early the next morning, we flew to Bangkok by Scandinavian Airlines and then on to Tashkent, Uzbekistan.

Back then it was a part of the Soviet Union. It was my first ever visit into the Soviet Bloc. We were in transit. I went to the ladies and was intercepted by a large, Russian-speaking lady who was in charge of the cloakroom. She handed me a pair of rather tatty old trousers and asked if she could buy the Levi jeans I was wearing. Then she jabbed her finger at my wristwatch and offered me more Russian roubles. I gently declined; this was met with exasperation on her part and a stream of Russian language directed at me. I was pleased to board the plane and get away from Tashkent.

From Tashkent we flew to Copenhagen, a large, modern airport with few English signs. We did not speak Danish, so we were very lost in the airport. What added to the frustration was that the overhead

Tannoy kept calling for "Miss Jane Yapp. Please come and collect your luggage from the carousel."

At last, we found the baggage hall and rescued our luggage. We found a taxi and travelled to a pre-booked hotel in the city, near the Tivoli Gardens. Leaving our luggage in our rooms, we made our way to the famous gardens before it was dark. It was the first European park I had ever been to. There were a lot of artists and acrobats performing in the park. I was fascinated by the ballet performance on a makeshift stage. They were so graceful.

The next morning, we flew into Heathrow.

My sister and four brothers were there to meet me at the airport, with a bouquet of flowers they had picked from their garden. They were fragrant red roses with lavender blooms - the scent still brings tears to my eyes.

After a week of getting my uniform and sewing the name tags onto every single item, I found myself at Queenswood.

Why would I need all these clothes? The thick, grey, woollen, pleated skirt of the winter uniform, with a pretty, lilac-coloured blouse, were all I needed, but no, I had to wear a burgundy-coloured, woollen jumper over it, plus a red flannel jacket and a grey felt beret jammed over my head. I felt so hot and flustered. It was a miracle that I did not faint with the heat. We never had to wear such heavy and thick clothes back home.

The Lower-Sixth-formers shared rooms in the beautifully renovated attic, four flights up, in this large, mock Tudor mansion. Climbing up the stairs with all my newly-acquired uniform was an unforgettable experience.

From the freedom of light cotton dresses and open sandals, I went to a thick winter uniform on a hot September's day - it was such a contrast.

There were lots of lessons to be learnt in the next two years, besides my A-levels.

Boarding school came with a rule book. There were exeat weekends and laundry etiquette; the food was so different, and the weather was so unpredictable that I never knew what to wear.

The food was so bland. After our home cooking from the spice islands, where were the soya and chilli sauce?

As winter set in, it was so very cold that I used to run a hot bath and stay in it as long as possible to warm up. Chilblains? What were they?

Lights out at 10pm! Who could ever finish all their work by then, if you wanted to make friends and have time to chat?

Language! I could understand everyone, but few could understand me. I spoke slowly and grammatically. They smiled, laughed and giggled.

It did not take long before the thirteen- and fourteen-year-olds sitting at my dining table decided that it would be great to make me say certain words that would make the entire table heave with laughter! One of those difficult words was "bread" - it sounded more like "blate" when it came out of my mouth.

After six months of being the school clown, I decided that enough was enough and I went to see the Headmistress, Miss Esme Gray. She looked very old to me but, in truth, she was probably just around sixty-five years.

I explained to her about my difficulty. I could write all my essays for my A-levels without any difficulty, but my Bruniean accent was giving me a hard time. No one had taught me colloquial English, so I did not understand their jokes or puns.

"I have the perfect teacher for you, Jane," said Miss Gray, very kindly. "We have a new teacher called Miss Sarah Kennedy, who teaches Speech and Drama. She will help you."

Indeed, Miss Sarah Kennedy, fresh from RADA, was my saving grace. For my first lesson, she gave me a short passage to read while she listened.

"Oh yes," she remarked, "I know what the problem is. You are taking in too many short breaths, mid-sentence. Try to hold your breath for the whole sentence."

It was like a diving lesson. I had to hold my breath for the whole spoken sentence but, like a goldfish, I kept coming up for air in between. She explained that, when speaking Chinese, I had learnt to take short breaths in between words to get the right tone. I was trying to use the same technique for speaking English. It was like putting lots of commas and exclamation marks into my sentences.

Every week we would meet up and, over the next two terms, she managed to eliminate most of my extra breaths when speaking. Next came lessons on colloquialisms and puns. The English language is peppered with snares and mines for a foreigner like me. You feel too silly to ask what "You can't have your cake and eat it," "It's an ill wind that does nobody no good," or "Well, knock me down with a feather," actually mean.

The vowel sounds were different from Malay, which I speak as well. Then the French words that have crept into the English language may not be obvious to an English native, but they also had to be learnt.

At the end of my two years at Q School, my accent had changed beyond recognition. It took me another ten years to feel sufficiently confident to switch from one accent to the other fluently. I can now amuse my children and husband with my different accents, and laugh with them.

Thank you, Miss Sarah Kennedy from Radio 2.

In retrospect, one thing that came out of Q was my friendship with Lesley Bone.

We have stayed in touch for almost fifty years. Lesley went to read Arts at Sussex University. She became a curator at the British Museum and, later, at de Young Museum in San Francisco. Her speciality was Inca and Aztec artefacts. We write to each other and have met up with our families over the years. She is a sweet friend to me and a special gift from Queenswood.

With A-levels in Physics, Chemistry and Biology under my belt, I applied to read Dentistry at The Royal Dental Hospital, Leicester Square.

The pre-clinical course for Anatomy, Physiology and Biochemistry was taught at St Bartholomew's Medical School, Charterhouse Square, Barbican, while Dental Anatomy was taught at The Royal Dental Hospital in Leicester Square.

On the first day, we were at The Royal Dental Hospital, Leicester Square, for the orientation course. On the second day, armed with my blue folder, courtesy of *Lignostab*, a big local anaesthetics manufacturer, I set off for Barts on the Underground from Balham, up the Northern Line to Moorgate station, and had to change to get to Barbican, which was the station closest to Charterhouse Square.

At Moorgate station during the height of the rush hour, I was standing on the platform waiting for my train. A man dressed in motorcycle gear stood in front of me, with a crash helmet in one hand and an identical blue folder in the other. He looked decidedly overheated and cross. I debated whether to say hello to him because he was obviously on my course, or should I just ignore this grumpy-looking man?

Well, I decided to hold my folder up, and bravely asked him, "Are you on my course?"

A bright, cheerful smile lit up his face. "Yes," he said. The train arrived on the platform and we rushed into the carriage. It was packed with commuters.

There was nowhere to sit, so we stood close, hanging on to the overhead straps.

To a packed audience, Nigel said, "Hello, my name is Nigel Paget. What's yours?"

"My name is Jane Yapp," I answered.

A chorus of "Hello Jane!" came from some of the commuters.

I wanted the ground to open up and swallow me, I was so embarrassed, and so pleased when we arrived at the next station and the doors opened. We spilled out on to the platform and walked to Charterhouse Square together. After that, he used to wait for me at Balham Underground station and we often travelled into college together. The rest, as they say, is history.

Chapter 4

University Years

To save money and to have some transport, I had acquired a Suzuki 125cc motorcycle, and commuted up to Barts Hospital from Wallington.

Jane and I were to meet by what was, in hindsight, a bit of God's timing.

That day, I'd looked out of the window to see a miserable outlook; it was dark and wet, and it was tipping down with rain. Donning my full protective bike-leathers, gauntlets and helmet, I set off down Woodcote Road, through Hackbridge, straining to see through my rain-splattered visor. Conditions were atrocious.

By Mitcham, the engine began to misfire a bit, but nothing too troublesome; however, by Clapham North things went rapidly downhill and the bike completely packed up, leaving me stranded adjacent to Stockwell Underground.

If I were to get to the first lecture, the only way was to ditch the bike and go by Tube.

After a short hop, I had to change at Moorgate and, as everyone moved from one platform to the next, I found myself standing just ahead of a Chinese girl with long, black hair, carrying the same blue *Lignostab* case that I had sitting under my arm.

I have to admit I stood out a bit, standing there still dripping in my bike leathers and helmet, looking a bit grumpy because of my broken motorbike. But we chatted all the way to Barbican station and walked together to Charterhouse Square, where our lectures took place.

It was a cracked spark-plug. It only malfunctioned when wet, so it took me a long time to locate the problem with my bike and so I'd often take the train when it was raining.

Over the next five years we courted. This was helped by the fact that both my and Jane's journey into college followed similar routes from the south of London. After a few months, I decided that motorcycle travel during the rush hour was quite life-threatening and, after a few near misses, the bike went.

Commuting in by train meant that I could leave British Rail at Balham and meet Jane, so we could travel up together on the Northern Line.

A lot of our courtship was done around that Balham interchange, which is identical today to what it was back in 1974.

Forty-six years later, we found ourselves standing on the same elevated platform, looking down across the rail tracks at the town of Balham.

A new Sainsbury's car park now fills an area that used to be made up of old small workshops and local businesses.

We stood there for a while, wondering where the time had gone.

Time doesn't really 'march on', it tends to tip-toe. There's no parade, no stomping of boots to alert you to its passing. One day, you turn around and it is gone.

Yet, in that forty-six years, so much had happened.

Meeting Jane was to change the direction of not just my life, but hers as well.

After qualifying, she had been expected to return to Brunei to become the first English-trained woman dentist to work there. That had been the plan.

Her mother had lined up a series of prospective suitors, all vetted, all Christian. Meeting me had put a serious cog in the wheels.

When you encounter someone and spend time with them, you slowly begin to uncover and find out their heritage, their family, their experiences.

I was to discover that, with Jane, I had been looking at the tip of the iceberg. It was only over the next ten to twenty years that I would begin to understand the size and shape of the culture from which she originated.

She came from an extended family, a veritable dynasty. She had an explosion of Christian relatives; over a hundred and thirty first cousins, plus uncles and aunts. Spread all over the world.

She spoke English, Malay and Chinese in many dialects, and had a heritage going back four thousand years.

The most important quality of all, though, was that she was the first Christian person I had ever met to spend any time with.

Although from a Christian heritage, my family were really "nominal Christians", attending church for Christmas, Easter, weddings, funerals and baptisms. But God and Jesus were not mentioned in everyday conversation, and prayer and regular Bible-reading did not happen.

So, as an occasional "toe-dipper" into church and Christian life I was, literally, like an infant when it came to any true understanding of the Gospel.

Chapter 4

I quickly began to realise that this element of Jane's life was not just a big component, it was THE essence of her existence. I liked the outward signs; she had a sense of peace and confidence way beyond her years, a gentleness and compassion for others. So I was happy to watch and enjoy, but also happy to sit on the sidelines, rather than making any personal commitment.

Our dental course started in Barts with intensive Anatomy, Biochemistry, Physiology, Dental Anatomy and Histology, to be studied and passed before moving on to the Royal Dental Hospital in Leicester Square, at that time the oldest dental school in the world.

We were really fortunate to be taught by some of the leading professors and lecturers of their time. Every module we studied had two hoops to jump through: an internal test and viva and then, and only then, if passed, we were allowed to sit the external qualifying exam.

The building, opening up on to the square itself, was cramped and a bit antiquated, but its situation meant we had a ready and willing supply of patients to practise on. It also meant that we spent four years in the centre of London, having opportunities to visit art galleries, museums, the parks and the sights of London. The West End theatres used to drop thirty tickets into our hospital when starting a new production, so we'd get a chance to see plays and musicals for free.

Over the five-year training period we were transformed from long-haired children of the fifties and sixties into responsible professionals.

They were very intensive times, as we had to do our studies in all the areas such as pharmacology, dental materials, orthodontics, pedodontics, periodontics, dental materials, medicine and surgery, whilst learning the practical skills of denture construction and crown & bridge construction and actually treating patients of all ages. This meant that we had only four weeks holiday a year, unlike other university courses that allowed twenty-six weeks each year.

I used to somehow fit in a couple of part-time jobs to supplement my income. One was working on Saturdays at Simpsons of Piccadilly, selling sea island cotton pyjamas and cashmere socks, and the other was cleaning windows for a variety of small hotels in Bayswater. One memorable moment I had at the Simpsons shop was Susan George (the film actress) coming up to me at my counter and stating, "You're about my husband's size and shape. Can I use you as a model to choose some clothes for him?"

So I spent two happy hours going all over the store trying on shirts, jackets and coats for her to choose.

My window-cleaning job was quite simple; I'd cycle round to a few small hotels in Bayswater and offer my services. The Georgian window ledges were nice and wide, so I didn't require a ladder - I'd just hop from one ledge to the next, using my scrim cloth and windscreen wiper.

We had a lively group of fellow students in our year, from all walks of life, some having already done one degree, and some having worked in the stock market, or jewellery shops. One was the was son of a church minister.

There were only six girls in our year.

Once we had obtained our two degrees, by 1978/9, we were to disperse in every direction. Fred and Keith, good friends, I am still in touch with today. Others we hear about along the grapevine.

Jane stayed on at the Royal and did a houseman's job in pedodontics and periodontics.

I was offered a place to carry on and do Medicine at Barts, so as to become a maxillofacial surgeon. Initially I started my houseman's job at Hyde Park Corner and St George's Hospital, doing the Max Fax job and cycling between venues on my trusty bike.

A senior registrar at George's, Mike Lawler, took me to one side one day, put his arm around my shoulder and gave me a bit of advice. "Look at me, Nigel, I'm forty-three, married, with two young children, living in a small flat. I spend my life on call, doing the bidding of my superiors. This maxillofacial career is very interesting, but it is also very demanding. You'll not have much time left for anything else. Have a long, hard think before you head off to do fifteen more years of training."

After a few months considering and pondering, I took his advice.

Jane and I continued to court and, now that we were self-supporting for the first time, I wrote to Jane's dad asking if I could marry her.

He'd met me a few times when he and Jane's mother, Nellie, had come to the UK for a visit.

I was surprised not to receive any reply for three months.

Jane was to be one of the very few to want to marry outside their culture, so a family conference was held to decide the best course of action.

Their biggest concern was that I was not a Christian, though not being Chinese came a close second.

Apparently, about thirty-five uncles, aunts and associated relatives attended the meeting.

One of their problems in deciding, was due to their past experiences when dealing with, and watching the lives of, British expatriates working in Brunei, Singapore and Malaysia.

Regrettably, they were often rather poor ambassadors by their actions - behaving badly by drinking, hosting wife-swapping parties, treating the locals with disdain and referring to them as natives. Also, by isolating themselves in the Shell sailing clubs, or exclusive, whites-only areas, they had not endeared themselves and were regarded with deep suspicion.

How was their daughter going to be treated by this Englishman?

Was he like these other British they had observed?

Happily for us, permission was given, and we were married at St Mark's Church on 15th September, 1979.

Adjusting to two cultures was going to be a forty-year learning curve for the two of us.

Chapter 5

Jane - Gift of Tongues 1974

IN 1973, PAPA ARRANGED FOR US to have a house in Balham to share while we were students. I started attending a church called St Stephens Church, in Clapham Park SW12 0NU.

We were located temporarily above a laundrette on Weir Road, where we used to worship and study the Bible. The old church had been demolished next door in 1969.

The new church was completed in 1974. There was great rejoicing; Rev. John Hall, our Anglican minister, was very keen for us to welcome all the surrounding churches to join us in the inauguration of the new building. The new church was single storey with a modern, open-plan feel to it.

One Sunday evening, we assembled in a semicircle. There was a large number of people from the neighbouring churches who came to celebrate with us. There were representatives from Bonneville Baptist Church, a Pentecostal church and various other churches. Rev. Hall led an informal evening service. Then he invited anyone who wished to pray to stand and do so. Various people stood up and gave thanks for the new building.

Then a sweet, middle-aged lady, who was sitting next to me, stood up to pray.

She started to pray in what sounded like a different language. I remembered hearing about the gift of tongues, but I have never witnessed one so close by. In Brunei, where I had grown up, no one ever spoke in tongues. When I had seen it on TV, I had been sceptical and wondered if it was a sort of "Show off", as no one ever seemed to interpret, and we were left rather confused by the experience. Yet this lady did not look like a poseur.

However, as she continued, it started to sound amazingly familiar. Suddenly, in fluent Hobohak, a dialect spoken by my grandfather, she started to praise God. Her accent was accurate, and her words were fluent and clear. Her punctuation and tones were perfect.

I sat in utter disbelief. Had she been a missionary working in China? Or maybe she had lived among Chinese Christians

Chapter 5

so as to acquire such an impeccable accent.

The most common Chinese spoken in the UK were Mandarin, or Cantonese, and these might be spoken by Caucasian language scholars; but not Hobohak. This was a very rare dialect to speak.

When the service ended, I helped to pass the drinks and biscuits round. I was overwhelmed with curiosity to find out more about our lady visitor.

Sitting down next to her with our cups of tea, I asked her if she was visiting Balham.

She told me that she was a true Cockney, born within the sound of Bow Bells, and had never left London in her life. In fact, she'd lived in South London since the war. I discovered that she cleaned houses for several families in Weir Road. I asked her if she knew what she had been praying about.

"No," she said, "I feel a strange joy coming over me and I just have to pray; it pours out of my mouth, and I wish that someone would interpret what I am saying."

Then she looked at me. "Did you understand what I was saying?" she asked me.

"Yes," I replied. "You were praising God for sending His son, Jesus, to save us. You were thanking Him for loving us so much."

I told her that she had been speaking in an old Hobohak dialect of Chinese which was spoken by my grandfather. It was quite rare.

She exclaimed "Hallelujah! At last I have an interpretation."

It suddenly occurred to me that I should have stood up to interpret to the church. I was the only Chinese person in the gathering that evening and, almost certainly, the only one to have understood and interpreted what she had been saying.

Even if you had had a hundred Chinese people there, it was a rare dialect that only one or two would have been able to understand.

My prejudice against the gift of tongues had prevented me from testifying to others about the gift, and the interpretation sent by the Holy Spirit.

If only I could have my time again, I would shout it above the rooftops. What a missed opportunity, when I was caught up in my own disbelief. I failed to give God the glory He deserves.

I had doubted about the Tower of Babel (Genesis ch.11 verses 1-9). So it is as if the whole gift of language and interpretation is just a confirmation that it is all true.

Right after Pentecost, the Jews who had gathered for the Passover in Jerusalem heard the gospel preached to them in their own language. There were Parthians, Medes, Elamites, and people from Mesopotamia, Judea, Cappadocia, Pontus, Asia, Phrygia, Pamphylia, Egypt, Cyrene, Rome, Crete and Arab areas.

I have been humbled by this experience.

Chapter 6

1979-1989 – A Challenging first ten years.

THE FIRST HOME WE LIVED IN, after we were married in September 1979, was a maisonette in Trinity Road, Tooting. It was a garden flat, tucked behind a huge hedge, opposite a fire station. From there, following our houseman jobs, we worked in two different dental practices.

I Joined a practice at 2 Gloucester Road, Teddington, owned by Peter Sinclair. He was a laid-back, calm New Zealander. His practice was an NHS, family affair, with four other dentists.

His words of advice to me were, "Kill your patients with kindness, don't hurt them, and make sure your fillings stay put."

Simple, really.

He was always around, and very generous with his time and advice.

Jane joined a practice on the Ridgeway in Wimbledon village, with just the principal, Clive Moyes, as the other dentist.

We worked away, learning our trade and discovered each other.

Marrying a non-Christian had been a step of faith taken by Jane. My family and friends were all, without exception, nominally Christian. That is, they might go to church when necessary, for baptisms, weddings and funerals and, perhaps, Easter and Christmas as well. But that was the sum of it.

Jane's family and friends were pretty much all signed up, baptised, evangelical Christians, so it was not long before frictions and tensions began to develop over certain issues and ways of doing things.

For Jane, God was at the centre and she took all decisions and actions based on "what would Jesus do?"

For myself, at this stage, I was happy for her to spend time with her Christian friends and to go to church. Hey, I even went along from time to time. But God and Jesus were just another part of life, and I could not understand what all the fuss was about.

This tension continued for the first ten years of our marriage.

When we had family birthdays or Christmas events, and both sets of friends and families were invited, there were noticeable cultural and faith differences.

It got to the stage when I would inwardly dread the possible embarrassment of Jane's Christian side talking about Jesus, or going all "holy" when chatting with my side.

I look back on it now with a sort of open-mouthed shame at my resistance to the call of Jesus. I was blinded, and blocked from seeing who Jesus really was.

I am convinced that, before dropping to my knees, asking for forgiveness and inviting Jesus into my life, I was obstructed and deafened by the world, which was keen to prevent me knowing and truly seeing who Jesus is and why He came.

Jane, for her part, was wondering where she had gone wrong.

Since her earliest days, she had prayed with her grandmother for a Christian husband in her years to come. She had continued with that prayer right up until the day she married me.

So, she was asking God: what had gone amiss?

In 1981, we bought a house in Manor Road, Wallington, and started our surgery. On 3rd November of that year our son, James, was born.

A very special event for any young couple.

We lived over the practice and, whilst we were building up our patient numbers, both of us still worked part of our time in Teddington and Wimbledon, as well as in Wallington.

To pay the mortgage (In 1981, the interest rates were around 16%) we used to see any people in pain or trouble, out of normal working hours and at weekends.

This turned our work into a 24/7 set-up, with little or no rest time.

By 1984 we were established, and had an extra dentist to help us.

We were now both working full-time in Wallington.

James had been baptised at our local Holy Trinity Church, his Chinese name being "Tsyap En", which means "Receiving Grace".

We moved church to St Patrick's, about half a mile away. Jane felt the Sunday school was very good there. I was attending now and again, but would drag my heels a bit, rather enjoying the chance of peace and quiet for an hour to

Chapter 6

read the Sunday paper whilst Jane took James and herself off to church.

Sophia was born in October 1985, and we were still rushing about, seeing patients at all hours and arranging school for James.

In 1986, we went to a one-day conference entitled "Making a Good Marriage Better," run by a man called Rob Parsons, who started the charity *Care for the Family*. He was a Welsh, Christian, retired solicitor. He spoke very well, regaling us with anecdotal stories of his role as a parent over the years and how, in hindsight, he would have done things differently. It was an excellent day, and truly transformational for Jane and me.

We came home from the talk and totally reset our work-life balance, creating more space in our work weeks and establishing holiday fire-breaks throughout the year.

Rob had pointed out that, as parents, we are so preoccupied with earning a living, keeping house and dealing with day-to-day problems, that the very people who are nearest and dearest to us very often get the least amount of time and attention - leading to unhappy marriages and unhappy children.

Looking back, that event gave us a huge push and changed our life-direction in such a positive way. I am eternally grateful for his ministry.

I think it also nudged me closer to understanding the joys of knowing Jesus.

By 1989, Sophia was four and James eight; they were keeping us very busy with their respective school lives and our surgery now had four working dentists and a hygienist.

Jane had been attending a Bible study with with some friends: Andrew and Ruth Miller, also Bob and Joyce. One evening, when they were asking about things to pray for, Jane mentioned that James had a high fever and wasn't well, so she'd like prayer about that.

Joyce and Ruth took her to one side and prayed.

Joyce told Jane that she'd just learnt to pray in tongues, and asked would it be OK to do that? Jane said that she was happy for her to try. Joyce rested her hand on Jane and prayed in what, to Jane, sounded like Arabic. All she can remember is that her shoulder began to get really hot. So much so, that she was glad when Joyce finished.

Returning home, Jane ran up the stairs to see how James was.

She had lifted him out of his bed, and was changing his fever-soaked pyjamas, when I came down from my office.

"He seems better," I suggested.

"Yes, the fever seems to have broken, I'm glad to say," she replied.

"By the way, did I hear you running up the stairs?" I asked.

"Did I just do that?" Jane asked.

"Yes; go and do it again," I suggested.

Jane tucked our son back into his bed, and then proceeded to run up and down the stairs two or three times.

We both sat on the top stair next to each other.

"How did that happen?" I asked.

"I'm not sure, but I suspect something amazing happened whilst Joyce was praying over me this evening," Jane suggested.

You see, for the previous three years, Jane's knees had been getting stiffer and sorer. It had been getting to such a stage that we had considered moving to a bungalow.

At our practice next door, she had got into the habit of going over early and climbing the stairs on her bottom, gradually easing herself up step by step. She stayed upstairs until all her patients had been treated, then slid carefully down.

She had also collapsed in a shop in San Francisco a year earlier, with both her knees unable to straighten.

We had been to see the orthopaedic specialist, who had prescribed some anti-inflammatory tablets.

Her knees have never given her any problems since. That's now thirty-two years on.

Jane also prayed for the ability to pray in the spirit, and she used to practise this whilst driving home after dropping our son off at school.

After receiving the gift, she started praying for me.

Three weeks later, I asked Jesus into my life. Let me explain how it happened.

Billy Graham

ONE NIGHT IN JUNE, 1989, I was woken by my wife in the night, as she was crying.

Trying to comfort her, I asked if she was unhappy with our marriage, or was there a problem with our children or a member of her family?

She told me she'd just had a dream and that was why she had been crying. In her dream, she had been on a dockside and had seen a long queue of people leading up to a ticket office.

Chapter 6

When her turn came to see the ticket master, he'd said, "This is for you; this is your ticket to Heaven; you can board this ship alongside."

There was a huge, beautiful vessel nearby, with people boarding.

"Can I have a ticket for Nigel, my husband, please?" she'd asked.

The ticket master's face fell at this request. "I'm sorry, Jane, he has to come and ask himself. You cannot take one for him."

That was why she was crying. She couldn't bear the thought that she would make it to Heaven, but without me.

Up to that point, I'd dug my heels in about making a commitment, but things were about to change.

That very morning, when I was treating a man in our surgery, I happened to ask him what he was doing that summer's evening in June.

"Oh, I'm glad you asked," he said, "I'm going to Crystal Palace sports ground to hear Billy Graham speak."

"Will many people be there?" I asked.

"Well, I think they are expecting somewhere between twenty and forty thousand tonight. Why don't you come?"

I rushed home and told Jane to arrange a baby-sitter if she could, because we were going out.

That night, we drove up to Crystal Palace, only a short drive from where we lived. It was a beautiful summer's evening and, as we walked towards the stadium, I was amazed at the crowds of people gathering.

We entered the arena and found some seats. We sat there watching, as groups of people gathered, some carrying church banners in front of them as they walked in.

By the time the event was ready to begin, there must have been twenty-seven thousand people assembled. I can remember thinking I didn't realise there were so many Christians in South London. Songs were sung, one or two people spoke, and then Billy Graham stood up.

His message was very simple: "You need Jesus. Without him, you have nothing. It's quite simple; get out of your seat and come down, and ask Jesus into your life. Do it now; don't put it off any longer."

Well, I'd sat on the sidelines for thirty-five years. I felt my seat getting hot, and I jumped up and walked down on to the grass arena, with Jane in tow.

The rest is a bit of a blur, but the upshot was that, having asked for forgiveness for my sins and asking Jesus to take over the management of my life, everything began to change.

It was as though a thick net curtain had been peeled away from my eyesight and, for the first time, I was able to see Jesus for who He is.

Over the next few months, I attended a "New Christian" course arranged by the event organisers, and was able to ask the 101 questions that had been troubling me over the years.

My wife was ecstatic, as were all her Christian friends, many of whom, unbeknownst to me, had been praying for me over the years. My own friends were cautious but, over the years, they have watched and witnessed the change that knowing Jesus has made in our lives.

Jane's Capon Story

On Christmas Eve back in 1982, I was out shopping for last-minute items. We had the family coming over to us for Christmas Day and I was rather nervous about putting together a traditional Christmas lunch. We had just got our surgery up and running, and we had moved into the old house next door. James was just a year old.

The Wallington Sainsbury's was pretty full with last-minute shoppers, everyone in coats and hats, pushing trolleys like mine around the aisles. I had already bought a turkey, which was sitting in our fridge back home, so I was very surprised to hear a voice say, "Pick up that capon," just as I was passing the frozen meat section.

I stopped with a start and looked around, but there was nobody close by. Peering into the chest freezer, I could see it was pretty empty. Typical for a Christmas Eve.

"Pick up that capon," the voice repeated.

Right at the bottom, tucked into the far corner, I spotted one frozen capon.

I hesitated. I'd never bought a capon before, and I couldn't think why I needed one now.

Nevertheless, I lifted the lid, leant right into the tub, and just managed to reach the large chicken (I'm only five feet four inches tall).

Placing it into my trolley, I worked my way towards the checkout wondering what had just happened.

Having paid for everything, I stepped out into the cold and gently snowing evening and said, half to myself, "I have all I need, Lord; who is this capon for?"

Immediately, the voice said, "Sylvia".

We had been running our practice in Wallington for only eighteen months, so I was not familiar with all the names of our patients. But it seemed to ring a distant bell. As I walked towards my car carrying my two heavy bags, I was so preoccupied with the name that I almost bumped into a couple of other fellow-shoppers.

Loading the car up and quickly sliding into the driving seat, I slammed the door to keep out the cold and the snow. The car interior had that special, wintertime feel. Cold, quiet, still.

"OK, Lord, I'll go back to our surgery and find her address. I don't know where she lives."

"St Michael's Road," the voice came loud and clear.

Now I was new to Wallington, but my father-in-law had told me they'd used to attend a church called St Michael and All Angels, where he'd sung in the choir.

That must be on St Michael's Road, I decided.

Setting off up the high street and turning left into Stafford Road, I carried on for a half mile or so and turned into the road with the church.

But this was called Milton Road.

Getting out of the car, I was looking at the church and mumbling to myself when a gentleman wearing a thick, dark coat and hat walked towards me down the road.

"Good evening; you look lost, can I help at all?" he asked kindly.

"Well, I'm looking for St Michael's Road," I replied.

"Ah, I see," he continued. "That's not here, it's over the other side of Stafford Road. Tucked round the back. It used to be there before the war; they have built lots of houses there now. Confusing isn't it?" He doffed his hat and walked away.

Getting back into my car, I turned round and headed back the way I had just come, windscreen wipers beating away against the snow, my headlights illuminating great flurries of snowflakes.

Five minutes later I turned into the narrow St Michael's Road. It was bordered by rows of small, terraced houses.

"Now what, Lord?" I asked myself. "I know it's Sylvia and I know the road, but what's the house number?"

Just as I was thinking and slowing, edging along the street, a front door suddenly flew open and two ladies came out on to the pavement.

I parked the car and watched, as one lady waved goodbye to the other.

Opening up the boot of my car, I grabbed the capon and slowly approached, walking through the snow. At the last minute, Sylvia turned and saw me.

"Oh hello; who? Oh, let me see; yes, I know, you're my dentist. That's right, Mrs Paget, my new dentist. What brings you here?"

I wasn't sure how I was going to explain the last thirty-five minutes to her.

Was she a Christian?

Would she laugh at me?

In the end, I just gave her the capon and said, "Hello, you are Sylvia, aren't you?"

"Yes," she replied.

"This is from Him," offering the capon.

"Sorry, this is from who?" Sylvia asked.

I decided I'd just have to come out with it: "This is from God," I stated, pushing the chicken into her hands.

She gave me a long, hard look and then burst into tears.

"You won't know this, but my husband has lost his job, three of my four children have had whooping cough, and we have six sausages for Christmas Lunch tomorrow.

"About half an hour ago, I was kneeling on the kitchen floor with my children and we were praying that God would send us some food for tomorrow."

I gave her a hug and set off back home.

We have a living God.

Forty years later, they are all grown and love the Lord. Two of her sons are preachers in churches.

Chapter 6

Our Wallington Surgery, 1982

Jane with her mum, 1978

James and Sophia, 1992

Jane with her mum and dad, plus her four brothers and two sisters

Living next door to the surgery worked very well

Our family, 1997

Chapter 7

1990-2000 – Family life and learning about Jesus.

By 1990, James was nine and Sophia five, and we were getting into a routine of working at our practice, organising our kids with their schoolwork and outside activities like swimming, and double bass and piano lessons.

Every other Christmas, we would try and travel to Brunei to spend some time with Jane's parents, brothers, sister, aunts, uncles and cousins. It was good for our children to learn of their rich heritage from across the world. We would also spend two weeks down at Furze Farm, in Cornwall, in the summer and would try to take them off to visit parts of the UK.

The pressures of running a practice took a lot of our energy, coupled with our parenting responsibilities, so friends had to be what we termed "low maintenance." We would often get opportunities to meet up with them only once in a while. People like Andy and Heather, for example, whom we've known for over forty-five years, live on the Western Isles of Scotland, and so visiting them would only happen now and again; and yet their friendship has been a very special one. Vincent and Hakima we have also known for forty years, and have shared many happy times in Cornwall together.

James's birthday is on 3rd November, so it became a bit of a tradition to hold a firework party in our garden. His friends and their parents would be invited, as well as other friends who had children. I'd put on a display of Catherine wheels, roman candles and rockets, and then we'd all have loads of sparklers, carefully lit from an old Bunsen burner. The children, wearing gloves, would then happily wander about the garden in the dark, their faces illuminated by the brilliant, glowing, sparkling wands.

We'd all then retreat indoors for an amazing Chinese feast, cooked by Jane.

The most recent birthday celebration we had in our home was for James's thirtieth birthday. He had invited thirty-four fellow medics, friends from university and his school, for a dinner. It seemed a good idea to make it an event so, to revive an age-old tradition, we asked them each to bring one firework with them. This resulted in a pyrotechnic extravaganza that lasted for twenty minutes.

I'd carefully arranged everything with safety in mind. Goggles, emergency buckets of water, gloves and secure firework storage. However, it transpired that they all wanted to let their own fireworks off themselves. The result was rockets, multiple mortars and Catherine wheels all being lit simultaneously, resulting in a display that would have looked good on the Sydney Harbour Bridge.

Christmas time was also a gathering of family and anybody without a home to go to. Jane's family being so extensive meant that there were usually four or five over in the UK studying; others would be just be an isolated one or two, so they were invited to join and, as my parents were getting older, my sisters and their families would join with us, too. So, twenty-seven for Christmas Day was the norm. It was busy but, in hindsight, well worth the effort and time. It was always pretty chaotic, but there were memorable moments of *Pictionary*, construction games, pantomimes, puppet shows and food.

When we happen to meet up with people, now living in Hong Kong, Brunei, Singapore, Malaysia and other parts of the world, they often remark about the wonderful English Christmas Day they spent with us twenty-eight, twenty, fifteen or eight years ago.

My life as a Christian really began with me attending St Patrick's Church, with Michael Rigby as the minister. He was a thoughtful, quietly-spoken man, who loved the Lord. His preaching was often quite challenging and used to "ruffle feathers", as they say in the trade.

Brian Brown took over from him and he was a warm ex-librarian, who had become a minister later on in his life, thereby having his "life experience" to add to his ministry.

Jane and I became involved with Pathfinders. This was the Sunday school that worked for the eleven to fourteen age group. Since space was needed for games and study, we used to meet in the church hall for 9.30, an hour before the church service.

Initially there were six youngsters, plus Jane, Nick Devine and myself. We'd play some lively games and then have a Bible study.

The church service started at 10.30, so the young people met up with their parents after Pathfinders, as they arrived for the service.

We began to realise that parents found it hard to get up early on a Sunday to drop their children off. So Jane and I started a collection service, picking them up from their homes.

Then we realised that they were often hungry, having not had any breakfast, so their attention span was pretty hopeless.

Jane had the idea of cooking pancakes, with toppings of cheese and ham, or ice cream and chocolate.

Gradually, numbers increased over the years until we had about sixty youngsters coming each Sunday morning. Nick and I would organise dodgeball, team games and rounders for the first twenty minutes or so, whilst Jane cooked up sixty or more pancakes in the church kitchen. We'd then all sit down for our breakfast together and then file into an adjacent room for a thirty-minute Bible study.

It worked really well.

Once a year, the Pathfinders would design and prepare the Pathfinder service, a morning worship run entirely by them. It was always a risk, and it involved a lot of rehearsal and preparation, but the results were often moving and it used to fill our church to the brim, full of parents wanting to see their children in action.

For half term weekends, we'd try and take them off somewhere. I owned an old, long-wheelbase Land Rover at that time; it was before we had all the health and safety rules and regulations, so we'd pack fifteen kids in the rear of the vehicle and let them rattle about in the back, whilst heading off to Oaks Park or Headley Heath for a camping trip with games and Bible study.

In the summer we would take them further afield, to Christchurch, Dorset; we'd stay in an old church and do rock climbing, go karting, and pot-holing in Cheddar Gorge.

It was exhausting, but rewarding.

Many accepted Jesus into their lives.

Some Sundays, Jane and I would return home, slump into a chair and wonder, "Did they take anything in from the Bible study today?"

We used to comfort ourselves that, if only one had learnt and understood something, it was all worthwhile.

One boy was a total handful, always causing trouble and, one memorable time, getting lost during our late-night walk on Box Hill.

He was exasperating.

Twenty years later, Jane and I met his parents whilst browsing through Woodcote Green garden nursery. After some pleasantries, they grabbed our hands and said how much they wanted to thank us for helping their son.

I was thinking prison, reform school?

But no; he was now a minister for a church in South Wales.

We have an amazing God.

Chapter 8

Holidays in Cornwall

My father being on duty 24/7 resulted in our family being tied to our house in Wallington.

Once a year, by friendly arrangement, Dr Ian Gurner, a colleague nearby, would cover for my father for two weeks so he could take us all on a family holiday.

The only place we ever went was Cornwall.

There would be a great sense of anticipation in our household prior to departure, and instructions were issued left, right and centre.

No one was allowed to sprain, break or damage a limb, eye or any other part of the body. Viruses were banned.

Bags were packed, surfboards painted, the garden tidied, bills paid, and the cat and other non-transportable pets were dropped off at their allocated, temporary homes. Dad would have monster surgeries as word spread that he would be away for a couple of weeks. The only bag he packed was a small, black suitcase full of emergency drugs, dressings and potions he felt might be required for the trip.

The evening before departure would see the last patient closing our front door around 9pm, and then we would help load the car ready for the trip.

We, as children, would go to sleep, to be woken around 2am and ushered or carried into the back seat of the car. Mum and Dad were in the front, with the dog in the footwell under Mum's feet.

There were no motorways, so the journey down to the West Country would usually take eight hours. Dad would perform heroic overtaking manoeuvres to pass three or four cars plus caravans, only for a small voice to request a toilet stop; he then had to repeat the passing process a few miles along the route.

Our destination was Upper Cory Farm in Morwenstow, owned by the Tapes.

We would negotiate the last few miles hidden between the huge Cornish hedges that lined the twisting lanes. Five-bar gates would provide only fleeting glimpses of fields and pasture.

Our heavily-laden car would, at last, turn into the lane leading up to the farmhouse and yard. Mary Tape would step out to greet us, drying her broad hands on her work apron.

A plump, giggling lady who would smother us children in a friendly hug.

"Come in, come in me dears," she'd exclaim, in her broad Cornish burr "You must be tired after your long journey. I've got drinks and sandwiches for you all; welcome, welcome."

She would lead the way into her front room, armchairs covered with white lace head-protectors, the family best china displayed in a glass cabinet, the room feeling pristine and unused. There, sitting on the table, would be an enormous tea of cakes, jam sandwiches, biscuits, orange juice and a pot of tea with matching teacups.

We had the whole farm to explore, its straw-filled barns, cowsheds (it was principally a dairy farm), chicken runs and pigsties.

Mary's operation centre was the kitchen, with a warming, wood-and-coal Aga, a huge rectangular table and slate flooring. Various pots and pans were hung from a wooden rack suspended from the ceiling. Off the kitchen was their dairy room, where we would be allowed to turn the centrifugal milk-separator for making butter and cream. Their back door housed an area for kicking off muddy work boots and for the hand water-pump that we all fought to use to replenish our water jug at dinner time.

There was no mains water and no mains electric. If we wanted to witness Henry Tape's wrath, all we needed to do was to inadvertently turn a light switch on late at night, whereupon the "chug chug" of the outdoor farm diesel generator would start up and wake everyone in the farm. Dogs would bark, sheep would baa, chickens crow, and then a huge, windblown, ruddy face and shoulders would thrust round our bedroom door.

"Woos thaart you?" he'd demand, in his thick, Cornish burr.

"Sorry Mr Tape," we'd whimper, "I was bursting to go to the toilet."

"Thars why ye ave a pot under ye bed. Use aart next time," he'd thunder.

We all learnt good bladder control after a few stays.

From this base, we would set out each day to explore the northern coast of Cornwall.

If it was sunny a beach would be chosen, and the day would be spent rock-pooling, crabbing, shrimping, building dams and constructing sand castles, surfing on traditional wooden boards, and exploring adjacent coves by hopping and jumping over the barnacle- and mussel-covered rocks.

Dad would sit with some huge book or other, leaning against a rock, sporting a floppy hat, and catching up on the latest medical advances. Mum and my sisters would be working out the best way to get a tan (vinegar and cooking oil was the preferred method). There was no protective sunscreen in those days.

On wet days, we would go for walks along the coast paths, or visit Clovelly, Boscastle, Padstow or Port Isaac.

Whatever the weather, we went in the sea every day, surfing with our wooden boards. Each was painted a different colour. Mine was red.

We would go to the local Morwenstow church on Sundays. It was a Norman church with a Celtic font. There were sixteenth-century wooden pews, which had seated families over hundreds of years. In the 1950s and 60s the place was pretty full, perhaps ninety to a hundred souls. But, as the years went on, the numbers decreased until, today, the church is part of a cluster of five, with one vicar, Teresa, serving all five parishes.

It was a very special time for our family.

Perhaps the only time we had to chat, talk, play board games and see our father.

As the two weeks went on, he began to relax and get fitter. It was always difficult to return to the pressures and lack of privacy of our normal home life.

After twelve years or so, Mary Tape announced that she was retiring, and so a new farm was found just a mile away, in the small village called Shop.

Furze Farm was run by Barbara and Arthur Wickett and, like Mary, they provided bed, breakfast and evening meals for a modest sum. Just like before, there was milking to watch, eggs to collect and fields to explore. Over the years, our family grew up and diversified, so my siblings began to do their own thing. But when Jane and I had our family, we, too, stayed at Furze Farm for our summer rest and recuperation between 1980 and 2000. It was always a special time, when we could relax, get a bit fitter and enjoy family time.

Chapter 9

2000-2010

By 2000, James was nineteen and was off to St John's to begin his Medicine studies, and Sophia was fifteen and was working hard for her GCSEs. My bowel operation had been successful and so, with renewed energy, we looked forward to what the new century would bring.

Moving churches, from St Patrick's Church of England to a free Evangelical church at Banstead, had raised the bar for Jane and me. It moved our lives into a more everyday-with-God approach to life, in place of what had been a mainly Sunday existence.

Our dental practice was now at its most successful and was very busy.

Whilst keeping all the plates spinning on their sticks, as seen in a circus act, we were trying to work out what we could do that would be acceptable and pleasing to God.

You had your place of work, and you brought biblical principles into having an honest and open approach with everything. You paid your taxes. You didn't swear; you kept your temper. By the way we behaved, we were conscious that we were ambassadors for Jesus. Yet there was a calling to both of us that our skills could be used more for God's glory.

It was around 2002 that we became aware of *Mercy Ships*, through some Christian friends of ours. Their daughter set off to work on the *Anastasis*. It triggered a desire in both our hearts to go there. But how and when? How do you look after all those spinning plates and go off and away?

In the meantime, we threw ourselves into our new church life with Paul Adams, the minister, giving us challenges and arranging Bible education with an energy and passion.

We attended weekend talks from David Pawson, who was lecturing on every book in the Bible, and Dick Lucas on Hebrews. In the summer there was a mission week at our church, with guest speakers and events every day. One fantastic evangelist was Roger Carswell, who had the gift of engaging with non-Christians and then explaining the Gospel to them.

Chapter 9

In the autumn, we as a church would go to Ashburnham Place, a Christian conference centre where one hundred and eighty of us would spend the weekend, relaxing, studying The Bible and getting to know one another.

We spent some New Year weeks staying up at Capernwray Bible College near Keswick. There was some excellent Bible-teaching given and it was a great way to start a new year.

We, as a family, would also continue to go surfing in Cornwall, and would endeavour to travel to Brunei, which was a good thing to do, as time will always march on.

Jane's father passed away in 2000, after a difficult illness. It was through God's timing that Jane was able to be with him at the end. My dad died suddenly, aged eighty-eight, in May 2009. He had been seemingly hale and hearty the days before he passed away, but my mum found him one morning, when she came downstairs, simply lying on the floor.

As he had been a doctor in Wallington for forty years, a lot of people attended his funeral.

Losing one's parent takes a lot of adjusting to. One minute they are there, as they have been all your life; the next minute, they are gone.

You now become the patriarch.

Until that time, you were unaware of the load that they had carried.

Now it's your turn.

Having our faith was so good at those moments of loss. Leaning heavily on Jesus, you discover how broad His shoulders actually are.

Knowing that we have an eternal God, with His promise through His son, Jesus, that whosoever believes in Him is promised eternal life (John Ch3 v 16.), transforms our understanding of death.

Returning to 2005 for a moment; Sophia had won a place to do Medicine at Imperial College and so, for the first time, we realised that our parental school responsibilities were no longer needed in the same way.

We began to research how to apply for serving with *Mercy Ships*.

It was a lot more onerous than we had expected. About twenty forms, references from our church and friends, dental certificates, immunisations, doctor's letters, money guarantees.

A lot of applicants fall at this first fence, we were to discover, declaring, "Surely, if they wanted us to come and help, they would pay our expenses?" and, "What's with all this paperwork? I can't be doing with this."

I see it as a test to discover how keen you are to serve. A few fences to jump. Weeding out the wheat from the chaff, perhaps?

Our minister was very encouraging. "It'll be life-changing for you both," he declared.

He was right.

So, come 2006, we were off to Liberia, and again, in 2007.

It became evident that running a dental practice with 15,000 patients and disappearing off to Africa was going to cause difficulties. Staff need constant attention. Dr Ko had always told me this wise saying:

"What is the best lubricant for a successful business?"

"It's the sound of the owner's footfall walking about."

In 2007, we had the opportunity to sell the practice.

So, we did.

It transformed our lives and allowed us space to use our skills in different parts of the world, and it allowed me to be more available to help at our church.

We also had more time to re-engage with our longstanding friends.

Both Jane and I felt called to use our training and experience for God's work. But how to do that when we were looking after fifteen thousand patients at our practice and had two teenage children, plus the usual clutter of everyday life?

The answer came in the concept of short-term mission.

Chapter 10

Liberia with Mercy Ships.

So, early one February morning in 2006, Jane and I found ourselves pushing our luggage along a rather convoluted and unusually long walk.

It seemed that the authorities at Gatwick Airport had decided to place our flight and its passengers at the most remote spot it could find.

As we rounded the corner and found the correct zone for our flight, we were overwhelmed by a scene of total chaos and a wall of noise. Groups of people were standing about in clusters with uniformed airport officials, gesticulating and arguing over half-opened suitcases, boxes, and kitchen pots and pans. Personal possessions were spread everywhere. Family relatives handed baskets and bundles of clothes around, often over the heads of others. Agitated humanity crushed together. A veritable sea of people, pushing and squeezing towards the check-in desks.

Each barrier was manned by two or three aircrew and managers. Everything was overweight, hand luggage was incorrect in size and shape, and raised voices and flaring tempers overpowered the airport's Tannoy.

It was unusually chaotic at Gatwick, however my wife was pretty calm. She has more or less seen it all before travelling to remote areas on her way to and from Brunei. But we were to find that Liberia was going to be different. Very different.

Astraeus Airlines had bravely opened regular flights to West Africa, and it was immediately popular. But when folk had had to save for three or four years to make the trip, they wanted to carry home as much as they could in their luggage.

This was to be our first taste of Africa and its people. We stood, with our bags beside us, a little bit like a couple of rabbits in the headlights.

We finally made it to the front of the queue and checked in our bags. Boarding passes in hand, we jostled with Africans and squeezed into our seats.

We had agonised over what to pack. What do you take when you do not know what you might need? We had brought along a lot of dental kit, jungle-fever sprays, antibiotics, anti-malarials, Bibles, toys and gifts for children we hoped to treat, cameras and a lot more. Much, we were never to use. Many things we did need were left behind.

The *Astraeus* Boeing 737 was jam-packed; every seat filled.

Somehow, passengers still managed to board the plane with huge, multi-stacked, wheeled suitcases with side-slung bags, coming under the misnomer of "Hand Luggage". Overhead lockers were straining to bursting-point, and the aircrew were asking passengers to allow items to be stored in the aircraft hold.

Two passengers failed to board, delaying us for 3 hours while the crew tried to find and offload their belongings from the plane.

Unlike the usual rather subdued, quiet, pre-flight atmosphere, there was a cheerful buzz of excitement throughout the plane. Photos were being taken, and there were cheerful exchanges, waves and calls back and forth down the length of the aircraft.

At last, we took off and settled into the eight-hour flight.

As we crossed over Mali and Guinea, the aircraft flew through a huge, extended, tropical thunderstorm. The plane lurched, dropped and bounced about for over half an hour, accompanied by an ever-increasing chorus of wails, screams, moans and cries. It felt as though some giant two-year-old had grabbed our plane and was trying to shake its contents of passengers and luggage free. From my cabin window, I watched as the wing-tips flexed up and down, flapping like a bird.

Then a fearful silence engulfed us all. Could the plane really survive this maltreatment? Once or twice, the plane plummeted as if we were in freefall.

It had been unnerving, scary and so troubling, many of us had been praying. Hence the huge celebration on landing safely (described in chapter 1).

The *Anastasis* was the largest vessel run by the Mercy Ships charity. Formerly an old Italian cruise ship laid down in 1953, it had been bought as scrap for $1m US in 1978 and converted into a hospital ship.

American founders, Don and Deyon Stephens, spent four years transforming it to accommodate a 40-bed ward, three operating theatres and a dental clinic, along with laboratories, X-ray facilities and space for personnel. Nobody was paid to work on the ship. The whole crew, medical staff and technicians were all volunteers, supported by church groups, families and friends.

The *Anastasis* was later decommissioned at the end of 2006, to be replaced by the much bigger *Africa Mercy* - a converted Danish car ferry. The two large train decks made it possible to construct well-designed operating theatres, wards and accommodation. More recently (2021), the massive *Global Mercy* ship has been purpose-built to be the world's largest charity hospital ship, with a fifty-year expected life-span.

The Numbers

SINCE ITS FOUNDING IN 1978, the *Mercy Ships* Christian charity has impacted 2.7 million people, delivered more than $38million of medical equipment, hospital supplies and medicines, and completed nearly eleven hundred-plus construction and agricultural projects including schools, clinics, toilet blocks, orphanages and water wells.

Mercy Ships has provided services and materials in developing nations valued at more than £1.2billion. Fifty-six developing nations have been visited, 592 port visits by their ships, 445,000+ dental procedures provided, 42,250+ professionals trained in their field of expertise, 95,000+ life-changing surgical procedures provided, and 6,315+ healthcare professionals trained to train others.

It's hard to describe to you the sense of newness and wonder when you arrive in a country that is so very far removed from our own, yet to see the amazing things that can be achieved when God has His hand in it. So let me continue with our trip to Monrovia.

Almost all the people I spoke to on the ship had either their church or individual people praying and supporting them back home.

The ship's crew was totally international, members coming from all over the world. The average number of countries being represented on board was usually 36.

The agreed language was English, which we were very happy about.

The force of God's love was everywhere. We started and ended each day with a prayer meeting and a Bible thought.

Besides the on-board hospital operating work, teams of people set out each day in different directions. The ship had sixteen vans and Land Rovers that took the teams to various projects.

I chatted to a road builder, who was off with six other men to repair drains and roads by a small village outside Monrovia. He had come from Norway, especially to help.

Mission teams also went to schools and villages. There were daily lists to sign up and join the groups visiting the prison, orphanages, churches and centres for disabled people.

Don Stephens, the founder of *Mercy Ships*, was coming to Liberia whilst we were there, his primary purpose being to arrange the next date that *Mercy Ships* could visit Liberia. He had not yet got an appointment with the new President (Ellen Johnson Sirleaf), only the Vice-president. We, as a ship, had therefore been asked to pray that his visit should be well-received.

Also, prayer was requested for the new *Africa Mercy* ship, which was to be in operation in June/July 2007. It was to take over from the *Anastasis*, which was to be decommissioned after twenty-five years in service.

Our day started off early, at 6.15. We'd pop down to the laundry area situated on one of the lowermost decks and collect our scrubs, which we lived in for the day. The refectory area was midships on the *Anastasis*, and the crew would assemble there for its meals, served galley-style. The tables were fixed to the deck, so people would sit in clusters of blue, green, or white surgical kit and chat and share about what was planned for the day.

At 7.30, we would head up a deck to the assembly room for a thirty-minute presentation, prayer and worship.

Heading down to the gangway area, we'd pick up our water and dental supplies, check through the Gurkha security and then board our two Land Rovers. The dental team usually consisted of nine or ten of us in two vehicles. Heading out along the jetty area, through guarded, wire-mesh gates, we entered the town outskirts, with its hubbub of human activity.

Dodgy-looking yellow taxis, smoke belching out of their exhausts, potholes to be avoided, motorcycles, men pushing wheelbarrows along the roadside with their cellphone numbers painted in white paint on the sides.

Crowds of people sat near the port entrance, hoping for some casual work, and stalls selling petrol in screw-topped jamjars and old lemonade bottles lined the road. United Nations concrete blocks, covered in barbed wire, sat at random intervals in the middle of the street, evidence of old checkpoints.

Our trip, to the Redemption Hospital in Kru town, took about twenty minutes. As we turned the corner leading up to the building, the road seemed to erupt with bodies as men, women and children leapt from their sitting and lying positions and charged across the road in front of and behind us. Was this a riot? Were we being attacked?

No; it was the morning dental queue erupting into formation by the hospital entrance. People started jostling and pushing for a place and a chance to be seen that day. There were about four hundred in the disorderly line. Some had been waiting for two or more days, this being a Monday.

The dental work was continuous and extremely tiring. It was very hot and humid. We gave thanks to God that we were both in good health and had good energy levels.

Almost all the patients had never seen a dentist in their lives. Most required two teeth being removed just to get rid of their immediate pain. A lot of them had had toothache for weeks, months and, sometimes, years.

On top of that, we endeavoured to repair and fill other teeth. This we would do whilst waiting for the anaesthetic to take effect, prior to carrying out minor oral surgery in virtually every case.

Their diet was very poor, consisting of a lot of sugary energy drinks, sugar cane, rice and occasional protein, so their teeth were often heavily decayed and rotten. As a consequence, they often presented with severely swollen faces due to abscess infections.

We often had some good opportunities to pray with patients. When asked, "What can I pray with you for?" they would come out with a long list. It was very moving and very special to be able to pray with these people.

Some of the young men had been child soldiers. They had very dead eyes and seemed almost impervious to pain.

During the civil war, rebel leaders would arrive at a local village and round up all the young men and children. They were given AK47 guns and were instructed to shoot their parents and families. Failing to do so meant they, too, would be shot and killed.

So, at the end of the conflict, these young men had nothing to return to. No relatives, no home, no village. For ten or more years, they had learnt how to kill and to use their guns if they wanted food, or anything.

That had been their education.

At the end of the civil war, there were 80,000 teenagers and young men left homeless, without family and heavily traumatised.

When treating them, they were unresponsive, totally insensitive to any pain, and looked almost detached from their surroundings.

One young man, called Adan, slipped silently into my treatment chair. He was fifteen years old, strong and wiry to look at. I tried to engage him in conversation, but met with no response, his dull eyes looking into some distant nightmare.

He allowed me to look at his teeth, and I could see three totally broken-down molars. Giving the local anaesthetic produced no reaction, and removing his bad teeth, no response at all. I may as well have been working on a lifeless person. It was so very distressing to see someone so damaged.

Our hearts went out to these devastated young people. They really needed to find Jesus, the true healer.

One lunchtime, Jane and I explored round the Redemption Hospital in which our dental clinic had been set up. It had around six hundred beds, and dealt with every sort of medical problem, from malaria and cholera, to trauma and cancer. From children to old age, from births to deaths. Their operating budget was miniscule and the whole area was very basic.

The man who showed us round was Dr Thomas (see photo). He looked tired and worn out. A gentle and kind man, dedicated to his job, he was the only doctor there, looking after the whole hospital that day!

We gave everyone we met - patients and their families, plus the staff - the pens we had brought with us with John 3 v 16 printed on the side. Also, they received a tract explaining the Gospel of Jesus and, of course, a toothbrush!

When we returned to the ship it was wonderfully cool, with the ship's air-conditioning.

We usually showered straight away and ate supper at 5pm. After that, we'd sometimes walk along the dockside, a safe, fenced-off area by the ship.

In the dry evenings there were often superb sunsets, and the sea breeze was cool and refreshing. Groups of people flowed out from the ship, and sat and talked about things and people they had seen in the day.

Whole families stayed on board (the long-termers), so their children were often running about, happily enjoying the freedom to play ball, ride a bike, or play a game or two.

The fellowship was very good.

The following Saturday, a group of us explored central Monrovia. We went with our interpreter, Henry, round a massive, open market. It was very lively and colourful, with lots of goods for sale, from food, to shoes, to hair-braiding, African style. It was 34°C and 95% humidity, really very hot. Meat was in short supply, with just hooves, heads and tails of animals being sold. The main meat cuts had gone off to the army. Large Banana Snails, all bigger than a tennis ball, were popular. The smell and the flies were a shock, so we returned to the ship after a few hours.

On Sunday, groups of people all went off in different directions to attend various church services. They ranged from high and formal, where everyone was dressed in suits for men and crisp whites for women, to extremely lively, four-hour praise services.

The church we attended was The Liberia Gospel Church, only a short walk from where the ship was docked. It was well-attended, with around five hundred people there. The gospel choir was quite amazing. It was very moving to see forty men and a few women come forward following the message, to ask Jesus into their lives and to seek forgiveness for things they had done during the civil war.

Without fail, all of us attending had a superb welcome.

Jane and I were invited by Henry, our interpreter, to a children's Bible study session in the afternoon. He collected us in the usual run-down, yellow taxi with split seats and doors that didn't quite shut, no aircon and one shared window-winder handle.

It was hot and very humid. We travelled for twenty minutes, away from the city centre and into an area called George Town.

Turning off the road, the car bumped along a progressively narrowing track, over a derelict railway line and along a potholed footpath, past shacks, overhanging trees, bushes and farm smallholdings. We arrived after another hour, and only just made it, as the taxi was overheating and steam was pouring out of the engine.

The plot, cleared from the surrounding trees and undergrowth, consisted of a small church and a two-roomed schoolhouse, just breeze blocks and a simple tin roof. The area really felt a long way from our ship.

The children were all ready and waiting for us. All one hundred of them! Plus another forty or so who turned up once we had arrived. We could hear their excited chatter, laughter and squeals as soon as we stepped out of the steaming car. Their teacher, Toni, introduced us and then asked me to give the talk for the day!

This, I was to learn over the next few years, would happen very often, the lesson being - always be prepared to give a Gospel message!

The temperature in the room felt like 40°C, and I was soon drenched in perspiration. I taught them a song called *When the Storm Rolls*, which we all sang with great hilarity.

The sun continued to beat down on the rusty, corrugated, tin roof; I could feel all my clothes sticking to me. They then sang some superb praise songs in three-part harmony! Many took it in turns to recite verses from the Bible.

We held a lively Bible quiz with pencils, books and bouncy balls as prizes.

It was absolutely wonderful. Really very special. Praise God for all those children.

We returned to the ship a bit dehydrated, had supper at 6 and attended a very good service on board in the evening.

Our time in Liberia, on that first visit, flew by. There was so much to see and absorb. A myriad of impressions, a multitude of conversations but, most importantly, a sense that God was at the centre of everything that we and the ship's company did. There was so much more that we were to discover and do, on later visits but, after our three weeks, it was time to go home.

Revelation 7 v 17: *"For the Lamb on the throne will be their Shepherd.*
He will lead them to springs of life-giving water. And God will wipe every tear from their eyes."

Chapter 10

Astraeus Airlines

Anastasis

Dr Thomas and myself. He was the only doctor at the Redemption Hospital

Our first day in Liberia

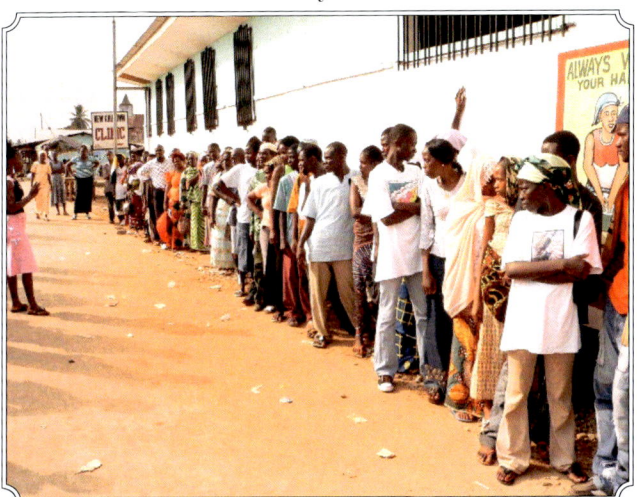

Dental queue in Monrovia

Sunday school visit, Liberia

65

A Step or Two of Faith

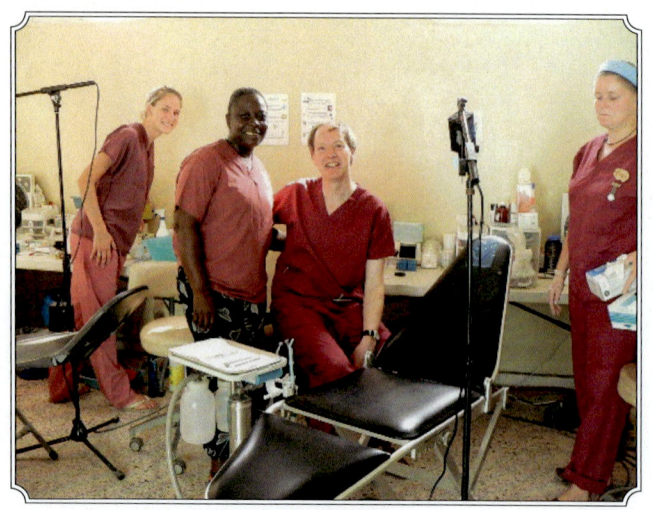

Getting ready to start our day

Jane and her nurse with some of the children with skin burns

Orphanage visit to the ship

The Captain showing the ship's bridge to the children

https://Youtu.be/i87jaHHxqlo
Short video of Liberia trip 2006 QR code

https://youtu.be/BsYCegllJcg
Cataract repair on *Anastasis* Mercy ship 2006

Chapter 11

Re-Entry to Wallington

ON RETURNING TO THE UK, our first readjustment took place at Gatwick Airport.

We had spent a few weeks living, and sharing our time, with fellow Christians from around the world, helping others to the best of our ability.

It had brought home to us how lucky we were to live in a part of the world with a free health service, free schooling and emergency services, a safe and secure environment to live in, a roof over our heads and food on our table.

On arriving at the airport, we were rather overwhelmed by the mass of people everywhere, mostly setting off on, or returning from, holidays. The usual mix of Brits, some in flip-flops, shorts and sunglasses, others in loose tracksuits and trainers. People sitting about, mobile phone wedged against ear and shoulder whilst heaving bags; some dressed in ski gear, with heavy ski-boots slung over their shoulders.

You would have thought they would have been happy and cheerful, thankful for a chance to get away and have a rest from their daily lives, but there was an air of agitation and disquiet. Customers were complaining, people were looking anxious and upset, and tired officials were trying to keep the peace, with people queuing and shoving.

What a contrast!

What a difference from where we had just been!

We felt we had been experiencing a slight "taste of heaven" on board our Mercy Ship and, suddenly, we had returned with a bang to the reality of our secular, selfish, fallen world.

It took us a few weeks to comprehend what the experience had done to us. Had we been altered somehow? Were we any different?

As we returned to Wallington, resuming the running of our dental practice, seeing our regular patients and looking after our staff and family concerns, we realised that we had changed.

Perhaps what I mean to say is, the mission experience had done something to us.

I kept thinking of the people we had met, ones with huge difficulties in their lives, their trust and thankfulness in the Lord, how impoverished they were and yet so grateful for any small amount of help and prayer. I thought about the crew on board the ship, giving up their time to do God's work. Some had been staying on the ship for years. Our small offering of three weeks with them seemed pretty paltry in comparison.

Behind everyone serving on the floating hospital there were churches, family and friend groups, financially and prayerfully supporting them so as to make their service possible.

There were many doctors, surgeons, dentists and nurses but, for every one of those, there were six others willing to give their time and effort.

Barry and Cheryl were a couple we met on board the first time we were there. They had no particular qualifications, Barry being a retired police officer. They were in their late 50s and felt called to serve, so they left their house in Bristol and signed up for 6 weeks.

When I first saw Barry he was in the kitchen, cutting cucumbers and muttering, "I'm not sure I bargained for this when I signed up to do God's work. If I see another cucumber when I get home, I'm going to go crazy."

But they stayed the course and helped wherever needed.

When we returned to Liberia the following year they, as a couple, had agreed to run the Hope centre off-ship. There, people booked for surgery on the ship, and were able to wait, stay and sleep, prior to going on board. It was a huge responsibility and a great staging-post of peace and calm for potential patients to get washed and prepared, in an environment of safety and pastoral care. Barry and Cheryl had positively blossomed into the role.

It seemed to us that God is able to use people of Faith. All they need to do is give Him their full, uninterrupted time.

Then amazing things happen.

I am sure, in hindsight, that people must have got a little tired of hearing about our trip. We were excited to have "taken the risk", as we saw it, and come back in one piece.

Many things could have gone awry but, by God's grace, they did not. So, we told lots of people of the things we had seen, amazing surgeries, churches visited, people and fellow Christians we had met.

We started to give talks to groups like Probus, Rotary and the Women's Institute about Mercy Ships. We had an article published in a local magazine.

Chapter 11

Then, out of nowhere, the opportunity came for us to sell our practice in Wallington. In fact, after only one advert, we had 40 different groups or individuals wanting to buy it.

We had started the practice from scratch in 1981, buying a house, putting a surgery into what had been the dining room, and living upstairs. It went from nothing to full-time in 6 months.

During that first year Joe Ball, our neighbour, a very kind, elderly man, used to lean on the adjoining fence and ask us if we'd like to buy his house, a rather decrepit, Edwardian redbrick affair, that he rattled around in.

We were fairly recently qualified, and buying the first house had been a major financial stretch, so the thought of getting a second loan had been just too overwhelming.

But he was persistent, persuasive and patient.

"It makes sense, you know, living next door to where you work."

"You'll never regret it," he reasoned.

He'd invite us into his living room, where the sofa was nudging the hearth, almost touching the gas fire (there was no central heating, and a lot of damp); he would give us some tea and a few pearls of wisdom.

Jane's father came to stay with us for a bit and he, too, thought it made sense.

We borrowed from Jane's brother, Fred, from a mortgage broker and, amazingly, from Joe Ball himself. We bought the house next door and called it *Panacea* (a cure for all ills).

Within a few years, the practice had grown from one to four operating surgeries. We had 15 staff and a lot of patients.

26 years later, we realised that it had become a taskmaster of its own.

It was a hamster wheel we were tied to, a demanding, exhausting and endless treadmill, that compelled us both to keep running inside it, with no let-up.

When you are inside the wheel, dashing, hurrying and sprinting, it is hard to visualise what you look like.

Others, observing from the outside, would say to us:

"I don't know how you do it."

"How do you fit it all in?"

"What, no time to stay and chat?"

"What are you trying to achieve?"

Our two children: James was twenty-six at that time and had just finished medical school, and Sophia was twenty-two and she was in the early stages of studying Medicine at Imperial College.

It became evident that running a dental practice with 15,000 patients and disappearing off to Africa was going to cause difficulties. Staff need constant attention. Dr Ko's advice came back to me regarding the owner needing to be there for a business to run successfully.

We therefore took the decision to sell the practice, and had the privilege and opportunity to choose who to sell it to. It was sold in September 2007.

We had built up a relationship of trust and care with thousands of patients over the years, so we wanted and hoped that the surgery would keep the same caring ethos once we had relinquished the reins of ownership.

As I write this, fourteen years on, we still live next door to the practice and we do see patients from time to time, as we have retained our dental registrations.

Selling the business transformed our lives and allowed us space to use our skills in different parts of the world, and it allowed me to be more available to help at our church.

We also had more time to re-engage with our longstanding friends.

So, having cleared the decks, as it were, we signed up to go again with *Mercy Ships*.

It was to be Liberia for a second time. On this trip we were to find out what prison life was like in Monrovia, we attended a cluster of baptisms in a really remote spot, and we were to see how God's hand touched our antibiotic supplies.

Chapter 12

Return to Liberia
Friday 19th April, 2008

The flight out to Monrovia, Liberia, via Brussels and Abidajan (Ivory Coast) was pretty good compared to the first time.

We arrived at 7pm, to endure the usual chaos at the airport arrivals terminal.

They had improved the interior arrivals lighting, but our bags were still grabbed by a sea of willing helpers trying to earn a dollar. After forging a path through the swirling mass of humanity, we found the *Mercy Ships* Land Rover and with it, Henry, our Liberian driver.

He worked as a translator and general problem-solver in the *Mercy Ships* dental section. He had had a very tough time during the civil war.

When Jane and I first met him, the year before, we had clocked him as being in his late 60s, but we later found out he was, in fact, only forty-two years old.

The toll on him during the civil war had been horrendous, and he really appreciated the work offered by the dental section of *Mercy Ships*.

The Chinese had been in the country repairing the roads, so Henry now felt it was OK to drive at full speed, overtaking anyone and everything in the pitch-black Liberian night.

I was sitting in the front and, after two near misses, suggested to him that there was no particular hurry and started to pray for protection. His overtaking technique was very consistent: accelerate at full tilt towards intended victim, keeping hand on horn; the car/lorry/wheelbarrow/pedestrian then leapt to one side or the other, we swerved to the open side (could be left or right) and overtook. If something happened to be coming from the opposite direction, then headlights were turned on at full beam so as to blind the opposition. I began to think that the potholes (now repaired) had accomplished the same purpose as speed bumps.

Thankfully, after one hour of this breakneck pace, the new Chinese road repairs ended and it was back to the good old 15 mph and giant craters in the road. (It was interesting that all the roads repaired by the Chinese led to copper or cobalt mines).

Driving through Monrovia, there seemed to be a slight improvement since we had last been there, in that there were actually some street lights working and a few buildings had electric light inside. There was also slightly less rubbish and plastic everywhere, but the streets were still alive with a sea of humanity.

We received a very warm greeting from people on our arrival at the ship. It felt like returning home.

At breakfast, we met up with a few friends from the past trip and familiarised ourselves with the general layout of the new ship. It was very different from the *Anastasis*.

The *Africa Mercy* was a totally refurbished vessel and had a "new smell" about it. It was much larger than the *Anastasis*, more spacious and with less outside deck space.

It had five operating theatres, and beds for eighty patients. There was accommodation for all 450 crew members. Having cost $35million, it is amazing what could be achieved when people put their faith and trust in God.

Our first day was a Saturday, so there was no dental clinic to go to. Jane went off with a group to the *Francis Drake Refuge for Orphan Children of Miners* (there are a lot of iron ore, copper and cobalt mines in Liberia, with associated work accidents). This was just the other side of Monrovia, where a husband and wife looked after thirty-three children. The *Mercy Ships* group sang songs, played games, told some Bible stories and brought some food for the children.

I met up with Keith Chapman, the dentist who was in the process of setting up a permanent base in Liberia to provide a clinic when the ship left at the end of the outreach.

Keith had been on the *Mercy Ship* for two and a half years, with his wife and children. He played guitar, surfed the Atlantic waves and had a heart to serve the Lord. I still keep in touch with him, fourteen years on.

I went out to ELWA (Everlasting Love Winning Africa) mission station to meet Keith and his wife, Christine, to have a look at the four-surgery dental clinic he was renovating and also a house he hoped to live in.

I actually went surfing as well! The water was so hot I was sweating.

I caught a couple of huge waves, then crawled out exhausted.

We had some lunch and then returned to the ship.

Chapter 12

Keith and his family remained in Liberia and worked in the mission after the ship sailed. A courageous move, as the security and police services were pretty ineffectual there. Supplies were very difficult to get, and just plain living was difficult.

Jane and I spent some Saturdays just staying on board. It was always a good time to sit in the canteen area and do some Bible study. It was usually nice and quiet, there being few interruptions. Most long-termers would be keen to get off the ship and visit churches or orphanages, or go to the beach. So we worked on the first 7 chapters of Revelations.

In the evening, we went with the whole dental team to a new Chinese restaurant, *The Great Wall*, a totally new experience for most of them. Jane organised some interesting dishes. We sang Christian songs between each course, and got other customers to join in.

The Chinese restaurant has now heard about what the *Mercy Ship* does.

The *Mercy Ships* family creates quite an amazing worldwide network, so we kept meeting up with folk we had seen the year before.

On Sundays, a lot of the 450 crew fanned out from the ship and visited local churches. It was a good way to develop friendship and fellowship with brothers and sisters in Christ.

We went to a service at The Monrovia Christian Fellowship. Started by an American couple in 1995, it had a congregation of 500 to 600. The worship was wonderful, everyone sang so well. Probably a more western format than a lot of the other Liberian churches.

We had travelled out to the church with the crew doctor, Greg, and his family.

Whilst having a snack on the way back to the ship, Greg explained that he was the ship's doctor, and how many on board required prayer, counselling and help, as well as the normal run-of-the-mill treatment of illnesses. He said his job was really exhausting. There were long-term problems of living on the ship and from the stresses that can build up in a closed community, even with those who knew and loved Jesus. He was serving for two years.

Interestingly enough, although it costs a huge amount to have a ship moored for ten months in a country with unlimited needs, the ship had a strict weekend policy of resting and Sunday worship. Every sixth weekend was extended to include the Monday. This helped to prevent burnout and exhaustion. It was no good trying to help others if the helpers were tired, stressed and exhausted themselves.

On Monday, following the breakfast scramble and the morning medical team meeting of worship and prayers, we loaded our Land Rovers and set off to the Redemption Hospital.

The roads were just as bad as ever.

We had to fuel-up the vehicle and also fill two 5-gallon containers for the generators we used at the hospital. The petrol station that the *Mercy Ships* transport fleet used was one of the few certified stations. It had normal, fairly modern petrol-pumps, rather than having the petrol stored in bottles or other random containers. The difference with filling up here, rather than in the UK, was that there were forty to fifty men sitting about, ready to assist, with the hope of getting some wages. It was such a hard existence there in Liberia.

We were met by a large queue of potential patients waiting outside the hospital, since it was a Monday morning.

As usual it was warm and humid, about 31°C and probably 90% humidity. Quite stifling and close.

We seemed to have plenty of helpers this time. Three dentists, one dental therapist, one hygienist, five dental nurses, three receptionists, five interpreters, three on sterilisation and two on generators, compressors, etc.

Jane and I had a good time catching up with the people we had worked with before.

After setting up, and a prayer time, we were off at full-steam. We both managed to pray with every patient about a topic of their choice.

I had one severe case, Eric, who had swollen up like a balloon on the left side of his face.

He came back the following Wednesday for me to check:

1) That he was still alive and

2) to remove the plastic drain I had placed in his cheek.

He lived a two-day journey away and had four children. He scratched a living growing vegetables and selling them in the market.

There were lots of severe swellings at our dental clinic that day.

Jane unfortunately stuck herself with a needle, so she had to go back to the ship to test the patient and herself for hepatitis, AIDS, etc. This created a sense of anxiety, but we trusted in our Saviour to watch over us.

She returned to the clinic to carry on with the patients. "Needle stick", as it is called, was a constant worry and a risk we all shared.

Chapter 12

On our return to the ship, we found out that all the tests were negative, praise God. (More about Jane's blood test and God's hand in her health later).

We took it in turns to prepare a short Bible-talk each morning before starting our dental clinic, and I was the one leading the next day. So, whilst being almost drowned out by the sound of the torrential, tropical rain clattering down on the metal roof outside, I went over Romans Chapter 10 with them:

[12] "For there is no difference between Jew and Gentile — the same Lord is Lord of all and richly blesses all who call on him, [13] for everyone who calls on the name of the Lord will be saved.

[14] "How, then, can they call on the one they have not believed in? And how can they believe in the one of whom they have not heard? And how can they hear without someone preaching to them? [15] And how can anyone preach unless they are sent? As it is written: 'How beautiful are the feet of those who bring good news!'"

Matthew, my second patient, had such a large facial swelling I had to incise his left cheek to drain the infection. He'd been ill for six weeks and looked really toxic. Cellulitis due to dental infection leads to 3% of deaths in Liberia and, indeed, West Africa.

It was so very refreshing to be able to wear one's Faith openly whilst working with fellow Christian staff, translators and patients. Something virtually impossible to do in the UK's restrictive and highly sensitive NHS environment.

The following Saturday, Jane and I joined a team to visit the Monrovia Prison.

This was quite harrowing.

In fact, it was very traumatic.

There were 754 inmates living in a series of blocks designed for two hundred souls. There was no funding from the government, so food was supplied by charities, or they could pay about 50p for a single meal. This was served from a large, metal cauldron into basic, small, clay bowls.

It looked like a scene from Oliver Twist.

Of course, most inmates had no money.

Out of the 754, forty-six were serving an actual sentence following a court trial. The rest were called detainees.

They were being held until they could raise funds to pay for their trial or hearing. Some were being jailed until fines or debts were paid.

The one thing we were able to do to help was to bring cellphones in, so that they could contact friends and family to try and arrange their aid. A lot of their families simply did not know where they were, communication and life in Liberia being so chaotic.

We met Francis, who led the Christian ministry with the thirteen prisons in Liberia. He showed us around, and Barry (from Bristol) and I went with Ralf, a freed prisoner, into one of the blocks.

This was the junior block, where youngsters aged from eight to seventeen were being held! Their prison accommodation consisted of concrete floors, tin roofs and rusted, barred cages to enclose them.

Francis' ministry was a simple one. These young people had lost everything, and had no hope of being released by normal means.

So, they needed Jesus.

We explained to them about Jesus, we shared worship with them and we prayed with them, asking them to put their lives into Jesus' hands.

And here is the amazing thing:

As the prisoners accepted Jesus into their lives, incredibly, release notes trickled in! It was a true answer to prayer.

However, sometimes they were held for two or more years.

How the releases occurred is not known, since it usually took a few hundred US dollars to get someone freed.

I was walking back from the prison block when a man called Emmanuel asked me to look at his neck. He had a large swelling, the size of a small satsuma, on the left side of his neck, causing him difficulty in swallowing. There was no hospital attached to the prison, and the pharmacy had run out of medicine.

I arranged to get him to the *Mercy Ship* to biopsy the lump. It certainly looked like a tumour.

He did not know that I was trained to diagnose lumps in the head and neck.

I truly believe, having had this happen so often on our trips, that God answers people's prayers by sending Christians their way.

If we had been unable to see him, the swelling would have just continued to grow and he would, most likely, have died.

I am glad to say he was treated on the ship some weeks later.

On the Sunday we travelled to the Dowain church, where we watched as seventeen people were baptised in the local stream. A very moving occasion, songs being sung, African style, and people in the water amongst the reeds, clapping, as each person emerged from the murky water.

Chapter 12

It was situated, once again, about thirty-five minutes' drive from our ship, along a muddy track that passed through a tall, overgrown, neglected rubber-tree plantation. The minister, Matthew, had only one arm. He had lost his right arm when rebels cut it off as a punishment during the civil war.

He had built a church, having cleared a plot of land for the project. It had a tin roof and wattle-and-daub walls, with a good, dry mud floor. We attended the service there straight after the baptisms in the nearby river.

In the evenings, back on board, we had started to join up with a lady called Rosie Timms, from southern California.

She was in her early seventies, a grandmother and a true evangelist. She was an inspiration to Jane and me, as she was totally fearless in explaining the Gospel of Christ to anyone and everyone who came her way.

Her day job was working at the eye department, admitting patients ready for their cataract surgery, but she spent her free time teaching songs down on the wards that were filled with patients at various stages of treatment.

We sang songs and I taught them *When the Storm Rolls*, which caused so much noise in Ward A that we had to go and do the same again in Ward B.

After supper, Rosie Timms, Jane and I had prepared some whiteboards, and took them down to the wards and repeated the song session. we added *Blessed Be the Name of the Lord*, with hand actions to "What can wash away my sins." There was lots of noise, children, visitors, nurses and drums. Quite different from the usual studied and hushed tones of a hospital in the UK.

We continued to join her on the wards for a lot of our time there. It was very rewarding chatting and explaining about Jesus, as well as just praying with the nurses and patients.

Now and again whilst working for God, things or events happen that are hard to explain. Jane and I are both scientists; we are trained to evaluate and challenge the unexplainable, yet we have witnessed many incidents which have taken place that only Faith in a living God can rationalise.

Along with our own experiences there have been, and still are, thousands of eminent scientists who follow Jesus, and have no problems squaring the Christian and science circle.

Recorded by Jane during the trip

IN THE BEGINNING OF APRIL 2008, my husband Nigel and I were working with *Mercy Ships* in Monrovia.

Let me take you to a hot, humid waiting-room full of patients who had one thing in common - dental pain and huge swellings on their faces (see photo page 80). Their eyes mirrored their sufferings, and their posture was one of resignation. On any one day there would usually be twenty out of one hundred patients with severe infections.

Our remit was to try and get them out of pain and pray for them.

The usual treatment would be to anaesthetise the area, remove the cause of the swelling, clean out the abscess, drain the infection, which could be a spoonful of yellow discharge at this stage, and, finally, put in a few sutures to hold the tissue together to prevent food from getting lodged. We would then send the patients home with antibiotics and painkillers.

Sometimes the swellings were so large that Nigel would insert a small rubber tube through a slit in the jaw or neck, to drain the pus for a few days. The patient would also be given a course of antibiotics. Usually, after a week, we were able to remove the infected tooth.

Towards the end of the two weeks that we had been there Vicki, the dental co-ordinator, asked me if we could give out less antibiotics to the patients, as we were low on the drugs and the new shipment had not arrived.

She showed me the seven packets of Amoxycillin left in the narrow drugs drawer. I told her that it was not possible, as the patients were swollen with infection and they were also poorly nourished; this latter can lead to noma as their healing process is abused.

That morning, we prayed for the shipment to arrive quickly.

Half way through the morning I had a sudden thought. I remembered reading somewhere in the dental journals where it had mentioned that, with good drainage of an acute abscess, we could lower the dosage of Amoxycillin 500mg, three times a day, to possibly three or four days, rather than seven. I went up to Vicki to share the good news; excitedly, I took a packet and I broke up the seven days' supply into four-day supplies, thereby producing an extra five packets. We set Jacki, one of the helpers, to the task of dividing up the rest. This way, we now had twelve packets of Amoxycillin. I wrote the first new dosage on these new packets as an example.

We prayed that our paltry supply would last us out and, heaving a sigh of relief, I went back to work.

Three days after that, I was hunched over my patient as usual when Vicki tapped me on my shoulder and asked if I had managed to source any more antibiotics. I said I had not, as the shipment had not arrived. But I was very happy to give

Chapter 12

some intramuscular injections of the drug if need be, as there was likely to be some in the ship's pharmacy.

All she said was, "Come and have a look."

So I followed her to our little drugs cabinet, and Vicki then said, "Open that drawer."

So I did. In it were seven packets of Amoxycillin, one of which had my writing on it for the four-day course.

Her next words were, "But it's not possible."

Being the dental coordinator, she had to document the patients we had seen each day, the work carried out and the prescriptions given. She showed me that, on the day we had originally divided the doses up into smaller quantities, we had seen forty-eight patients between the four of us and given away forty-five packets of antibiotics.

On the second day, we saw forty-seven patients and gave away forty-five packets. I am not sure how many we had given away that third day as well, but what we do know is that we had given away in excess of ninety packets to date. I am sure that I would not have been able to fit the ninety packets back into that narrow drawer if I had them.

Vicki looked at me and said, "What do you think?"

I wanted to cry with a mixture of amazement and joy and, after gathering myself together, I said to Vicki, "Well, I can't explain how, Vicki, but I think this is by God's Grace. This is God's mathematics, not mine. From now on, until the next shipment arrives, we should just put our hand in the drawer and take out a packet if we need it for a patient, and Praise God."

We had to leave at the end of the week, but Vicki e-mailed me three weeks later to give me an update.

Their supply of antibiotics had lasted two more weeks, until the new shipment arrived from the USA.

We have a Living God. Nigel and I are so thrilled to work for such a Gracious God. Let's give thanks and Praise to this Living God.

Matthew Ch 19 v 26: *"Jesus looked at them and said, 'With man this is impossible, but with God all things are possible.'"*

Liberia, second visit

Redemption Hospital

Rosie Timms - a true Evangelist

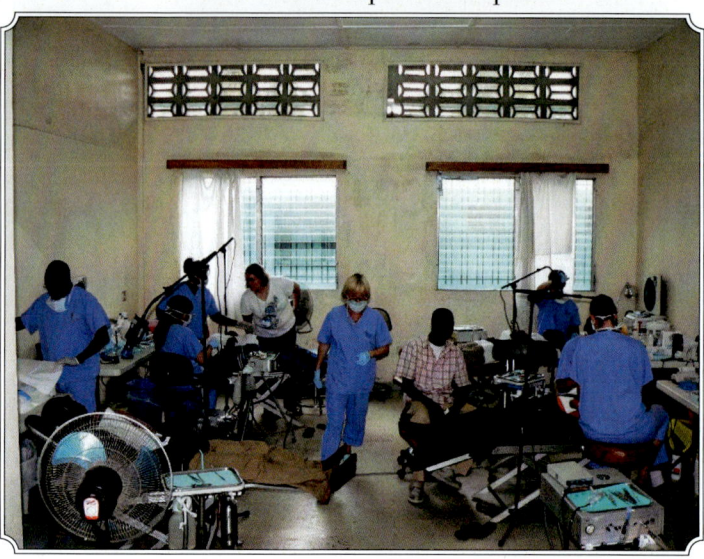

Clinic in Liberia

The New *Africa Mercy*

Many benign tumours

Chapter 13

A trip to Burma is suggested

On our return to the UK, and having a similar re-entry experience when arriving at Heathrow Airport, we readjusted once again to our home routine, the difference this time being that we were not overloaded by things to sort out in the dental practice.

Jane and I continued to work part-time, but we no longer had the responsibility of running the surgery. This, therefore, freed me up to help more at our church and to catch up with long-overdue household repairs and maintenance.

On returning from a short-term mission trip, there are a lot of e-mails, *WhatsApp* and *Messenger* contact details to sort out, messages to forward, photos and notes to file away, requests to remember, and people to phone and write to.

This usually takes about three weeks to settle down, then everything that had been going on UK-side had to be sorted and dealt with as well.

What we really began to appreciate, though, was having more time to talk with people.

Now, when I bumped into someone in the street, it was no longer "Sorry, must dash," it was "Fancy a cup of coffee?"

Building relationships is what allows the Gospel of Christ to be explained to others.

That vital question, that one comment, can be the key to open someone's door.

With the reduction in stress, my health and energy improved and, as a consequence, the quality of life improved for my wife, Jane, and for those I was involved with.

A low point in my own health had occurred in the year 2000, when a longstanding health issue came to a head. For the past twenty years, I had been getting episodes of obstruction and twisting of a rather elongated large bowel. This rendered me incapacitated and had me doubled over in pain, often ending up in A&E.

Various treatment regimens had been tried, but the frequency of the episodes increased, from once or twice a year, to agony every five or six weeks. We prayed and prayed over this and, in answer, we had a phone call, out of the blue, from a doctor friend of ours.

"Nigel needs to see Mr Roger Leicester," she said.

For years I had done the rounds, seeing various clinicians who had given me helpful advice, but nothing to solve the recurring problem. The consultation with this new man lasted three minutes.

"Your large intestine is way too long. I'll shorten it for you and remove the sigmoid curve," he suggested.

"Will this help?" I asked.

"Yes, you'll not have a problem after that," he replied.

So, I had two feet of my intestine removed!

Not a pleasant operation but, praise God, I have not had a recurrence since that time.

One passage of The Bible kept coming to mind whilst I was in hospital:

"If your right eye causes you to stumble, gouge it out and throw it away. It is better to lose one part of your body than your whole body be thrown into hell and if your right hand causes you to stumble, cut it off and throw it away." (Matthew Ch 5 v 29-30)

I am not sure if my intestines had been causing me to stumble, but the process certainly made me pause and think about the consequences of not trusting in Jesus in my life.

Jane and I continued to give talks about *Mercy Ships* to church groups, and we kept in contact with some of the many people we had met whilst serving abroad.

Next door to where we lived was a general medical practice run by a good friend of mine, called Dr Ko. He is Burmese and, both being owners of a practice, with all the responsibilities that go along with the task, we'd often meet up on a Tuesday evening after work, have a Peroni and listen to each other's tales of woe, share advice and arrange to have the odd meal together with Jane and Molly, his wife.

He'd heard about our Africa trips and was intrigued.

Ko was born in 1944 in central Myanmar, in a town called Shwebo, and was the eldest of eleven children.

He grew up in what was then known as the rice bowl of Burma. His mother and father owned and ran a large rice mill. He attended an English-speaking Catholic school and then went on to the Yangon medical college. At that time, Burma had the best educational system in South East Asia.

Chapter 13

After the military junta took over in the 1950s, an Army major and some troops arrived at Ko's parents' rice mill one day and announced that it was now owned by the state. They confiscated their whole business.

They lost everything.

Ko and Molly arrived in the UK in 1971, with one suitcase.

He asked if Jane and I might be willing to travel to Myanmar to help set up a surgery to treat patients in a similar fashion as we had been able to do on the *Mercy Ship*. He had been living in the UK for thirty-five years, but felt a desire to help his fellow compatriots back in his own home country.

After some consideration, Jane and I said we would be happy to travel out with him and Molly to, first of all, assess what and where we might be able to help.

As long as we could wear our Christian hats whilst doing so.

So, that August, we set off for Burma on a fact-finding trip. This time there was to be no large, established *Mercy Ships* charity arranging everything.

We were on our own and, as a consequence, we had to place our trust more in God.

At the time of writing, Myanmar is a country of fifty-four million people in South East Asia which shares borders with Bangladesh, India, China, Thailand and Laos. It was ruled by an oppressive military government from 1962 to 2011, either directly or indirectly, leading to international condemnation and sanctions.

Aung San Suu Kyi spent years campaigning for democratic reforms. A gradual liberalisation began in 2010, though the military still retained considerable influence.

A government, led by Ms Suu Kyi, came to power after free elections in 2015, but a deadly military crackdown on Rohingya Muslims two years later sent hundreds of thousands fleeing to Bangladesh.

It triggered a rift between Ms Suu Kyi and her previous supporters in the international community, after she refused to condemn the crackdown or describe it as ethnic cleansing. But she has remained hugely popular at home, shown in her party's landslide win in the November 2020 election.

However, January 2021 has seen the military once again seize power, and the elected government has been suspended.

When we travelled out there in 2009, Burma (Myanmar) was in a very depressed state. The country was mostly closed to visitors, and NGOs (Non-Governmental Organisations) and a lot of international charities were not welcomed.

We were able to get access because Dr Ko had contacts and connections in Yangon and Mandalay. He was able to use that local knowledge to obtain the necessary entry permits and visas.

We flew to Yangon (Rangoon) via Singapore and, from there, to Mandalay via a small, internal airline.

Mandalay is a large, bustling city set on a square grid layout, with the old royal palace at its centre. At the time we visited, it suffered from many power cuts. City funding was very limited for normal maintenance of roads, street lighting etc. All the shops, restaurants and businesses had their own huge generators installed on the pavements outside their premises, so the noise, and smell of diesel fumes, were terrible.

The hospital we were heading for was across the Irrawaddy River, in a nearby town called Sagaing (pronounced Sah-guy). This river is a huge waterway that runs virtually the length of the country, from north to south. It is the country's irrigational lifeline.

The hospital was set over a ten-acre site, all single storey, whitewashed and very clean, run by a Dr Zaw with calm efficiency and good humour. He is a general surgeon in his seventies, and managed the hospital by himself, with one secretary. There were three hundred and fifty beds, and lots of nurses.

This Sitagu Hospital offered free treatment to people in the surrounding area; however, donations were accepted and very much needed.

Our role, this first time, was to assess the dental clinic and to treat a few patients.

We had a fascinating three days there, with Ko and his family acting as interpreters for us. The patients came from a variety of areas, but particularly from the monasteries surrounding the hospital.

The accommodation facilities were clean, and set within the hospital grounds. A whitewashed bedroom with solid wood beds (good for preventing bed bugs), a non-itchy, brightly-coloured Chinese blanket and a rubbery pillow that was impossible to compress or indent with one's head.

There was occasional hot water, but most washing had to be done in a shower or using a ladle for water, at outside temperatures. It was one aspect of all our travels that I found hardest to adjust to. Perhaps my childhood days spent surfing in Cornwall in 15°C sea temperatures had been preparing me for these times.

The hospital's existing dental facility came out of a 1930s brochure. It was situated in a room only a little bigger than a small bathroom. There were one or two hand instruments, but no wash basin, no gloves, no anaesthetic, no filling materials; there was a Victorian pump-up chair, and an old wooden storage unit as might be seen in the V&A museum.

So, over a bowl of noodles, I drew out an ideal surgery plan. A sort of wish list.

The ideal would be: a spacious room, well-lit, air-conditioned, tiled and easy to clean. Wash basins, steriliser, x-ray machine, storage cupboards, and three dental chairs. Reception desk, filing for records.

It was drawn pretty much on the back of a large, A4 envelope.

I gave this to Dr Zaw, with little expectation that it would be constructed. He said he would try and arrange the construction of the new dental clinic for his hospital.

Heading down to Yangon, we visited nearly all of the dental supply companies in the city, to get prices for equipment and instruments. They were about one tenth the cost of getting similar items in the UK, which I found very heartening.

We also attended two services at two different churches in Yangon. The Baptist church had a large, very active Sunday school and youth section. It was good to see that the members were free to worship openly, with no obvious friction between themselves and the Buddhists. We also visited the Holy Trinity Cathedral.

There was a huge amount of cultural input that Jane and I had to assimilate. The language, the customs, the peoples, their expectations and hopes. It was really good that we had carried out this first scouting visit.

Before we knew it, we were setting off with *Mercy Ships*, this time to Benin and once again having to go through the usual remit of form-filling and vaccinations.

Chapter 14

Benin 2009 – A different country with unique problems.

We travelled via Paris to Cotonou and, due to a delay from London, Jane and I had only twenty minutes to navigate ourselves round Charles De Gaulle Airport to locate the connecting flight.

We desperately searched for our departure gate. This ended up with me travelling up one enormous escalator and seeing Jane travelling down another, in the opposite direction!

We made the plane with minutes to spare and we were escorted to our seats by the air steward whilst he pointedly looked at his watch.

The aircraft door was slammed shut, whereupon we had to sit and wait on the runway for one and a half hours!

A large proportion of Benin seemed to be on the plane, which made for a lively flight.

In Contrast to Monrovia, Cotonou airport was well-organised and busy. Nevertheless, with the hubbub of people, it took us an hour to locate the *Africa Mercy Ship* crew trying to find us.

Benin is a small country lying along the western border of Nigeria. In comparison to Liberia, it seemed relatively prosperous and secure. There were plentiful street lights and lots of cars. Most people got about by motorbike, which did not need a licence, hence the total chaos on the roads. Back in 2009 it had a population of seven million. Income was generated from some offshore oil, agricultural products such as palm oil and cotton, and it was a safe haven for shipping wishing to avoid the Nigerian pirates.

The Cotonou port that the *Africa Mercy Ship* was docked in had fifteen to twenty ships moored offshore awaiting a chance to dock, rather than risk being attacked.

We arrived at the ship by 10.30pm, had the welcome meeting, and crashed out.

It was good once again to meet up with a lot of familiar faces. The work had been going on with enormous energy in Cotonou.

Benin is the centre for voodoo in western Africa, so the need for Jesus here was

Chapter 14

massive. (voodoo is a religion practiced by the Aja, Ewe, and Fon peoples of Benin, Togo, Ghana, and Nigeria. Its fundamental principle is that everything is spirit. Humans are spirits who inhabit the visible world. The unseen world is populated by *lwa* (spirits), *mystè* (mysteries), *anvizib* (the invisibles), *zanj* (angels), and the spirits of ancestors and the recently deceased.

We went with a group to worship at a church in Cotonou town. It was very lively, with the visiting Bishop speaking for about eighty minutes, a common problem in west African churches, along with the second issue: volume.

The PA system was set using the theory that, to be heard, understood and remembered, go for maximum volume. The sermon could probably have been heard in the UK.

(From then on, I have always carried some earplugs with me when visiting an African church. As a guest, you get placed right at the front and, usually, right next to the loudspeakers).

There were about three hundred and fifty people inside the tin-covered church, with only a few electric fans; so it got very hot. The message was given in English and was translated into French. The prosperity gospel was being hammered out with great gusto, plus some unsettling moments with people rolling on the floor.

The streets were reasonably passable, crowded with people milling about and hundreds of motorbikes weaving in all directions. The place seemed to be safer than Liberia, where rapes and murders were common during the night.

But the poverty was still everywhere to see. Many homes were just one-roomed shacks, tumbled together by the roadside.

There was a high incidence of all diseases in Benin, particularly AIDS, hepatitis, malaria, typhoid, polio, yellow fever, cholera and tuberculosis. Once again, we needed to trust in God's care in keeping us safe, whilst getting up close and personal with patients and when seeing so many each day.

The journey to the Ministère De La Santé Dental Clinic took about half an hour, the last mile or so along a sandy, potholed road lined with basic shacks and teeming with people.

It had rained heavily in the night, so the temperature was lower; some of the potholes were, therefore, full of water and it was good that our vehicle had a snorkel, otherwise we would have got stuck in the chest-deep water. Quite a few motorbikes advanced merrily into the same water, only to vanish, except for the heads of the driver and passenger. The bikes were called "zemijohns" and usually had two or more people/animals/cargo on board. No helmets were worn, hence we had two to three broken jaws coming to the clinic to be mended every week.

The clinic we had "borrowed" was brand new! It had been built quite recently, but had never been used. It was clean and spacious, and there was even electricity!

Due to a recent donation, we had new autoclaves, generators and compressors, and updated chairs. As a consequence, we saw and treated eighty patients on our first day. Apparently a record for the outreach.

French was the second language, with Fon being the main tribal dialect spoken. My O-level mangled French seemed to be understood in places, but it limited our ability to talk, and pray about other issues the patients had in their lives besides their teeth. Those attending were mostly adults requiring multiple extractions. Some had come from Nigeria, some from Togo; all had had severe pain for ages.

When on board the ship, we always had to locate the finance department and pay our crew bills. The *Mercy Ship's* crew model was unique in that it required all volunteers to not only pay their own way, but settle fees for staying on board ship (around £350 per week).

Everyone, from the Captain and First Engineer to deck hand, from top surgeon, to nurse and washing-up assistant, all paid crew fees.

After supper, Jane and I joined the "Jesus film" (based on the Gospel of Luke) team and we set off for the Papanu district, which was built on sand near the coast. We parked the Land Rovers in a sandy, open area and, gradually, people filtered out of their homes. As the sun went down we sang some songs, and a local choir-cum-dance troupe performed. By this time, about one hundred and fifty people had gathered, benches were found and a few chairs appeared. At dusk, we started up the film, The Gospel of Luke, translated into Fon, the local dialect.

After half an hour, the numbers had swollen to four hundred and fifty. It was a beautiful evening, with a full moon and a warm, onshore breeze to keep us all cool and free from flies.

When invited to come and give their lives to Jesus, about a hundred and thirty people came forward, of whom fifty were children. This was encouraging, especially since a new church plant had been started in the region only three months ago. We met the pastor and their family, and saw the basic, sand-floored church with a partially-covered roof. We hoped and prayed that some of those who came forward that evening would

Chapter 14

appear at the church on the following Sunday.

Jane was quite amazing with the youngsters. They had things done without a peep or sound coming out. Within a couple of days, the other two dentists and I were sending the children to her. She emitted a peace and calmness that permeated throughout the clinic.

Children, just like the adults, arrived with horrendous decay, swellings and pain. They were usually pretty scared (the country usually had no local anaesthetic for dental work), so getting their treatment done took a lot of time, patience and skill.

On our way home, we got blocked in a queue of vehicles that were waiting for access to the docks. The small roundabout at the harbour entrance was totally jammed with articulated lorries facing in all directions, and even across the traffic island itself!

After thirty minutes of going nowhere, and seeing the drivers setting up their hammocks for the night, we managed to negotiate a way across the central reserve, drove through a five-foot hedge and quietly trundled down the wrong side of the dual carriageway and back to the ship. Not quite orthodox, but spending the night there was not too appealing.

Back on the ship, we had supper with a couple of people, one of whom happened to be the Captain, John McDonnell. He had travelled to over one hundred and forty sovereign states, served in the Vietnam War, and met presidents and dignitaries from around the world. As a Christian, he wanted to use his skills for the Lord. He had an amazing testimony on how he became a Christian after being captured by pirates off Columbia. It was during that period his prayers were answered.

Occasionally the ship required some major repairs, which would necessitate the power being off all day. This meant no light, no hot food, no air con, no toilets. The general advice was usually to go somewhere else.

We set off at 7.50am to locate a small boat that took us to Ganvie, a village further up-river. The trip took about one hour, and we travelled across a massive lake that was at its height during the rainy season.

Ganvie was a village/town built on stilts and people could get about only by rivercraft. The main occupation was fishing, with some crop-growing. The dental team hoped to come out to this village for two or three days to treat people there. It was a shame we would not be there to join them as we were scheduled to return back to the U.K.

before the outreach to Ganvie could take place.

The locals got about on ferries. These were open, wooden, clinker affairs with side- and cross-bench seating, fitted with a large outboard motor at the stern. Designed to carry fifty people safely, every one that went past us contained about one hundred individuals, also carrying their belongings. The result was that the gunwales were only inches from the waterline. We were told that sinkings were common events.

My first patient, Oziegbe (meaning "he who is patient"), had a fractured jaw, so I sent him back to the ship for an x-ray. (I managed to fix it on the following Thursday, using the titanium version of Meccano, metal plates and screws.)

He had broken it falling off his zimejohn (motorbike) a month before. He had been miserable as, every time he tried to eat, the centreline of his mandible flexed and grated as the opposing edges rubbed together.

Jane had a miserable two-year-old with swollen cheeks, and teeth all over the place in his upper jaw. She suspected Burkitt's Lymphoma and sent him for a biopsy and blood test. It was confirmed he had got Burkitt's, and the medical team started chemotherapy. It is the only known leukaemia to be carried by mosquitoes. His early treatment meant that the prognosis was very good.

Jane and I worked with two other dentists, Dag and Simon. Dag was from Norway and was on the ship for a year with his wife and two daughters; Simon Crew was from Dorset. He was a regular volunteer and also used his skills in Vietnam and Cambodia. Simon sported a beard and played guitar; he was a lively, very intelligent character, providing great energy to the dental team.

We are still in touch.

The remaining time in Cotonou continued with working every day at the clinic and spending time with other groups when the opportunity arose, visiting orphanage projects, prison visits and church support.

The ship had a café area, appropriately named *Starbucks*, where people would gather in groups and socialise. Prayer time was always going on, and many used to sit about with laptops, e-mailing, and chatting with friends and family back in their respective homelands.

The four hundred and fifty crew were continuously changing as people came and went. Yet the ship managed to have a continuity and consistency about it that allowed the vessel to function.

The humility, dedication, unity, purpose, and faith of the crew inspired us beyond words, renewed our faith, and changed our perspective for ever.

On the *Africa Mercy*, we found a community of faith in action - not preaching or exercising superficial spirituality - not basking in dogma or flaunting their beliefs - not revelling in banners or engaged in conflict - but, rather quietly, serving the least among us, in an environment of unconditional love.

A community of volunteers from forty countries and, whether you were a janitor or a seasoned surgeon, everyone knew that they were an essential part of something much bigger than themselves. And that only together could we go far.

At its centre was Jesus.

We were once again heading home. There was always a wish that we could have stayed a few weeks longer. The welcome and community fellowship was very special.

Jeremiah Ch 17 v 14: *"Heal me, Lord, and I shall be healed; save me and I shall be saved, for you are the one I praise."*

Chapter 15

A return to Burma

WHILST OUT IN BENIN and serving on the ship, we had had some processing to do with regard to what we had seen whilst visiting Myanmar. It was very different from the highly-regulated *Mercy Ships* organisation. If we were to do our dentistry in Burma, it would be totally under our control and responsibility would be ours.

If we were to have a problem, say a patient collapse, how would the country's authorities respond and react?

What were normal local dental services like?

How would the indigenous dentists feel about us coming to treat patients in their territory? Would they feel threatened, be angry, welcome us?

All sorts of thoughts came to our minds between the first and second visit.

The country was run by the military junta, and so everything was controlled and run by the Army. It is hard to imagine, but here are some of the things NOT provided by the state and if you were NOT connected to the military:

No free state schooling, no free and independent legal system, no free hospital treatment, or GP treatment. No ambulance service, no mandatory car insurance (accidents have to be resolved there and then on the roadside), no old-age pension. No independent banks (so every transaction has to be in cash), no credit cards, no welfare state, no housing benefit, no unemployment benefit, no free higher education. No undertakers (families were responsible for burying their dead), all land purchases overseen and controlled by the military. Anyone can be arrested at any time, so no right of appeal.

Makes you think, doesn't it?

The main religion in Myanmar is Buddhism, which is very widespread around the central regions and major cities. However, amongst the population of fifty-four million, over six million are Christian. They are mostly from minority groups or tribes, and tend to live in the poorer, outlying districts, around the edges of the country. There

Chapter 15

are over one hundred and thirty-five ethnic groups in Myanmar.

Jane and I felt there was a huge need in the country; their people had been totally cut off from the rest of the world for over fifty years. Most of the regions were very, very poor and undeveloped. Yet they were a gentle, kind, honest and open people.

After praying over the issue and doing a bit of research, we told Dr Ko we were happy to return to the Sagaing Hospital and treat patients, providing we could, once again, wear our Christian hats.

During the coming months, we heard that Dr Zaw had started the construction of our new dental clinic in a courtyard area of the hospital.

Second visit to Burma, 29th Jan to 14th Feb 2010

Dr Ko and his son, Thura, were there to meet us when we arrived in Yangon.

Thura Ko was born in the UK, went to Wallington Boys Grammar School, on to university and then worked for Rothschild Bank for a time. He moved from there to Hong Kong and then moved to live and work in Myanmar. He had a wonderful sense of humour and a great compassion for his fellow Burmese countrymen.

The following day we revisited the *Cathedral of the Holy Trinity*, a large church in the middle of Yangon. It was well-attended and the message was from Genesis. Dr Ko came with us, and I had an opportunity to explain about Jesus as our Saviour and the differences between Anglican, Baptist and Catholic worship. It transpired that he went to a Catholic school in Yangon.

The service was in English and the sermon was given first in English, followed by a Burmese version. There were probably around 400 people attending, with a full choir.

We managed to have a chat with the minister, Rev. Reginald Bennett. He was a true evangelical, and had a huge amount of energy and life about him. We hoped and prayed we could keep in touch and encourage one another.

The following day, we left for the airport at 5.45am and caught the local flight to Mandalay. The terminal for the local flights was an old building teeming with people, all rushing about.

Unlike our African experience, there was an orderly bustle and enthusiasm about getting things done so, before we knew it, our bags were weighed, tagged and scanned, and so were we.

No computers, just paper tickets and lots of staff. The process was all over in a flash.

Our boarding tag was a bright blue colour and, when our flight was ready, we were called aboard our plane by a man walking about the departure area ringing a bell whilst waving a blue flag.

Fifty minutes later, we landed at Mandalay Airport.

It had a massive runway and a huge, empty terminal, designed to take Boeing 747s.

All ready and waiting. But to no avail.

There were no other aircraft that day, just our one small plane containing forty-five passengers.

We collected our bags directly from the plane and ambled across the airport apron and through the huge, virtually deserted building, where we were met by Dr Zaw and Dr Ko's wife, Molly.

Apparently, the airport had been built by a Chinese contractor to cater for large groups of tourist flights. But the international travel industry felt uneasy dealing with a military-controlled country, so only eight thousand foreigners had entered Burma in the last year. (Over the next ten years, this was to increase to three million a year, prior to Covid and the coup in 2021).

The journey to Sagaing Hospital took us through fertile flood plains surrounding the Irrawaddy River. The bumpy track ran along a raised embankment. We travelled in an old, rather worn-out truck, weaving our way through a continuous flow of ox carts, motorcycles, goat herds, bikes laden with farm produce, chickens and groups of people carrying a multitude of different things.

After having an Indian-style chicken omelette and some tea in a bamboo-and-rattan roadside café, we arrived at the hospital.

Our accommodation, once again, was basic. There was evidence of electrical activity, because there were light fittings and plug sockets. However, there was no current flowing. If we opened the windows to get some air, then we became vulnerable to mosquitoes. No electric power also meant no fans or air con.

Dr Zaw proudly led the way through the winding, bed-filled corridors of his hospital, greeting patients, staff and visitors along the way. This was his fiefdom. There was a spring and bounce to his step.

He carried great authority, but you could see that his staff really respected and were fond of him.

We reached the spot that, on our first visit, had been an empty quadrangle and, with a flourish, he spread his arms wide with a big grin on his face.

"Well, what do you think?" he asked.

Chapter 15

Absolutely superb comes to mind. The new dental unit filled the entire area.

Inside, it was bright, large and spacious, well-lit and very clean, all newly-tiled throughout. There were three new dental chairs, and lots of storage space. It had an autoclave, state of the art panoramic OPG x-ray, good handpieces and hand instruments and, most importantly, air conditioning!

All completed since last year. Compared to the rest of the hospital, it resembled the *Starship Enterprise*. We were quite amazed.

Word had already got out and there were already fifteen or sixteen patients waiting, so we got stuck in and treated them before lunch. We had two newly-qualified local dentists working with us. They were excellent at assisting, and helping with the translation. Their training was fairly basic, so we were able to help them along a little whilst we were there.

Eating supper whilst being observed by one hundred and fifty nuns was a little disconcerting, but more about that later.

Still jet-lagged, we woke at 4am and decided it was a good opportunity to do some more Bible-reading. With no telephone, internet, TV or radio, it was refreshing how much time there was to read uninterrupted. We read through the book of Exodus and about the lives of Joshua, Gideon and Samson.

What patience God shows us.

The morning temperatures in Sagaing in January were quite cool first thing but, by midday, the temperature reached 25°C, the weather being very similar to early autumn in the UK.

I was interested to see fifteen or more nurses busy sweeping the paths that criss-crossed between different hospital buildings, wiping down windows and generally tidying everywhere. Their efforts created a plume of dust that filled the courtyard area, the early morning sunlight creating beams of light. Their red, ankle-length skirts, crisp white shirts and starched hats stood out in the fragmented and sparkling sunshine. Small, quiet words of encouragement to one another, a laugh, a mopping of a brow. No sullenness, no reluctance, just a desire to get the day started well.

They repeated this exercise every morning we were there, so it was obviously the start to their day. It seemed everyone was expected to help in the running of this charity hospital. No empires of self-importance were allowed to exist.

We were working away in the new clinic, dealing with a few teething troubles, when it transpired that some information had been passed on to the authorities that there was someone from the BBC staying at the hospital. (As I was the only Caucasian for miles around, I suspect they thought it was me.) As a result, there was a call from the military regarding our visit.

Three army jeeps swept into the hospital compound, screeching to a dramatic halt, soldiers springing out of their vehicles, with a senior officer in charge.

Passports were copied, questions asked. Dr Zaw was summoned and, eventually, they disappeared off.

We trusted that God would smooth things over.

After work Tun, a young dentist helping us, took us for an exploration round the town.

Sagaing rested alongside the Irrawaddy River, and sprawled along a wide, intricate network of roads and dusty tracks. These were lined with a huge variety of wooden houses, shops and other buildings, all teeming with life, animals, motorbikes (often ridden by three or four family members squeezed together), oxen, chickens, people sitting about and others walking in groups. The whole place, from top to toe, was covered in a layer of pale dust, a product of the dry season. This created a hazy atmosphere, enriched by strong smells of cooking fires, spices, motor fumes and animals.

Every ten or twenty yards, there were rather gnarled-looking trees, providing shady areas where locals set up their businesses. Tyre repairs, fax machines, iced drinks, snacks, and welding workshops with large cylinders of oxy-acetylene sitting on the kerbside.

We asked Tun to take us to see the three churches in Sagaing. The largest was the *Centenary Baptist Church*, established one hundred and twenty years ago. The Pastor, Rev. Kyaw Win, was very welcoming, showing us around, and explaining that they had lost their school due to the present administration, but that they were still getting converts and had a vibrant Sunday school. The other two were independent Baptist churches, planted some hundred years ago by missionaries from the UK.

Once it got dark, we returned to have supper at the adjacent nunnery. They'd insisted we come, since we had treated some of their number during the day. It was hard to refuse food which was especially cooked for us; once again, we were observed by the one hundred and fifty nuns - particularly tricky when one chokes on a piece of chilli. All this whilst trying to sit cross-legged on the floor beside the very low-lying dining tables. It turned out to be almost a daily event, so we had to get used to it.

These were Buddhist nuns, all dressed in pink, heads shaven. Welcoming and gentle. Spending their days studying and bowing to a false idol. Something so upsetting to God.

Not only that, we were to discover that the hospital we were working in was surrounded by about one hundred such monasteries and nunneries. It was the university centre of Buddhist study.

Why had God placed us there, we wanted to know?

What could two Christian dentists achieve for the Gospel of Christ?

Jane had had rather a severe stomach upset in the night, and was rather pale the next morning. We went for breakfast with Dr Zaw, who kindly arranged some medication which worked very well. Thanks must go to God for watching over us.

It was good to meet up with Dr Zaw, since we had a chance to talk about what we believe in and why we are here. He also had a chance to explain about the workings of the hospital and how he managed it.

In truth, he is seventy-three years old, he works a seven-day week, and has one break of two weeks away each year to visit his home town in north Burma, where he acts as an examiner for the potential new medics. He has seventy-five staff, and three hundred and fifty beds full of patients. He looked tired. Jane and I felt he might collapse at any time.

It turned out he went to a Christian mission school as a child, and so we had a good discussion over breakfast regarding values and beliefs, and where they come from. He quoted us a verse from The Bible that he had found to be very true. We found it in Titus Ch 1 v 15-16! *"15 To the pure, all things are pure, but to those who are corrupted and do not believe, nothing is pure. In fact, both their minds and consciences are corrupted. 16 They claim to know God, but by their actions they deny him. They are detestable, disobedient and unfit for doing anything good."*

He found time to see us three or four times a day. I spent two hours sorting out a dental problem for him that afternoon.

Patients attending the hospital, and their friends and relatives, would wait in a tree-covered area, these providing shade. Around the trees, they had built a network of raised, wooden platforms for everyone to sit, sleep, chat and wait. It worked well in the dry season. There was also a little wooden hut that acted as the hospital café in the waiting area.

There were usually quite a lot of people in this zone, and there was always a happy but subdued atmosphere about the place. The families were expected to provide food and clothing for their relatives when staying in the hospital.

We had opportunities to talk about our faith in Jesus, which was good.

The whole area was steeped in Buddhism, the region having been Buddhist since 1013 AD.

It was very tranquil, nothing like the African voodoo we had found in Benin, which made my flesh creep. But they were seeking eternal life through study and good works. Without Jesus, all this would become dust in God's eyes.

It felt as if we were staying in the focal point of their belief system. Only God knew how He could use us there.

I wanted to try and get a message out using the internet. At lunchtime, I was taken to a building in one of the monasteries, where they had some computers attached to a phone. But after sitting there for three quarters of an hour, waiting for the first *Explorer* page to appear, I realised that this was obviously a different computer world.

After work, Tun took us in his rehabilitated car, through the teeming streets of Sagaing, to a small internet café amongst the network of huts and lean-tos.

Our presence caused a bit of a stir and, with a fan club of about thirty people observing, Tun and I managed to send ONE e-mail and a few photos in the record time of two hours! Without Tun's help, it never would have happened.

Tun was twenty-four, the son of a doctor. He had finished his dental training. His English was coming on at a rapid rate. He was quick to learn. It was good to share the Gospel with him.

Whilst we were working in the new clinic, eight dentists suddenly walked in to observe and help! They had all travelled in from Mandalay.

So the day developed into a full-blown teaching session. Still, we saw about forty patients and explained everything as we went along. Quite tiring, with so many people in the room.

We had been invited out for a meal that night, with some of the hospital staff and the dental team. It was to be in Mandalay, which was an hour away.

We received good news though - we had become known as the "Two Christian Dentists" in the community, which made the whole trip worthwhile. It was a label we were happy to wear.

The meal was, thankfully, simple and in the centre of Mandalay city. There were sixteen of us. The journey there was along roads that were corrugated and potholed; so much so that the van we were in shook and rattled, and so did we. Everything was covered in dust, everywhere teeming with people. The city had a population of five million, no street lights and intermittent electricity.

The next day, six young dentists came and joined us again. We saw quite a few patients and reviewed some we had treated earlier in the week. My last patient of the day required a tooth removing; all was going well until she had a full-blown panic attack, with hyperventilation, rapid pulse and hysteria. It took Jane, myself and some of the others over an hour to settle her down and to finish her treatment. Jane and I prayed hard.

As she was leaving she had another attack, and so we admitted her to the hospital for glucose and observation.

Thankfully, she recovered and went home later that day.

That evening, we went with Tun to visit his family in Mandalay.

His father was a doctor, his uncle a karate teacher and his second uncle a retired head teacher. They all lived in a rambling cluster of buildings set around a large, dirt courtyard, with a big tree in the middle, just off one of the city streets. We were given a huge welcome and chatted.

They had all been to a mission school. Their family extended to about twenty-five people.

It seemed that everyone over the age of fifty-five had received a fairly good education and spoke English, and many had attended a Christian mission school.

We continued treating patients and working with the young dentists over the next ten days. It transpired that most were qualified, but had yet to find a job.

We suggested that it would be a good idea to perhaps use their skills to treat their community free of charge, perhaps one or two days a week.

This concept took off and, fourteen years on, the clinic in Sagaing Hospital was open four days a week, run by volunteer dentists.

We travelled with Dr Ko and his wife up to Shwebo, the town Ko grew up in. It was situated in the rice-growing area of Burma, about four hours west of Sagaing.

Today, 2021 as I write this, Ko is the only surviving child from his family of eleven brothers and sisters.

We stopped off on the way to visit a brand-new, one-hundred-bed hospital that was due to open shortly. Dr Zaw was there with twenty of his team, assembling beds and fumigating the operating theatres.

We were able to design a suitable dental surgery and fittings with him, the plan being for us to visit the hospital following year to run and test the new clinic.

We were pleased that we had got to know quite a lot of people at the hospital. They, too, were getting to know us. We really needed a month or two there.

After a bit of research, we tracked down a Dr Mang Cin Pau, the man who had contacted Christchurch Banstead via word@work (this is a daily devotional sent by e mail to 30,000 people around the world from *BeaconLight* – see page 264). He was a doctor working with The Myanmar Compassion Project. They were based in a small building down a side road in the outskirts of Yangon. They provided medical and dental cover for one hundred and eighty orphanages and monthly financial support for sixty-eight homes.

The director was Prof Dal. He was a gentle, small man who worked tirelessly for this community of children.

The organisation was totally Christian and was licensed by the government. We still help support them (at the time of writing this book 2022). We spent a wonderful time with them, and hoped to visit again.

Returning via Yangon, we were able to meet up with Rev. R Bennett for a Sunday service before flying home.

Psalm 119 v 105: *"Your word is a lamp to guide my feet and a light for my path."*

Chapter 15

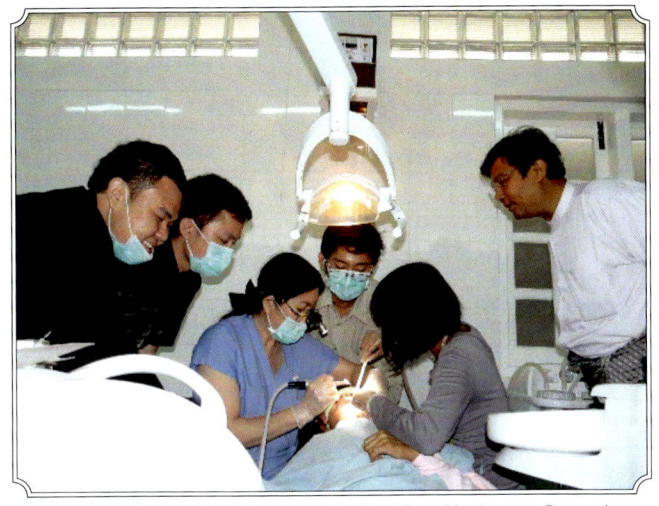

Jane working in the newly-built clinic at Sagaing Hospital

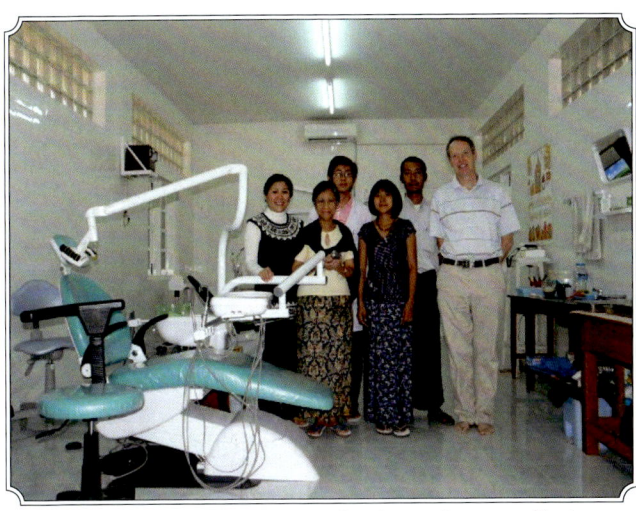

All set for patients in the brand-new clinic

Meeting up with Reverend Tin Win

Centenary Baptist Church, Sagaing

https://youtu.be/xh1yHQATONo
Video of Sagaing Hospital, 2011, near Mandalay Burma

Street life in Sagaing

101

Chapter 16

God Provides

ON REFLECTION, IT WAS QUITE incredible that Dr Zaw had planned, arranged, and built the new dental surgery unit for the hospital in such a short time. Everything worked, and it had a really clean and bright appearance. In fact, set amongst the other facilities in the hospital, it was like stepping into Dr Who's *Tardis*. A small entrance door from a rather grim concrete corridor opened up into this wide, bright, cool, quiet clinic.

Since word had spread about our mercy dental trips around the world, fellow dentists and medical professionals had very kindly begun offering bits of second-hand kit they thought might be useful for impoverished areas.

Their desire to help was much appreciated, and their generosity welcome. But, whilst working with *Mercy Ships* and now, in Myanmar, we had learnt a few essential truths:

When doing work in the Lord's name, you have to try and give of your very best. Everyone doing nursing, medicine and dentistry should be qualified for the task.

Surgeons working in third-world countries need to be skilled and experienced.

It's not a place where we should go to try and improve our own skills, albeit that we are always learning.

Otherwise, it gives God a bad name.

We had heard tales of medical teams arriving from other countries with only rudimentary qualifications, treating patients for cleft lips and other defects and leaving a trail of very poor results and damage behind, then disappearing back to their countries.

Equipment being donated from, say, the UK, would usually be working to a degree, but it was often old and flawed, hence the reason to give it away.

This donation then needed packaging up and dispatching, and then receiving at the destination country. It then needed installing in the correct part of the surgery, be it clinic or hospital.

Chapter 16

Almost always, especially with temperamental dental kit, there were spare parts needed. Almost always, these were unobtainable, so some form of adaptation had to be performed to get said piece of equipment to work. Very often, it was never got to operate properly and would sit, like a white elephant, for all to see but none to use.

On our travels around the world, Jane and I have seen more donated dental chairs not working, than working. They are probably still sitting in the back rooms of medical and dental units as you read this.

The same goes for sterilisers, cautery equipment and, especially, dental delivery systems.

We have, therefore, developed the method of buying new materials, new instruments and new equipment. In Myanmar, these were usually bought in Yangon itself, often manufactured in Korea, China or Vietnam. The local suppliers installed the equipment themselves, and it came with a guarantee. The cost, overall, was often less than shipping secondhand kit from home.

The impression given to the visitor or patient was that the very best was being given in the Lord's name.

We did the same with all the filling materials, antibiotics, anesthetics, hand instruments, sutures, disinfectant, cotton-wool rolls, toothbrushes and toothpaste.

Everything was new, in-date and well-packaged. These latter items we usually brought with us from dental suppliers in the UK.

Why? One of the difficulties we have encountered, when buying antibiotics and local anesthetics abroad, is that many were fake and did not work.

How was all this funded? Well, here's the truth: God funds it.

I can hear your mind racing away at this point. Oh yes, sure, it says, I've heard that one before. The money has to come from somewhere. God doesn't provide a golden money-tree in our back gardens.

Well, you are correct about that last thought. A lot of working for God is about resetting the framework we wish to live in.

If we believe that we follow a Creator God, One who built the Earth, the mountains, seas and the trees, a God who built you and I, then surely it follows that everything belongs to Him?

We are only transient in this world.

God is eternal.

So, all money that comes our way, be they donations, earned income, savings, gifts, or inheritance, ultimately, they are God's.

We are simply caretakers.

Just as in the parable of the talents, we will be held accountable for how we used the skills and funds provided to us by God.

Interestingly, for the majority of trips we undertook, we had to book, arrange and pay for them ourselves first. Only then would some funds arrive to support the journey.

I think and believe that God wants us to take a step of Faith first. He then tells us, OK, good, you are doing this for me; here are some funds to support your efforts.

After our arrival back in Britain we had had a month or two to sort ourselves out after Burma and, before we knew it, we were off to Togo with *Mercy Ships* once again.

Chapter 17

A sea of patients await us in Togo

TOGO IS A COUNTRY in West Africa, bordered by Ghana to the west, Benin to the east and Burkina Faso to the north. The country extends south to the Gulf of Guinea, where its capital, Lomé, is located. Togo covers 22,008 square miles, making it one of the smallest countries in Africa, with a population of approximately eight million, as well as one of the narrowest countries in the world, with a width of less than seventy-one miles between Ghana and its slightly larger eastern neighbour, Benin.

The main language spoken is French, but there are many local languages. It is very poor, just like the majority of West African nations.

One of the common problems with, not just Togo, but also the group of West African nations, was their lack of qualified medical and dental staff. If local children received the education, the funding and the support necessary to become qualified, they invariably moved to work in countries that offered better pay and prospects. This resulted in a huge shortfall of doctors, nurses and dentists that each country needed to look after its own population.

So, one of the main ambitions of the *Mercy Ships* organisation nowadays is not just to see and treat patients in need whilst visiting, it is to encourage and train local doctors, midwives, nurses and dentists so that, when the ship sails away, people are left behind who can continue with the work.

We headed off to join the *Africa Mercy* in May 2010.

A diamond can create a lot of emotions; from amazement, to wonder, from happiness, to fear of losing its very possession.

Jesus has been likened to a diamond by some commentators: total clarity, pureness, inspiring, a transmitter of light and incredibly valuable.

So it was that our trip started off with a diamond. This one attached to a ring of platinum and gold. It arrived, two days before our departure, by courier. Our job was to take it to Alex on board *Mercy Ships* so he could propose to his girlfriend. He had not yet asked her, we had never met Alex and, at the time, we did not know the name of his potential wife.

There was a trust here, unique to Christians working together, and with it came a responsibility, namely - not to lose the thing!

I'd thought about wearing it for safety, but it was better off in the depths of my hand luggage.

Apparently, Alex bought it on the internet from *H. Samuel,* but could not get it shipped or DHL'd out to Togo.

After a smooth journey out to Lomé, we reached the *Africa Mercy* and got all our crew paperwork completed, attending the on-board service that evening.

We had a good time talking with a lady called Cathy, who was out on the *Mercy Ship* for the first time. She had one twenty-two-year-old son, her husband had just retired from the US Air Force, and her "dream" had always been to come out and serve. She had no particular skills or training, but was having a wonderful time helping with all the catering that was needed on the ship.

"I get to meet all the crew," she enthused, "my challenge is to remember all their names as they come to the restaurant area; so far I am up to one hundred and sixty," she told us.

Cathy was on the ship for six weeks and felt the trip had truly touched her since she had been there in Togo.

Our Lomé dental clinic had been set up in the corner of a small hospital about twenty-five minutes' drive from the ship. About one hundred and eighty people were waiting when we arrived, so obviously there was no shortage of business (see photo page 112)!

We had one other dentist with us, a young lady from Holland called Marika. She had been serving for three weeks already and had one week left. Her home church were supporting her and had been vicariously enjoying her adventure in Togo, sharing in regular newsletters she sent them.

Dag, the Norwegian resident dentist, was away in Manchester presenting a paper on osteomyelitis, something we saw a lot of out here in W. Africa.

The clinic the ship had refurbished and equipped was air-conditioned! This was wonderful and a real blessing, since it was extremely hot out there, 39°C.

We treated many patients, a typical example being a lady called Akoko. She had travelled fifty-five miles, had been in pain for five years, and required eight teeth removing. She had heard about *Mercy Ships* from the local TV and had got her nephew to bring her on his zimmejohn motorcycle. She was

Chapter 17

very thrilled to get everything sorted in one visit.

We met up with Alex Williams and gave him the ring. He was on the ship for two years and hoped to propose to his girlfriend, Sharon, by the waterfalls in Ghana that coming weekend.

Our workday was very busy, with lots of tricky surgical work mixed in with showing two teams of visitors round the dental building, something that was quite common and tended to disrupt the general flow of patient care. We also had quite a few children to treat, all needing permanent molars removing, all very apprehensive, all quite exhausting. Still, the reward was to achieve the desired result without scaring off the rest of the Lomé population. Once again, Jane was the star performer. God has given her a special gift when it comes to little ones.

That evening, Jane and I shared a hot chocolate with a lovely, unassuming, quite senior couple called Ian and Jean McColl. He had been on the ship for eight weeks as a general surgeon, with his wife working in recovery. It turned out that Ian was on the Board of Governors for Mercy Ships, as well as a plethora of other organisations. They were an amazing example of humble, kind, compassionate Christians. (see footnote at the end of this chapter)

Whilst we were arriving at the clinic one day, the heavens opened. There was a tremendous thunderstorm, accompanied by lightning and stair-rods of rain.

All the generators got soaked and wouldn't start, so some of the interpreters and I jerry-rigged a plastic rainshield two floors up, with thunderbolts and winds blasting about. At one point, the wind was so strong that the plastic sheeting we were grappling with lifted two of us completely off our feet, like rag-dolls at the end of a rope.

We eventually managed to cover things enough to get started and had an exceptionally busy time, with all of us having a day of difficult surgicals. The other dentist, Marika, had to fly back to Holland that evening, since her mother unexpectedly had to have cancer surgery.

At supper, we met up with Barry and Cheryl from the Liberia trip (see photo page 191).

They took us over to visit the Lomé hospitality centre they ran, which was situated on a compound of about an acre. There were eighty people staying there, and about twenty care-workers.

They were all happily sitting about, singing worship songs, eating and sleeping.

Every Friday, they held a "celebration of sight", where all the patients treated for cataracts the previous week had a final eye-check before discharge. Usually there were about two hundred people plus their families, and they all danced and sang celebrations, giving praise to God for their new sight. The joy was overwhelming.

Cheryl and Barry had no experience in running such a set-up. They had no medical background. There was staff management, rosters to arrange, transport, plumbing, 1500 meals to provide each week, generators, and security issues. With God's help, they have coped with the challenges thrown at them.

We attended a presentation on the *Mental Health Outreach* and the work being done for deaf children. Two teams were running six-week programmes to help build up groups with some experience in Togo for when the ship left.

After our day's clinic we returned to the ship, had supper and ended up talking with the ship's engineers, Dave, Phil, Peter and Al. All were master mariners who tended to hang about together, reminiscing about previous ships, journeys past and memorable events.

They would normally be retired and pruning roses at home (ages ranged from sixty-four to seventy), but God had other plans and here they were, fixing generators, ship's drive units, aircon units, cranes, and electrical fittings, plus loads more.

I was fully briefed on the relative merits of the proposed new 2.5MW generator and the current 1.2MW which was so problematic on the ship. Not to mention a host of technical minutiae that made up the average day of the engineers on board.

All wanting to serve the Lord.

When Saturday arrived we were just getting our picnic lunch when, lo and behold, there was a girl we had met on the flight over, called Marienne. She was a Dutch water engineer, and was working with a separate mission group north of Lomé. She was trying to get on the ship with three other friends to look over the vessel, but had been barred since she had no pass.

They were just about to leave. God's timing is amazing.

We obtained visitor passes for them, and gave them a tour of the ship and explained all the activities.

On the Sunday, we went with a group to the "Fishing Village Church" planted by *Mercy Ships* back in 1996. The church was set amongst a host of sandy shacks with rusty zinc roofs, right by the sea. The Sunday school had about one hundred children in it and the congregation numbered about eighty-five. They

Chapter 17

were currently building a new church and school as funds came in.

As we sat there, with open sides to the church, the ocean only a hundred yards away on one side, fishing boats pulled up onto the beach on the other, people strolled by, stopping to observe the service and our worship for a while. Lots of goats sauntered about, the odd rusty pickup truck, or motorbike, and plenty of children. The Christian message was vital, since the fishing village was known to be steeped in voodoo tradition.

As always on these ventures, my turn came. I talked about Matthew Ch 8 v 23 - Jesus calming the sea - and got everyone to sing *When the Storm Rolls*.

The message preached was from Jacob through to Joseph, ending with people being asked to check with themselves where they were going when they died: Heaven, or Hell. Jesus, or No Jesus. Quite simple, really.

When we got back to the ship, we were invited by Anander and his wife for a Sri Lankan curry in his flat aboard ship. He was the ship's Chief Engineer. They had two children with them on board, who attended the ship's school.

His real heart was for the lost so, after work, he and a team of four or five would drive out to remote village areas and project the "Jesus film" from the rear of their Land Rover.

They would arrive, set up shop in a suitable area, and then go from house to house inviting people to watch the film. Most villages often had only one TV for the whole community, so any form of event was always welcomed. As the sun began to set, first of all the children would arrive, happily running and jumping about, followed by their mums, often with baby on their hip and, last of all, the men would stroll over, usually five or ten minutes after the film had started.

Most nights, three to four hundred would be there, arranged in a natural semicircle, watching the story of Jesus' life. When the film reached the part where Jesus was on the cross, it was stopped. At that point a local minister, working with Anander, would give a short Gospel message and ask people to repent and invite Jesus into their lives. Many would step forward, and those of us joining the group for the evening would pray with the individuals. Names were taken, and efforts made to invite them to their local churches.

It was an amazing ministry that Anander organised.

Question: How many people does it take to remove two small baby teeth from a five-year-old child who is in pain?

Answer: Eight plus one.

Four needed to give the local anaesthetic, plus one local care helper to translate. When all is numb, three more to hold arms, hands and feet, and pray, plus one dentist, who is the ninth. Total time taken: one and a quarter hours.

Happily the child, Sophie, was all smiles five minutes later, and no more painful nights. The dentist (me) needed a lie-down.

I found the workdays exhausting sometimes; it was only through God's grace that we completed the day. Still, the team of helpers were excellent, and the translators essential when trying to explain what we could and couldn't do.

I spent some time removing a large, oval, golf-ball-sized lump from the neck of a lady called Katossi. It had been there for five years. I had no idea what it was, so I sent the thing off for a histopathology test. The good news was that it turned out to be a benign growth.

There were lots of osteomyelitis cases, necessitating big dissections removing great lumps of necrotic bone. We had seven more children with all the associated difficulties in explaining and performing tooth removal. One child, Kossi, needed twelve teeth removing and was HIV positive.

We usually had about 4 HIV patients a day but, with God's help and careful instrument usage, we felt safe and as secure as we could be in that part of the world.

The road to our clinic, adjacent to the beach, was being totally rebuilt into a dual carriageway whilst we were there. The place was swarming with machines, teams of workmen, piles of sand, cement, concrete blocks, street traders, taxis, lorries going to the port and taxi motorcycles and, in and amongst all that, were we, threading our way to and from the clinic.

Some days, our journey was simple, other times it could take an age to negotiate the queues, the potholes, diversions, bulldozers and streams of people.

Jane and I never ceased to be amazed at the breadth and scope of help that was given out in Jesus' name every day of the week. Our contribution was small and quite short, but the ship changed the lives of all who came to serve.

I chatted with the new crew doctor, Dr Pangwa, from UK. He was given three days' notice to come out to the ship, and was there for eight weeks. He originally came from India and was a committed Christian.

He was wandering about the ship, looking a bit bewildered by all the streams of activity.

When you are new to a place, it is always striking how everyone seems to know what to do and where to go. You are swimming in treacle, whilst everyone else is rushing by, looking so very confident. He said he applied because he had felt God calling him.

In the ship's café area was a wooden, upright piano tucked away in a corner. Jane got into a routine of helping some of the children with their piano. She became a bit like the "piano Pied Piper", sitting in the snack area with a cluster of children round her, various tunes gently and carefully emitting from the keyboard.

Oh yes, about the diamond. Alex did pluck up courage to ask his girlfriend Sharon to marry him, by the waterfalls of Ghana, and she said:

Yes!

1 John Ch 3v 1 NIV:

"How great is the love the Father has lavished on us, that we should be called children of God! And that is what we are! The reason the world does not know us is that it did not know him."

Footnote: Lord McColl was born in 1933 and educated at Hutchesons' Grammar School, Glasgow, and St Paul's School, London, where he won a Foundation Scholarship in Classics. He studied Medicine at London University and was Professor of Surgery at Guy's Hospital until 1998. He was also Surgeon to the international charity *Mercy Ships*, and frequently operated in the poorest countries of West Africa. A committed Christian, Lord McColl was made a Life Peer in the Queen's Birthday Honours in 1989, for his work for disabled people.

A Step or Two of Faith

On our way to the clinic

Morning queue for the dental clinic

Showing the "Jesus film" out in the community

Being introduced at the village church

Our dental team in Benin

Precarious ferry transport in Ganvie

Chapter 18

Return to Sagaing near Mandalay

All this activity seemed a long, long way from Wallington, and returning to our home life, our church life and our family life always took a bit of adjustment after these mission trips.

I am sure many who spend years away at a time on mission trips would wonder what on earth I am complaining about. They would infer:

"You're only away for a short time. You should try signing up for a few years, like proper missionaries."

Well, they are probably right. Selling up everything and following Jesus is what He asked one man to do. But I would like to keep encouraging you, the reader, to try short-term mission. You get to see God at work.

I am not grumbling, just stating what happens and how important it is to rest on the Lord before, during and after each trip.

Just travelling to do our dentistry was good, but Jane and I began to realise that getting people who we were privileged to meet to know Jesus, was a better legacy for us to leave behind.

Sending yourself off to another part of the world can have a destabilising effect when you return. You find that you become a little fragmented. Bits of you are left behind, especially when you have made and found new relationships in Christ.

Parts of you are needed by your family, with their requests and demands for attention, and bits of you are playing catch-up with your church family. What is left over, is wanted by friends and acquaintances.

Whilst Jane and I were away, pretty much cut off from most news and current affairs, people at home got on with their lives.

Being short-term, the emphasis tended to be on trying to compress as much as we could into the two, three or four weeks that we had on the mission.

In our day-to-day lives, living at home, spending our days in our town, city and country, we absorb morsels of information from numerous sources. This is all filed away for storage and possible later use.

We began to find we had missing or blank sections of local knowledge. Events that had happened we were unaware of. The same thing at our home church. Special events and guest speakers might be missed, so references to those experiences we did not understand.

What we were learning was how to put our trust in the Lord and not worry about these lost pieces of local news. The Lord would keep His eye on that for us.

Each time we set off for a new excursion, God provided the funds, the safety and the health we required.

When you set off to a foreign place, it is crucial to dedicate the whole project to the Lord. As our trips progressed and we found ourselves doing more gospel work than dental work, having a Christian group of brothers and sisters praying for us became increasingly important.

Our next trip was a return to Burma, in January 2011. This was our third time, and things were beginning to happen. We were not to know this, but more and more items were going to take place each time we returned - helicopter trips, Buddhist monks turning to Christ, churches being rebuilt.

We have a Living God, always working and watching over us.

Burma, January 2011

I AM SURE GOD had a reason He wanted Jane and myself in Burma; already there had been an impact with an improved understanding of Christians just willing to help. We hoped and prayed that people living, working and being treated would ask why we had come, so that we would be unafraid with our Gospel and could be confident for Christ.

Our small motor-truck passed over the scalloped, British, post-war, steel bridge that crossed the huge Irrawaddy River and into Sagaing village.

The road serving the hospital was the same meandering, dusty, gravel track, lined with rather dehydrated, dusty, dishevelled trees. It now had a familiarity about it that created a sense of fondness. A delight in the simplicity and openness of local living. Nothing had changed in the year we had been away. It was as if we had stepped into the CS Lewis wardrobe, to return to Wallington with all its normality, only to re-enter twelve months later to find no time had passed in Burma. Everything was the same.

Every hundred yards or so there were the old buildings, set back from the lane, all looking ancient but which, in fairness, were probably no more than 170 to 190 years old.

Thoughts of "the land that time forgot" came to mind, as everything we saw had an overgrown, tangled and crumbly look about it.

These larger, senescent dwellings held communities of monks and nuns, and extended for about three miles in all directions. This district was bordered by a five-hundred-foot-high cluster of hills that separated the area from the Irrawaddy River.

The hospital backs on to the hillside and, as we drove in, it had the familiar calm, unhurried, peaceful air about it.

Dr Zaw stepped out from his hospital office, wearing the same rather tatty brown jacket he had worn during our previous two visits. He greeted us like long-lost friends, insisting we needed some food at once. He had been away for a few days, helping with the setting-up of another hospital in a predominantly Christian area in Northern Burma.

Meanwhile, we got ourselves settled into our lodgings, which were the same as before.

They had been advertising our impending arrival for the past month, so we were excited to see who the Lord was to send us.

A cluster of patients were waiting the next morning when went to our clinic. We worked our way through the list and stopped for some lunch at one. There was a Christian plastic surgeon from Belgium, along with his anaesthetist, doing twelve cleft-lip repairs a day on children of all ages. He was Professor Albert De Mey. This was his third time there as well. The hospital corridors were cluttered with parents and relatives looking after children in various states of repair, either pre- or post-op.

It is hard to describe how peaceful it was without the constant intrusion of telephones, mobiles, computers, e-mail, texts, TV, *iPads*, etc. After our work, we would talk and chat about things. People had time to eat and time to sleep. They had time for each other without interruptions.

After a couple of days, both Jane and I were feeling a bit under the weather, probably as a result of the extended trip getting there. We saw some patients, with Dr Ko and Molly translating.

In the afternoon, I set off with Dr Ko, a Dr Ong, two dental technicians, a driver and some builders, to check out the new dental clinic at The Byamaryu Hospital in Sitagu. It was about an hour's drive along a bumpy road. We planned to work there Thursday to Saturday each week. Apparently, there were a lot of people needing help in this region. Jane stayed on at the Sagaing Hospital to see patients.

It was just as well we went; the clinic was all topsy-turvy and had very little kit there. We checked over the new chair and compressor, mended a leak in the air-line, got the water running, and measured up for some more furniture and flooring. We had discussions with the hospital manager regarding patient flow, etc., and made a list of instruments and materials to bring up with us.

Although open, the hospital was not really up and running. Getting staff on a permanent basis was difficult, due to a lack of funding.

The local community lived in wooden houses with thatched or corrugated iron roofs, connected by earthen paths and decorated with a variety of farm animals wandering about.

The next day, we returned to the Sitagu hospital at 7am with a team of fourteen and loads of dental kit.

Why fourteen? Well, Jane and myself, Dr Ko and his wife, Molly (to interpret), two dentists to act as dental nurses, a two man film crew, a doctor, two student dentists, a driver and a dental technician.

We were met by a reception committee of a further ten people, plus the thirty to forty patients who were there to be treated.

For the past few days a truck, equipped with huge, metal, cone-shaped loudspeakers, had been going from village to village advertising our forthcoming arrival.

We had a pretty chaotic day. There were difficulties with new equipment that wouldn't behave, and frantic phone calls to Yangon to get technical advice. Everyone clustering around the clinic, eagerly/anxiously watching what was going on. The film crew mixed up in everything. Visitors and delegations coming to see the surgery in action.

All in all, quite exhausting but, praise God, all went well. Everyone was seen and treated, photos were taken, films made, hands were shaken.

We returned to Sagaing along the jarring road, all of us once again crammed into our van, weaving past the usual impediments of ox carts, horses, motorbikes, herds of goats being driven home for the night, bicycles and lorries. Everything was shrouded in dust and coloured orange by the setting sun.

We saw fifty-two patients the next day, and even more the day after that, all from the local surrounding villages. They provided a rich tapestry of colours and style, big straw hats, betel-nut teeth, suntanned, lined faces from working in the fields, wide, gap-toothed grins. Tough, sandpaper hands and feet.

Each one loved by God.

Chapter 18

The following morning, as we were having breakfast, the Chief Monk, or Abbot, made a surprise, grand entrance, accompanied by his entourage of helpers. He was, to the Burmese Buddhists, the equivalent of our Archbishop of Canterbury, and was able to diplomatically walk the line between the junta and the Burmese people.

He liked the concept of *Mercy Ships*, and had decided to try and organise a vessel to help the people in the southern delta area. There was only one hospital there, to serve an area the size of England.

We had a lively discussion about Compassion, God and Love, and he asked if we could come back next year to help with the ship project! So much so that, that very day, he sent Dr Zaw and a team of eighteen to go southwards to the delta region, to fact-find and assess the possibilities.

He told us that the seed for the idea of providing hospitals came from a visit he did to a Christian Mission Hospital in northern Burma forty years ago, and a visit to a convent near Ostend once, whilst stranded due to a storm in the English Channel.

The Abbot was quite excited about the ship idea for the delta region. He asked when we could come back to help with this. We gave that request to God, and we were to see what he had to say about it.

You will see, later on in this book, that we arranged for him to visit the *Africa Mercy* in Pointe Noire, Congo, a year or two after this meeting.

We were both getting tired after a week so, come the Sunday, we set off to find a church to have a day of rest. We explained that, although the clinic was open, we would not be there, since it is God's Sabbath day.

We went to the *Southerland Memorial Baptist Church* in Sagaing town. We were given a very warm welcome, and shook everyone's hand at least twice.

Jane and I then spent the next few days alternating our time between Sagaing and Sitagu hospitals, commuting up and down the dusty, bumpy roads. The need was greater up at the more rural Sitagu region. The numbers requesting treatment were doubling every time we went there, I suppose as our name spread.

Jane and I were both having dodgy tummies. I took four Imodium tablets on one day alone. It tended to knock the stuffing out of us and, just as we needed the greater energy, we were found wanting. But, with God's grace, we recovered.

Whilst going on our travels up and down the Mandalay roads, we had a chance to talk with a lot of different people. Quite a few had relatives or friends who were

Christian. The Gospel was at work there. We hoped that we were standing strong for Jesus in our time there.

We had been reading John's and Peter's letters. 1 Peter Ch 4 v 10-11 is a passage that inspired us:

"Each of you should use whatever gift you have received to serve others, as faithful stewards of God's grace in its various forms.[11] If anyone speaks, they should do so as one who speaks the very words of God. If anyone serves, they should do so with the strength God provides, so that in all things God may be praised through Jesus Christ. To him be the glory and the power for ever and ever. Amen."

Chapter 18

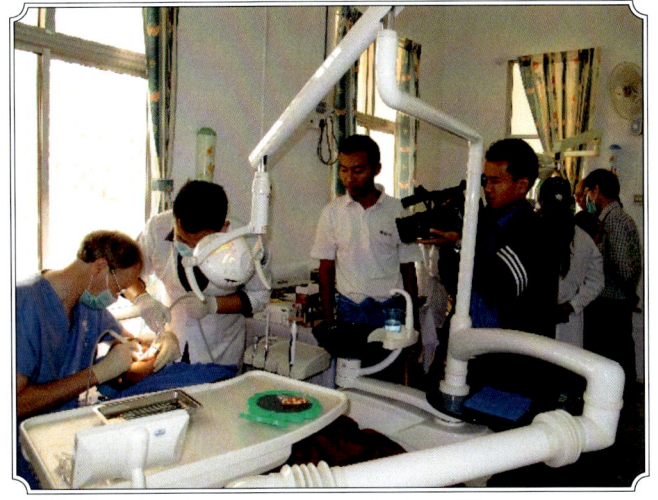

The Byamaryu hospital in Sitagu.

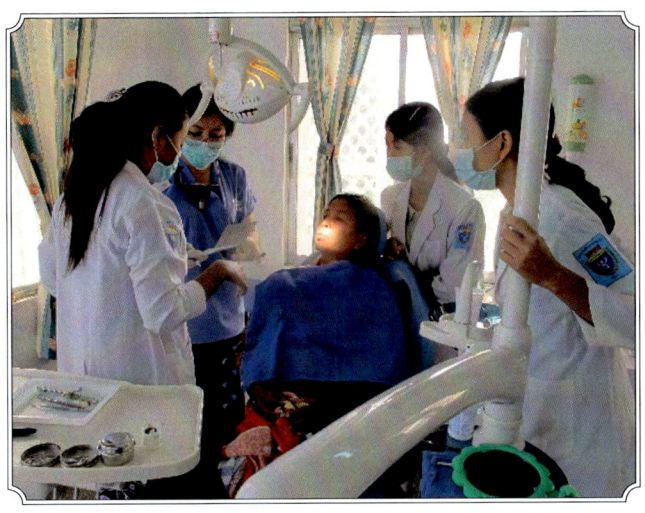

Jane with her team

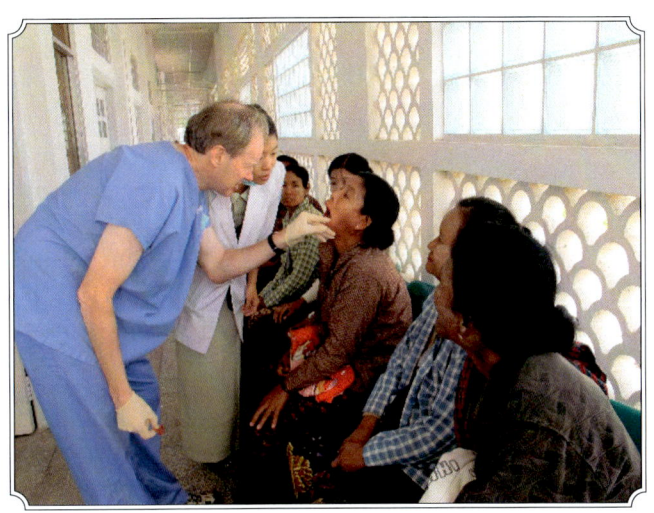

Checking patients after treatment

Patients arriving by ox cart

Meal time with the young dentists

Plenty of room on the roof!
A common sight in Burma

119

Chapter 19

August 2011 – Risks and Encouragement in China and Mongolia.

GOING TO CHINA, AND THEN on to Mongolia, came about via a friend, Cynthia Bong, whom we met whilst attending St Andrews Church in Brunei.

She spoke fluent Mandarin and had some Christian friends she wanted us to meet in Shanghai, and then also another contact in Ulaan Baatar in Mongolia, called Solomon. He was a minister working with the nomadic herdsmen who were living in yurts near the capital.

The result was that we found ourselves flying to Shanghai in August 2011.

Shanghai

I'LL BE HONEST WITH YOU, we did not really know what to expect on this mission trip. It was way outside my comfort zone and we had a very open agenda. Basically, it was to meet up with some Christians in Shanghai and then help do some dentistry in Mongolia. We had three weeks allocated. It was going to be interesting to see what God wanted us to do.

We were kindly met by Hwang and her son, Kevin (name changed for security reasons). They were from a local house church with two hundred-plus members. They drove us to a small hotel near to where they lived in Shanghai, and we crept into bed at 2am.

The next morning, they took us to dinner to meet up with some members from their underground church. They met on Sundays for a morning service and they then had a youth service in the afternoon. There was also a Bible study and prayer session on Saturdays. English was quite limited in China; written English even less so.

The couple we were travelling with, Cynthia and Ah Toh, her husband, arrived the next day and we all went for a meal with the house church minister, John and his wife, Glory (names changed for security). They worked full time, looking after their house church.

Were they successful at explaining the Gospel?

Chapter 19

That month, before we had arrived on July 14, they baptised one hundred and thirty-nine people, aged from fifteen to eighty!

Shanghai district has a population of… wait for it… two hundred million people. The locals call it the "city of heads", i.e. all you see whilst walking about are seas of heads packed together.

I gave John a stack of *CrossCheck* booklets and the DVD. He seemed to think they would be useful and translating would be no problem. (We have since translated the *CrossCheck* booklets into traditional and simplified Mandarin.)

We talked about the difficulties they faced and it quickly became apparent that everything was very sensitive and fraught with possible trouble. They were very worried about the attention I, as a Caucasian, might bring, especially when I asked if we could attend a home church service. There were worried looks, and a troubled silence descended.

Having explained that the last thing we wanted was to threaten their work, it was felt that Jane could be absorbed into their numbers without creating too much notice. She therefore went off to join a prayer meeting with the underground house church that Friday evening. Let her tell the story of what happened in her own words:

Jane:

I went at 9pm with our hostess to an underground car park near the city centre. We climbed up a stairwell to the third floor; this was above the shops on a main street. A man opened the wrought-iron gates and locked it carefully behind him. We were led into a large auditorium, where about four hundred people were standing without their shoes on. Foam matting covered the floor in front of a raised platform.

Everyone was singing hymns with the aid of a projection screen and a pianist. Being Chinese, I blended in and looked just like every one else. Some of the congregation greeted me warmly, like a long-lost friend. My Mandarin lessons really paid off. The praises they sang sounded familiar. Then we were invited to kneel and pray. There were open prayers and communal prayers. They prayed for the ministry of the word of God to be effective and spread through the nation. They prayed for the ministers and they prayed for their workplaces, that they would not lose their jobs should their employers find that they were Christians.

As we prayed together, so the prayers were raised with tongues almost in unison. We prayed as a single body, the rhythm rose and fell at the same rate. A cool breeze circulated around us, comforting us on that hot, humid summer's night in the heart of the city.

An enormous peace fell over the room. As the voices were raised to thank the Lord, so one of the men started to thank God in fluent Austrian - I could only understand the 'Danke schon'. Later, I discovered that he spoke only Mandarin. We left the worship at 11pm, but they were planning to carry on until 1am. Praise God.

They pray every Friday from 6pm to 1am, and the larger group meets once a month. Their prayers were so heartfelt, I felt honoured to be allowed to join them on this one occasion.

Nigel:
On the Saturday, we spent some more time with our Christian hosts, who showed us where they lived and their community areas.

Shanghai is an enormous, bustling city, filled to the brim with people. Everywhere you go, from pavement to viewing point, from restaurant to street café, you will be pressed from either side by fellow human beings. You feel quite safe; it does not have the undercurrent of edginess or tension you sometimes feel in West Africa, but the sheer weight of humanity takes a bit of getting used to.

On Sunday, we were up at 6am to give us time to pack our things, have some breakfast and to check out of where we were staying.

Hwang picked us up at 8.30am and took us to the Holy Trinity Church. Regrettably, we were not able to join her own church. It was very kind of her, since she would normally have been attending her own house church. The service was conducted in Mandarin and was similar to high Anglican. There were four to five hundred people there.

One of the problems for Christians in China is that there are very few officially-licensed churches available, so the formation of house churches keeps gathering apace.

Following the service, we went back to Hwang's flat and were able to ask how the growth takes place. She explained:

Once a week, every member of the church invites someone or some people for a meal, and they explain the Gospel to them. If well-received, they keep asking those people and keep explaining, answering questions and giving their testimonies. From this, many people come to Christ and join their house church.

They are only allowed to attend the church once they have asked Jesus into their lives.

They are increasing their numbers by a third every year.

We bade farewell to Hwang and boarded the bullet train for Beijing.

Chapter 19

Journey time: 1200km in five hours. Ticket cost: £45.00.

Although this train had crashed recently, we trusted that God would get us there OK.

A typhoon caught Shanghai. We had high winds and heavy rain, with some trees down. This did not, apparently, have an adverse affect on the train. Not like "leaves on the line" in the UK causing mass delays.

The train terminal resembled our new Terminal 5 at Heathrow, except it was a mile long and joined up with the airport terminals. The big difference was that they were completely packed with thousands of Chinese, all very good at finding the correct queue to be in.

I don't think I, as the only Caucasian, blended in too well.

We were severely delayed in the departure lounge at the Beijing airport, with a huge thunderstorm; lightning and thunder everywhere. We prayed for a safe flight to Ulaan Baatar. We had made contact with our hosts and would be staying in a small apartment complex whilst we were there.

As we stood in the check-in queue, we met a girl called Crystal, who asked if we could contact a Christian orphanage she knew of in Mongolia. This is how God often works, putting fellow Christians together at just the right time and place.

Mongolia

We arrived in Ulaan Baatar at 4am and were met by Cynthia's son, Jonathan, who had been there for three months, a man called James, who was PA to the Prime Minister, and his assistant.

James' father had spent a lifetime smuggling Bibles into China, despite great risk to himself over the years.

They kindly loaded our stuff into two cars and took us to our small hostel to stay.

We were not sure how information travelled in Mongolia, but we were surprised that the minister was taking an interest in our visit.

The capital city, Ulaan Baatar, resembled a partly-finished factory building site; lots of utilitarian, brutish blocks, with unfinished roadsides of gravel and earth. Power cables ran in a maze of haphazard directions all along, across and over the dusty, traffic-filled roads. Lots of people were walking about everywhere, carefully avoiding potholes and broken pavements. The men were strong and stocky, consistent with their four thousand years of wrestling experience; the women were tall and slim. Families had four or more children.

The men focused their time on wrestling, archery, horseback riding and protection. Still harking back to the Genghis Khan era of centuries ago. The women seemed to do pretty much everything else, from bringing in the wages, child-raising and house management. Most came from a nomadic heritage and so their roles were still pretty much unchanged. We discovered that adapting to life in a concrete apartment block was proving very difficult for many of Ulaan Baatar's citizens.

There were huge, five- or six-foot diameter, steaming, rusty steel pipes running alongside many roads, connecting one block of flats to the next. Part of the centralised heating system giving the suburbs an apocalyptic feel to them.

We met up with a pastor called Solomon, who was a very pleasant, gentle young man, aged thirty-three, married with two children. He had arranged for us to meet a series of people over the next few days, starting with two Christian men named Baaska and Badran. They were in their thirties, tall, strong and dressed like something from a spaghetti western - rough shirts, worn, tough boots, leather and fur coats, and a heavy five o'clock shadow. They worked with the thousands of herdsmen who were now encamped around the capital. Most had lost their means of survival when their herds of yaks, horses and cattle had frozen to death in a super-cold winter snap in 2009.

They took us to the outskirts of Ulaan Baatar, where these once-proud, independent people now scratched a $2-a-day living by sorting through the city's garbage.

Baaska and Badran worked with families there, preaching the Gospel and helping where they could.

The people lived in a collection of ramshackle houses and yurts, which are the Mongolian circular tents. Their homes were randomly spread on the rolling hillsides surrounding the city of Ulaan Baatar. No order to them, no water supply, drains, or electrics. How they survived in the winter, when the temperature dropped to -45°C for months on end, I have no idea.

We set up shop in a yurt tent, that normally acted as Baaska's church, and looked at children and adults (see photos page 130/1). They had a lot of dental problems.

As we were treating people, the word got out and, after an hour, a large crowd began to develop. We had only limited supplies of needles and local anaesthetic, so we treated as many as we could and hoped to return the following Friday. It was quite an experience, working with no dental chairs, lights, suction, assistants, materials, etc., but the people were very friendly and lent a hand where possible (see photo page 130).

The following day, we hoped to meet the head of the local dental school, Bazar Amarsaikhan. Solomon phoned him regarding our visit, and it transpired that he was a Christian and had been praying for some outside help to come.

Well, the meeting with the professor did not occur that day, and he seemed to have disappeared for the moment. We spent the morning with Pastor Solomon, and were chatting about Ephesians 6 when his phone suddenly went; it was a lady called Norah. She was the legal and special adviser to the current Prime Minister, and wanted to meet up with us!

We set off and had lunch with her and her husband; she was a Christian and was very interested about what we were up to. We explained about the people we had been treating, who live off the garbage dump, and she was totally enthralled.

She said she had always wanted to arrange a charity hospital for people who had no funding, and we discussed possible sources. She was meeting up with one of the world's leading mining companies the next day and intended to ask them for some help, in return for being in Mongolia.

Norah (see photo) has a great heart and compassion for her Mongolian people.

After her meeting, she planned to join us at our makeshift clinic on the outskirts of Ulaan Baatar. We explained that we were running low on materials and, within a few phone calls, she had located a source for us. So we went and stocked up with more anaesthetic, gloves, needles, tissues and filling materials.

We were bowled over by the way God had arranged our days and the people He has put us in touch with. It was very exciting watching His plans unfold. We prayed that nothing would get in the way of Norah's efforts (We are still in touch with Norah in 2021; she keeps well and continues to walk with the Lord).

Later on, Solomon took us to a large, peaceful and welcoming Christian café run by four local churches, including his own, where he said lots of people met up during weekdays. Over coffee, he told us of his ministry with the eleven- to seventeen-year-olds in the local schools. That year alone, he and his team had spoken to seventeen thousand teenagers. We prayed for his ministry, that it would touch the emerging generation.

We were greeted by a huge breakfast spread the next morning!

That night before, we had had some spare time, so Jane and I ended up showing the owner and staff of the Hostel some of the films and photos we had taken illustrating what we had been doing. We explained about the displaced nomadic folk and how they survived by foraging through the city garbage dump.

Because of the language difficulty, we were not sure how much was understood. I think God touched their hearts somehow, hence the feast. They kindly offered to launder our scrubs, clinical towels and linen covers every day, free, for the remainder of our stay there.

We had been expecting a transport pick-up by 12 midday, but nothing happened. After a few phone calls, it transpired that Norah, the minister's adviser, had arranged a reporter and a film crew to come with us. This caused a problem with Baaska, since the garbage community had had some bad experiences in the past with the authorities. He was refusing to take us.

We decided to pray and gave the problem to God and, by 12.30, we were collected; we met up with Norah, but her film crew got lost and so were left behind.

This time we were better prepared and had stocked up well on materials. We treated eighty-five adults and children in the circular yurt. It was full of families when we arrived, and the day was fairly chaotic. Norah made her film using my small HD *Flip* camera (see QR codes page 131). She was shocked and amazed at the number of people and how they lived.

She managed to broadcast the film and get an article in the newspaper. We prayed that God would be glorified in all this.

We returned from the city outskirts, and had to rush for a meal with the Education Minister and his family. Another first for us.

We spent some time with them, discussing why we had travelled to Mongolia, and our wish to help people in the name of Jesus. He was sceptical, trying to uncover some hidden agenda we might have had. In the end we parted amicably, since he realised we were not going to be any political threat to his Education ministry. Walking back, we dropped into a local restaurant run by an Irishman, Sean Henessey. We chatted about our mission here, and he wanted us to see the local orphanage that he supported, run by a Catholic nun. Which we did, later on that day.

Whilst attending a Sunday service, held in a large conference room in a hotel and organised by Solomon, we had a chance to meet some local members of the city community. A lot of the women and children were away on a weekend retreat. However, there was an exciting presentation by one of their missionaries who had been working in Tibet. She had just returned after working there for 8 months. Solomon gave a good message on the Armour of God (Ephesians Ch.6) and, following the service, we went with him for a Mongolian lunch and, finally, met up with Professor Bazar Amarsaikhan and his wife and daughter.

He was Dean of the Mongolian dental school. We spent the next day with him, and he told us he had his "Nehemiah Project", which was to build a new dental school and staff it with fully-trained PhD lecturers (completed in 2021).

He took us to the old dental school premises and then on to the new one, due to be opened in September that year. Every day, he declared to his staff of eighty that God led the project and would provide for, and watch over, all of them.

The new building was given to him as a result of prayer. It is situated in the poorer outskirts of Ulaan Baatar. There had been no government funding, so he was planning to charge patients a small token fee. We gave him Norah's contact details and prayed that these two Christian leaders could get together to work out some funding for the project. The new premises were on 4 floors, and was a stunning facility, right in the area where the need was greatest, on the outskirts of the city near where we had been working!

Norah arrived with her husband, Gant. We had a good talk about things, and I gave her lots of our photos and some films I had made of the interviews and dental treatments. We then sat down and did some Bible study on Exodus Ch 4 vv 2 and 3. I asked if Gant was a Christian and he said he was not, yet. So I gave him my testimony and also went through *CrossCheck*, and we prayed together. The time went quickly, so a breakfast meeting was arranged to carry on where we left off.

Norah picked us up from our hostel the next morning. She drove us to her apartment and cooked us breakfast! We did another Bible study, on Jeremiah Ch 2 v 13 (tending broken cisterns.).

Our prayers were answered as, ten years on, the dental school is prospering under the Christian leadership of Professor Bazar Amarsaikhan. We keep in touch on *Facebook*.

In Ulaan Baatar, getting about town was fairly easy. You stood by the roadside and waved a hand. Anyone driving by with a free seat, instantly turned into a taxi!

We went on from Norah and Gant to a small restaurant, to have lunch with the Deputy Prime Minister and his wife, who was the Deputy Health Minister. I am not really sure how this came about. They were not Christian, and were deeply suspicious of missionaries; we therefore had a very careful conversation.

It turned out that she was a dentist and had trained under Professor Bazar

Amarsaikhan. I explained what a superb facility he was building, and expressed my hopes that some funding might be possible so that the poor communities could be treated by the students, free of charge. As we chatted, the two of them began to relax, and even asked if they could show us round their country.

We took a drive out to see the wide open expanse of the Mongolian countryside. Miles and miles of grassland with mountain ranges bordering the plains. Very few houses, but quite a few yurts about. We were taken by John, a minister friend of Solomon, to a summer house just outside the city, and met his wife, three-month-old son and his mother-in-law. He was passionate about the Lord, and explained a lot of things regarding Christian life, churches and the Mongolian people.

He took us to the airport and we were seen off by James, Aggu, Jonathan, Scott and some further Christian friends.

Mongolia has a population of three million. It is the world's most sparsely populated country. It fought for, and achieved, separation from China in 1921 with Russian help. However, Russia signed a treaty with China in 1924, handing back ownership of the country. The Soviet Union officially recognised Mongolian independence in 1945, but it took another forty-five years before the "modest meeting", organised by the Mongolian Democratic Union on 10th December 1989.

This meeting landmarked the start of the Democratic Movement in Mongolia. A gathering of over one hundred thousand people took place on 4th March 1990, on the square at Cinema Yalalt, now known as the Square of Liberty where, sitting at one raised side, there sits a huge, dark-coloured statue of Genghis Khan (born Temujin around 31st May, 1162), and still a massive presence in the country.

The first democratic elections were held in July 1990. The People's Republic of Mongolia officially ceased to exist on 13th February 1992, with Mongolia becoming an independent country.

Major challenges for the government were employment, education and children's welfare. The very idea of the traditional, nomadic way of life is under threat. "Insider capitalism" yields great wealth for a few, but leads to gripping poverty for most others. Failing to address this adequately has already caused the collapse of one government. Pray that the leaders of Mongolia might rule with fairness and wisdom.

In 1989, there may have been only four Mongolian Christians. By 2000, there was an estimated community of eight to ten thousand. Today, there are over forty thousand believers, in hundreds of churches and groups, meeting in most parts of the country.

We did not return to Mongolia, which was a pity, since many amazing things happened during our short, three-week visit. The good thing, upon reflection, was that we had been able to keep in touch via e-mail, *Messenger* and *Facebook*.

We continued to encourage and share Bible verses with many of those we met whilst there. The country is very remote and quite cut off, so do keep it in your prayers.

Mark Ch 16 v 15:

"He said to them, 'Go into all the world and preach the gospel to all creation'."

A Step or Two of Faith

Ah Tow, Cynthia, Jonathan, James, Nigel, Jane and Tony

Jane, Nigel, Jonathan and Cynthia (back row) Baaska, Solomon and Badran (front row)

Rev. Johnny and his family, Cynthia, Jane and Nigel.

Our volunteer dental team outside our yurt clinic

Thousands living outside Ulaan Baatar

Our first, rather elderly patient

Chapter 19

Practising opening wide

Our youngest patient

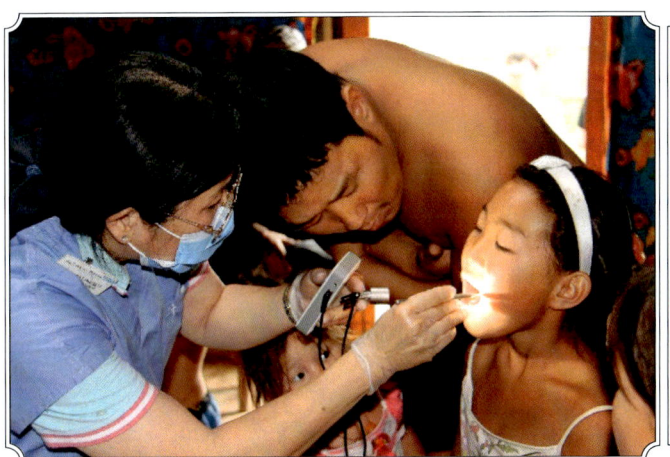

Working in a yurt with virtually no assistance or equipment, everyone lends a hand.

https://youtu.be/F7dZR5UPvHg
Ulaan Baatar dental outreach, 2011

https://youtu.be/fRZ3gm5Waul
Some testimonies in Mongolia, 2011

131

Chapter 20

1300 children to examine! Plus teachers.

Returning to Burma in January 2012 was filled with anticipation and excitement.

Firstly, we were beginning to form friendships, and remained in contact with these people whilst home in the UK, so we were looking forward to seeing them again.

Secondly, the country was seeing a total opening of communications since the military junta had relinquished some of its control, allowing an elected government to have a greater say in how things were run.

Aung San Suu Kyi, the Nobel Peace Prize winner and long-term figurehead of Myanmar, had been released from twenty years of house arrest and was the new face of Burma. As a result, international sanctions were being removed, and foreign investment, tourism and businesses were opening up for the first time in fifty years.

Flying out to Yangon this time, we had prayed that God would use us for His own purposes during our visit.

We had arranged to go to a town called Hpa An, in south-east Burma but, despite getting work permits from the chief minister of the Department of Health, the military, the town officials and their dental council, it was deemed that the area was not safe or secure enough for foreign nationals to stay there - there was a deep sense of suspicion between the Christian Karen people and the Buddhist groups in that region.

With so many different tribes and cultures in Burma, there has been endless friction and minor conflict in the country since it was liberated from the Japanese at the end of the Second World War. Many agreements had been made to different tribal groups to encourage their support during the war years, only for all these promises to be broken under the new regime. So there continues, even today, an atmosphere of distrust and non-cooperation from these disenfranchised groups.

Chapter 20

When we arrived at Yangon Airport, it was already twice as busy as it had been the year before. Cars everywhere, whistles blowing, crowds of people waiting to meet and greet. A calm but busy mix, all so characteristic of the Burmese way of doing things.

We stayed initially in a house with some of Dr Ko's family, which was just as well, as all the hotels and guest houses were fully booked.

The publicity about Burma's opening-up seemed to have started something; Burma was not ready, the roads were still bumpy and potholed, the streets were still busy and the electricity still prone to 'brown-outs.' There were way too few hotel rooms and no public transport suitable for travellers, and many of the background essentials, like health provision, insurance, banking services, and legal support, were non-existent.

On the Sunday, we met up with Rev. Reginald Bennett at the Holy Trinity Cathedral, which was packed for the morning service. He led the service and, at the end, removed his ceremonial cassock to be dressed in informal jeans and t-shirt. He encouraged us all to stay on for a twenty-minute Bible study with him. It was an excellent evangelistic talk, based on Romans 10, with a *PowerPoint* presentation. Over two hundred people stayed on to listen.

As a result of the security issue, we decided to return to Mandalay and Sagaing Hospital, to help with a charity school situated a short distance from the hospital.

We visited the mixed school on the afternoon we arrived in Sagaing. It had 1300 pupils, spread all around a rambling arrangement of wooden huts and buildings connected by a series of hard, caked-mud paths.

It was certainly a very lively place, the children being aged from four to sixteen. We found a suitable room and agreed to screen as many as possible on the Wednesday.

Wanting to see how our new clinic was doing, we travelled the two-hour bumpy ride back to Sadaw hospital, where we had established a surgery the previous year.

We managed to treat fifty or so patients, taking two young dentists with us, plus a good team of local helpers through the day. We had a wonderful welcome from everyone, and it was great to meet up with them all again. There were opportunities to pray with patients, and good discussions over lunch.

The dental clinic looked in good shape and was regularly used. In fact, it was the only part of the new hospital that was being used properly. They had no resident medical staff there, and so local people never knew from one day to the next when a doctor would be at the hospital. To have a resident doctor there would cost $140 US per month in salary, but the hospital had no funding and, therefore, no doctor.

Wednesday was our big screening day.

At 7am, we all set off for the school, only a fifteen-minute walk from the hospital up a dusty track.

It was all pretty chaotic and, I am glad to say, filled with laughter and happiness.

Children were collected, with their teachers, in batches of forty. They were given a ten-minute oral hygiene lesson. Next, they were sent over to us, in groups of twenty at a time, to be examined and given a toothbrush. Any child needing urgent dental treatment was given a numbered note which they took to their teacher, who logged them down. We had two people cleaning and sterilising instruments, two holding torches and heads, two interpreting and handing out brushes, two giving health education, and two sorting and organising the children (see photos page 141).

We also had one doctor travelling with us, who examined the children for ringworm and scabies. Out of 1300 children, six hundred had ringworm and one hundred had scabies. Ringworm creates round patches on the skin or scalp, with a red raised edge and a clearer centre - they are scaly and very itchy.

All we then had to do was to treat the one hundred and ten children whom we had found to be needing urgent dental care.

The next day, we returned to the Sadaw hospital to treat patients. Another two-hour trip along the dusty, bumpy road, and two hours back again. We took a member of staff back with us to the Sagaing hospital so that we could take a large, full-face OPG radiograph of her. As we had some time, and the excellent facilities at our Sitagu clinic, we extracted the impacted wisdom tooth for her and saw a few other patients.

Come the Friday, we started the day with prayer, as we did every day, as well as reading a chapter from The Bible. But it was essential, because we were starting on the one hundred and ten young patients who all needed urgent treatment.

I would often get up at 6am to go down to a nice old tree alongside the road, situated just outside the hospital grounds; it actually had an internet connection of sorts. I'd sit myself down on my now familiar wooden bench, and nod and smile a greeting to a couple of people who were crouched on their haunches nearby.

Chapter 20

It was very cool in the morning, even chilly, so the mosquitoes were not about at that time of day. I'd sit there with my *iPad*, a symbol of twenty-first-century technology contrasting with the morning traffic of cyclists, horse carts and pedestrians going about their day, much as they have for hundreds of years.

There was an ever-present plume of white dust in the air, kicked up by wheel and foot and it hung about, coating the trees, the walls, the people and animals with a fine, soft layer; almost giving the impression, to the observer, that he was looking at life through a piece of fine, white gauze.

Suddenly, thirty-eight e-mails would arrive with a woosh, from what seemed another planet, and I'd set about replying and sending. Whilst I was typing away, well-wrapped souls, with puffer-jackets and hats, would shuffle past, often carrying bundles of goods to sell. They would find their regular spot, beneath a tree or in the lee of an old wall, and would set up their stall for the day. Bags of nuts, satsumas, very small, but very sweet, packets of biscuits and dried fruit. Mobile phone accessories, cables, connectors and phone covers would be on another wooden table further along. All expectantly and quietly awaiting the day's trade.

Having sorted the mail, I would head back up through the throng of gathering patients and arriving staff, and go to the small canteen where we had our meals.

We usually had a breakfast of rice noodles and some local, traditional soup, plus some toast (my request) and tea or coffee.

We headed over to the clinic, through the enlarged cluster of patients and relatives once again, to get set up for the one hundred and ten young people set to arrive as a result of our screening. These were a lot of young people who had never received dental care before. Most had huge holes in their adult molars, principally caused by a sweet shop that was situated actually in the school grounds. Each morning, before the clinic started, we would gather everyone together and we would pray for the six 'C's : Compassion, Consideration, Care, Concern, Carefulness and Kindness.

The children had been told to come down from their school in groups of eight and, as we finished the first four, they would return to their school to send the next eight, and so on.

Some treatments were simple, some quite complex; some children were easy to treat, some very nervous. After two hours, we had treated twenty-three children from four to eighteen years old.

I was just getting into the swing of things when my stomach started cramping up every few minutes, like some annoying, ultra-slow, relentless metronome.

There was now a gaggle of twelve children outside in the waiting corridor; we had all three chairs filled, plus two extra patients going numb. Everyone was at full stretch, instruments being washed and sterilised, translators talking ten to the dozen, patient cards being filled in, teachers asking if they, too, could be seen whilst they were here. Meanwhile, my stomach was now cramping every minute; I was feeling cold and clammy, and prayed for strength and control.

We got to one o'clock and had to finish the last three waiting before lunch, having seen fifty-three.

I rushed back to our little room and loosed half the planet.

It was so frustrating having such a susceptibility to food poisoning. I felt very cold and washed out, so went outside and sat in the warm sun, praying to God to give me a hand in the afternoon. We simply couldn't let everyone down, not with all these eager young people and all this preparation.

I returned to the clinic to find Jane still working away, and entered the fray once more.

Someone gave me a strong, sweet coffee and I sipped *Coca-Cola*, which revived me a bit, so as to keep going until the late afternoon (it was a survival technique, plus endless Imodium, that I would have to adopt on nearly all our trips to Burma).

We had managed ninety-five patients, but were both very tired. I returned to the room, where the diarrhoea continued through the night. Jane gave me some rice and ginger, which also helped.

I woke feeling totally washed out. Fortunately we had planned a rest day, so I had a chance for a bit of recovery time.

In the afternoon, we visited a charity school in Mandalay with six thousand students! We met with the headmaster and his team and he took us on a tour of the place. It was like a small town.

We discussed the possibility of coming over a day or two later to see and treat some children. There were quite a few orphans from the huge tsunami disaster of December 2007.

Praise God I was feeling a lot better the following day. We had some food and went to church.

We visited the Centenary Baptist Church, situated right next to the Irrawaddy River. The young people were full of enthusiasm and sang some wonderful praise songs. The sermon was in Burmese, so we were none the wiser at the end, though we could, at least, read the passage from Luke 8 in our own

Bible. The greeting was very warm from everyone in the congregation, but the place seemed to lack the energy and joy found in other more vibrant churches we had visited, which was a shame.

We handed out a large pile of *CrossCheck* booklets and gave out pens to the youngsters which had **"The Earth is the Lord's and Everything in it"** - Psalm 24 v 1 - printed on the side. On each mission trip we ventured on, we wanted to leave some Bible scripture with as many people as possible. The pens were the simplest and best method.

Everyone wanted a pen, so everyone received one. With the Bible verse on it. We would usually bring two thousand or more different-coloured pens to hand out to patients, staff, airport officials, policemen, or shopkeepers.

Come Monday, as things worked out, we cleared all the patients at the hospital we were staying at by 11am so, having located the van driver, we loaded up our dental kit, our dental team and a huge bag of satsumas, and set off for the large charity school in Mandalay.

The traffic was always very busy on the road to Mandalay town. Our route took us down the dusty lane and over the giant, steel-girder road/rail bridge, built by the British just after the Second World War. The roads and byways were crammed with a plethora of varied transportation, each heading in their chosen directions, driving down slip roads the wrong way to avoid the toll booths that were dotted about, driving on the shady side of the road, stopping to buy some watermelons, loading and unloading baskets of goods, and vehicle repairs being carried out wherever they happened to be.

The river was at its lowest level in January, so the fertile riverbed became a hive of activity as tomatoes, greens, rice, etc. were planted and grown before the rainy season in May/June time, when the river swells and floods. A few broad channels permit the passage of the rivercraft carrying teak logs, people, industrial goods, etc., in an assortment of rather dodgy-looking boats.

We successfully navigated our way over the water and headed towards the city of 4.6 million souls. There were probably 350,000 Christians in Mandalay, but the Gospel outreach was very tepid.

As we got nearer to the city centre, the quantity and intensity of the traffic escalated. Road repairs were carried out by hand, with work teams of fifty to a hundred people, both men and women. They carried baskets of rocks and dumped them on the road, while others bashed them down; more gravel was added and levelled, then great buckets of tar were heated upon open fires and poured over the surface. All this was done on one side of the road whilst, on the other side, there developed a bottleneck of bikes, lorries, buses, pedestrians, oxen and street-sellers coming from both directions.

The horn was obviously the first and most important item to be installed when building a car or bike for use in Burma. All drivers developed their own horn technique, which I used to enjoy studying. The principle was to continually produce a rapid pulse of ultra-short beeps, mainly to indicate "important vehicle coming." These were then interspersed with a selection of extra beeps, depending on what blocked the way: four extra beeps for a motorcycle, which would swerve to one side, two extra toots for a bicycle, and a continuous horn for a water buffalo.

We slowly progressed, our driver expertly tooting and beeping his way along, until at last we arrived at the giant school, which was in full swing. The entrance gates were blocked by about fifty motorcycles waiting for children to finish their morning session. These had to be moved and their owners tracked down, before we could trundle through the opening and along the internal street to arrive at the clinic.

There were children there from all over the country; all ethnic groups, all ages. Quite an amazing variety of buildings. But one aspect became apparent here - the children and teachers were all very happy and outgoing. All keen to try out their English, all keen to show us around.

We waded our way through the throngs of youths and set up our stall in a third-floor room in their dedicated medical centre. There was lots of willing help and the patients were fairly straightforward to treat. They had two dental chairs, but there was a problem with both of them (no surprises there). Fortunately, I managed to take one apart and fix it but, as with all things dental, if the equipment is not working, we are very limited in what we can achieve.

We finished and were given some food, and had a chance to talk with some of the teachers and office staff. They knew that we were Christian and asked about the *Mercy Ship*. It was good to explain why we had come, and that we have a loving and caring God who cares for all people.

The return journey to our hospital was a repeat of the outward passage, except for the fact that the setting sun was now low in the sky and everything was bathed in a dusty, orange glow. This country has so much beauty and such a gentle people. It is such a tragedy they do not believe in an everlasting Saviour, but spend their energy tending their broken temples and false idols.

It was good to meet up again with Professor Albert De Mey, who had returned to carry out more cleft-lip

Chapter 20

repairs at the hospital. He stated that these three weeks were the highlight of his year (see his interview via QR code page 140).

Fortunately, the days were warm and the sun seemed to provide a soothing energy when we felt all cold and clammy inside, but our effectiveness waned. That weekend we rested and slept, just eating rice and ginger soup. We managed to attend an Anglican church, which was good.

We continued to work at the three clinics, seeing lots of young people, but regrettably, three of us developed upset stomachs and our energy levels were low. Fortunately, the days were warm and the sun seemed to provide a soothing energy when we felt all cold and clammy inside, but our effectiveness waned. That weekend we rested and slept, just eating rice and ginger soup. We managed to attend an Anglican church for Sunday worship, which was good.

The planned visit to Hpa-an in the Karen district was finally cancelled. Since the signing of the peace treaty with the rebels early in January, they were now hotly debating borders and territories, and so tensions continued. Perhaps another time we come to Myanmar, we might have a chance to go there.

Two opthalmic surgeons from the UK tried to go to the hospital there a month before we arrived, and had their passports confiscated. It took three weeks of negotiations to allow them to return to Yangon.

It had probably been our busiest visit to Burma yet; certainly the most tiring. But lots of conversations took place, many people helped. We prayed that we had been good ambassadors for our God and Jesus our Saviour. We hoped it was He who was seen as the compassionate healer, rather than ourselves.

When back in Yangon, we went to visit an orphanage situated about four miles beyond the airport. Planning a visit such as this was never as straightforward as you might think. We woke at 6.30am, not sure what time the visit was scheduled for. With little sign of life, we went for a walk in the cool air, returning by 8am. Then someone went with us to a small, streetside café, where we had some noodles and coffee.

By the time we returned (approx. 9.15), there were about fourteen assorted people spread about the house. Relatives of Dr Ko, drivers, some builders, a gardener, our hosts, and a doctor or two. We gently enquired if the orphanage visit was still on, and it seemed that it was, but nobody was sure when we would set off. Phone calls were being made, instructions written down, lists handed out, directions given. Jane and I went and put together a dental pack, in case there might be an expectation of our services once we arrived. With the language barrier, communication is not 100%, more like 50%. That creates the odd misunderstanding, so we try to be prepared for everything we can imagine.

By 11am it was now quite hot outside, and nine of us got into two fairly old cars and set off across Yangon City in search of the orphanage. The journey took about an hour. With no air con in the cars, it was a hot and dusty journey.

The orphanage was set amongst a cluster of large, shady trees, the compound being about three acres in size. All the orphans came from the tsunami disaster. Attached to the place was a school for about two hundred children. The buildings were single-storey and wood on stilts, with open sides to allow air to flow about.

There was a gaggle of younger children playing tag round one of the huge tree-trunks; shrieks of laughter and calls filled the air. The grounds were hard-packed mud, which gave off a puff of dust as you walked across it. The area had a dusting of crunchy leaves that fall at this time of year. We were shown around and introduced to some of the organisers. The lady we were staying with is one of their main supporters. We were taken on a tour around the place, but we were unable to do a dental screening, since they were not prepared for our visit.

Being guests in another country, it was not always possible to impose one's own agenda on to theirs. We tried to adapt and to offer help where we could and trusted that God would lead us to the places He wanted us to be. What we did now realise, though, was that we had no desire to visit pagodas, temples or other idols that cover Myanmar. It was its people we wanted to see.

John Ch 3 v16 was our driver: *"For God so loved the world that He gave His one and only Son, that whoever believes in Him shall not perish but have eternal life."*

https://youtu.be/4ui4bBob3BQ
Professor Albert De Mey interview.
Reconstructive Plastic surgeon from Belgium.

Chapter 20

Myint Myint Aye, aged eighty-six

Some of the 1300 children we screened

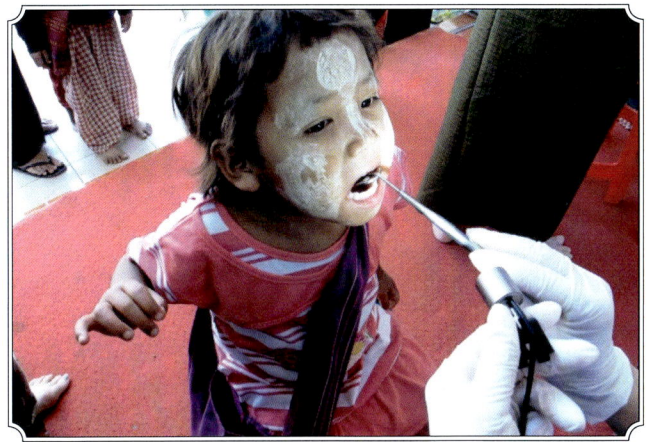

A three year old with Thanaka paste on her face to protect against the strong sunlight

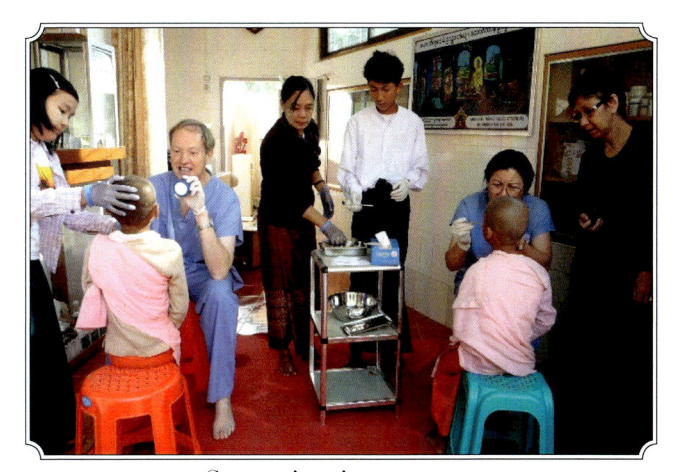

Screening in progress

https://www.youtube.com/watch?v=p6VPS31MI1I
School screening at Sagaing

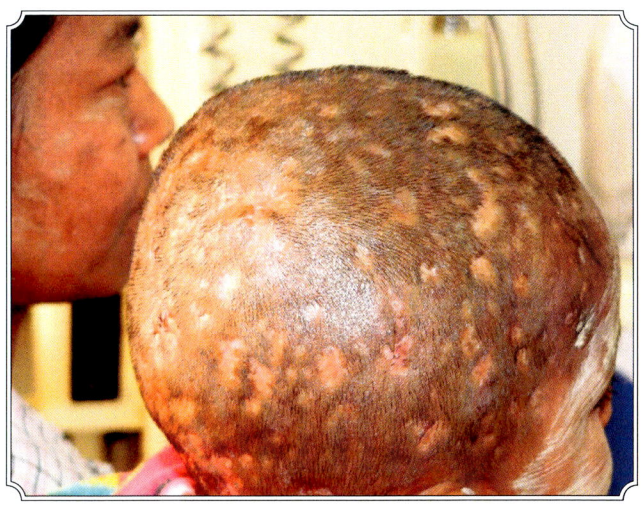

Scabies was very common with the pupils

141

Chapter 21

Mercy Ships, Conakry, Guinea, Sept 2012

We had booked to travel to Guinea in October 2012 but, as the date approached, Jane's mum had become more frail and her health was declining fast. We felt it best that Jane should head home to Brunei to be with her mum, whilst I would set off for Conakry on my own, for her to join me later, if the Lord saw fit.

I was driven to Heathrow at 4am by a young Indian man who was Hindu. After I had got him to explain to me his faith, and how it worked, he then asked me to tell him about my faith, so it was good to talk about the Bible, the Gospel and how Jesus is the Earth's saviour.

The *Air France* plane travelled via Paris and Nouvakchot (Mauritania) to Conakry.

Nouvakchot is a city on a flat, dry, sandy area of land: it is spread out far and wide. All buildings are single-story. The place looked as though it might have been a film set for Mars. Everything was covered in red dust. How people lived, worked, and existed there in 42°C, I could not begin to imagine.

On arrival at Conakry Airport which, for Africa, was reasonably calm, I was met by Phillipe, who drove the *Mercy Ships* Land Rover to and from the *Africa Mercy*. It took us two hours to negotiate the two miles to the ship! No traffic lights at junctions, no traffic police, no roundabouts. Just total gridlock. A vibrant mishmash of lorries, buses, cars, bikes, pedestrians and hand carts, all pressing to get through, round, past, in between and ahead of each other.

Guinea ranks 178th out of 187 on the UN Human Development Index. In 2010, Guinea held its first democratic elections, following twenty-four years under a dictator and two years of military control.

It has a population of 1.4 million and an area of 94,981 square miles. It is a predominantly Islamic country, with Muslims representing about 85% of the population. Christians, mostly Roman Catholic, make up about 10% of the population. It was going to be interesting

Chapter 21

to see how the Christian ship fared in a Muslim environment.

It felt as though my left arm was missing, with Jane eight thousand miles away.

It was a 6am start to the day. Once again, it was good to see all the crew getting ready for their day's work for the Lord. A general sense of purpose about the place.

After morning prayers, and a talk about agricultural education being an opening for the Gospel, we set off in two Land Rovers for the clinic. This was about ten minutes away from the ship. We had the use of four rooms on the ground floor of a two-storey building, built round a small courtyard.

The team were a little disjointed when I arrived. There was a slight lack of joy in their work. At lunchtime, I dragged them all outside for a team photo, and managed to get them laughing as I balanced precariously on the Land Rover roof to get a good camera angle, only to fall off twice.

The main language was French, but there were three or four local African dialects as well. This made good communication difficult. Fortunately, the local translators all spoke good English.

Before the ship arrives in any country, an advance team goes there to locate suitable buildings for off-ship work and, at the same time, it advertises for, and interviews, local graduates and previous *Mercy Ships* helpers, to apply for a selection of jobs. Mostly translation work, but also as drivers, security and for other jobs. These jobs were highly-prized and competitively sought-after for the opportunities they give.

The city was a bit jumpy, as there had been a number of demonstrations against the existing government, closing whole sections of the town. There were lots of soldiers in groups, dotted about on street corners. Two demonstrators were shot the day before I arrived, raising the tension level. Apparently, it was the anniversary of a large massacre that took place in Conakry in 1992 (four hundred people were killed and hundreds more injured).

After returning to the ship, and whilst having some food, I bumped into Rosie Timms. She, the seventy-four-year-old, was back again, a bundle of energy for the Lord. She was working in the eye department once again. We headed down to the wards, to visit a girl she had donated a pint of blood to. This ten-year-old had had a large, ten-inch growth on the left-hand side of her face removed that day, and had needed a large, two-litre transfusion.

We sang songs, played games with the patients who were there with their relatives and friends, and spent time chatting about Jesus to the mainly-Muslim patients.

Guinea is broken up into thirty-three districts. Nine of these districts had been affected with cholera and Conakry, the capital, had been hit the hardest. As of 4th September, 2012, 5,938 people across Guinea were reportedly affected with cholera, and two hundred and eleven people had died. Two thirds of babies born died before their first birthday.

Visually, poverty surrounded us. Rubbish was dumped everywhere and even on our dental site (a government hospital extension); rubbish, including medical waste, was just dumped on the ground. We incinerated all our medical waste on the ship, but the capital's hospital had very lax controls.

There was at least 60% unemployment. Most people who were working in government, police and security jobs, supplemented their small pay by accepting bribes, so getting things done in Conakry was often difficult for an organisation like *Mercy Ships*, which had to try and operate in a dark, black-market environment.

On the Sunday, for some reason, I was up at 6am and watched a spectacular sunrise. There was always an additional buzz in the canteen on Sunday mornings, as people worked out which church they hoped to visit and what they planned to do for the rest of their day off. I attended the ward service, held on Deck Three, between A and B wards, conducted amongst all the patients. We had 468 crew on board at that time, from thirty-seven different countries. Almost full to capacity.

The next morning, on arriving at the clinic, we had about 450 people queuing up for the dental screening. This made progress to the gates rather slow. A team from the *Mercy Ship* had come to help marshal the line.

We screened for large swellings and people in severe pain. It was not possible to see everyone, but the ship was there until May, so they would all be seen before the ship sailed away.

I saw a number of large, facial swellings, one man with what looked like a nasty growth on his face, from the salivary gland. I prayed with him and arranged for a histology test (see photo page 153). One of my lady patients insisted on tying her headscarf over her eyes so she did not have to see anything being done! That's a first.

It was mandatory for fresh crew to attend the "new crew" ship talks on safety, security, pastoral issues, fire drill, escape drill, IT protocol, health issues (mainly cholera problems), ambassadorial responsibilities of *Mercy Ships* crew regarding Conakry people, integrity, and faith sensitivities. Having staggered out of those presentations, I came across a

Chapter 21

Dutch lady, Josephine, who played piano duets, so we played in the *Starbuck's* café. There were only two pianos on board, and one was to be found in the ship's town square café zone.

After work, I visited the "Hope Centre" one evening, where Barry and Cheryl were again running the reception for people awaiting their eye, IVF and orthopaedic operations. I went with the ship's chaplain and her husband, plus Tim Brown, an anaesthetist from Dorset who was a regular shipmate. He was very good at playing sea shanties on his violin.

There were sixty beds in the centre, all arrivals requiring, feeding, washing, sorting and managing to get them ready for their surgery on the ship. It was always a major exercise to coordinate and manage all the different people coming from all parts of the country.

The following day, I received the good news that Jane would be joining me on the *Africa Mercy* on Tuesday, 9th October. The sad news was that her mum had gone to be with the Lord. Jane had been asked to write the eulogy, and she was keen to give praise to the Lord for her mum's ninety-three years. She discovered there were upwards of a thousand people attending the funeral.

After getting back to the ship, I met up with Rosie Timms and we visited the wards, explaining the Gospel with the help of the wordless book that has felt, coloured pages - yellow for the heaven God planned for us, black for the sin that blocks the way, red for the blood of Jesus given on our behalf, white for the colour of our souls once cleansed by Jesus, and green for our future growth in Jesus Christ.

There were about four of us who would go down to the wards. Rosie (74yrs), Diane (68), Judy (45) and me - a rather random group. Technically, the *Mercy Ships* administration was a bit cautious about proclaiming the Gospel to non-Christian patients, but we felt the worst that could happen would be to be thrown off the ship!

Bob Cairncross gave his life story to the crew on Saturday night. He was a Yorkshireman. He'd served in the Royal Navy for fifteen years, on various ships, as an engineering officer. He joined the *Anastasis* (earlier *Mercy Ship*) in 1998, and had been serving ever since. He was now Operations Manager on the ship. His wife, Anne, was in charge of pastoral care. They had their three children with them on board. I met them over the years on our travels, and spent a good evening or two with them catching up and hearing of their experiences on board the *Africa Mercy*.

On the ship, there were a lot of twenty- to thirty-year-olds, usually serving from six to eighteen weeks at a time, or more. A lot were nurses (you need a lot to provide

24-hour cover), but there were plenty of guys in engineering, agriculture, teaching, screening services, orphanage outreach, buildings repairs, well-digging, etc. This group provided a great amount of energy, which gave the ship its buzz.

I spent some time with a sixty-year-old lady, Barbara. Originally from South Africa, she trained and lived in the UK for eighteen years before moving to Perth, in Australia. She was working on the ship as a nurse. After chatting for a while, it became clear she believed in God, but was not sure of her salvation and her path to heaven. She allowed me to go through *CrossCheck* with her and we then prayed that she would accept Jesus as the way, the truth and the life, and allow His spirit to enter, rather than salvation by her good works, which had been her current understanding.

One Sunday, I travelled with eight others to the church, "God's Love". The minister there was Michael Cardgo. His spoken English was excellent. There was a long history of voodoo, witchcraft and other practices in Guinea, and his message was that this bondage has been completely broken by Jesus and by His blood shed on the cross. African men and women must completely break with these things, and entrust their lives to Jesus.

Guinea has a high mountain, *Pico Basile*, where, by tradition, people went to seek blessings on their children, marriages, birthdays, etc. Thus they were dedicating themselves to a mountain, rather than to God. Just as we, in the west, dedicate our lives to idols (be they cars, or houses, computers, TV shows, holidays, careers, etc.) instead of to God.

I managed to get a satellite call through to Jane. She had just got back to the UK, and was rather exhausted and a bit disorientated. She was coming out to join me on the Tuesday - we felt that some time spent here with *Mercy Ships* would do her good.

When we arrived at the clinic on the Monday morning, there were the usual 450 people waiting. We always prayed that God would help us choose those most in need of care.

My first patient was a thirty-year-old man called Mark, who, when asked, refused to open his mouth. This sometimes happens, due to fear and apprehension but, after some difficult discussion, I discovered that his upper and lower jaws were fused together. They had been that way for twelve years! He had managed to survive by getting food through a small hole where one tooth was missing. I sent him back to the ship for an x-ray and to see the maxillo-facial department. Possible causes were severe infection, fracture of the mandible, or a tumour of some sort.

I am glad to say that Mark was operated on a month later and his jaw was re-ar-

Chapter 21

ticulated so that he could eat, speak and laugh again.

I worked at the clinic until 1 o'clock the next day, then left early to travel with Phillipe, the *Mercy Ships* driver, to the airport to meet Jane. The plane was delayed.

After it landed, we stood around watching all the passengers meet their friends and family amongst the African hustle and bustle. After an hour or so, there was no sign of my wife. So, with some difficulty, I managed to persuade a series of security guards to allow me to progress into the arrivals section to locate Jane. Her luggage had gone missing, so she was the last person there.

She was OK wearing my shirts and scrubs for the next week, but leant heavily on the Lord. No clothes, no personal items and grieving over her mum.

Jane's flight over to Conakry had been interesting by the way the Lord touched it. Our son, James, had kindly driven Jane to Terminal 2 at Heathrow to catch the *Air France* linking flight to Paris, where she was due to join the longer flight to Guinea.

On arrival, they were told that her flight had been cancelled and she was number fourteen on the waiting list to board the next flight to Paris. She explained about her requirement to get to the *Mercy Ship*, and the luggage and herself were wait-listed.

"Mum, It doesn't look good," James said, as they parted at the immigration control gate, "I'll sit in the café out here and wait, in case you cannot board the flight."

"Not to worry, James," my wife told him, "If God wants me to get to Conakry and the *Mercy Ship*, He'll make it happen."

"OK, Mum, I'll be waiting," our son replied, not totally convinced.

At the departure gate there was a throng of people, all hovering around the stewards and check-in officials, wanting to know if they could board and saying how important their own personal trip was.

Voices were raised, tempers fraying.

Jane quietly slipped her standby boarding-pass to the lady at the computer terminal; it was the same African girl she had talked to at the original check-in desk. She took one look at her and said, "Follow me, please," and headed off along the gantry, Jane in tow. She stopped by the aircraft door and said, "Bless you; have a good flight," and promptly shut the door. She was the last person on the plane, and the only spare seat was in Business Class!

What an answer to prayer, and a good witness to our son that we have a God of the impossible. That is what the

Scriptures mean when they say, *"No eye has seen, no ear has heard, and no mind has imagined what God has prepared for those who love Him."* - 1 Corinthians Ch 2 v 9.

God works outside of the box! His plans go way beyond our short-sighted view, and He is working in ways that may not make sense to us. We can take comfort in the knowledge that His plans are ones laid out by a loving Father. He has prepared a way for us because He loves us. He goes beyond what we can imagine and, even when we don't understand it, we can trust that He loves us.

Our day started with the discussion topic of "Spending our day doing things that please the Lord," and how we try, and often fail, in that aim.

We all travelled to the clinic, driving in our two Land Rovers through the busy Conakry streets. There were always lots of soldiers hanging about in groups of three or four, some camping on roadside corners. Lots of street-sellers were walking amongst the traffic selling peanuts, hand tissues, soap, phonecards, bread rolls, fruit, kitchen knives, or sunglasses. A veritable cornucopia of items.

On the pavements were a myriad of stalls and small businesses, spread along both sides of the road; these obstructed the way, so pedestrians were forced to walk in the road itself. The road was filled with cars both parked, double parked and moving. Into this mix were added an assortment of yellow taxis, aggressively pushing their way into and out of traffic jams. There were obviously no traffic lights at junctions and roundabouts were used as good places to park or set up yet more market stalls. No traffic Police to keep order.

Result: total jams often occurred, with shouting matches, waving of arms and honking of horns. We were often marooned like white, floating, *Mercy Ship* icebergs sitting amongst all this hubbub.

The patients attending seemed to be having bigger and bigger dental problems to solve. People with eighteen or more teeth to be removed were common. There were only around twelve dentists, in a country of one and a half million people. Most patients attending had never had dental treatment before in their lives.

Jane and I shared a meal together with Mark and Gretchen and their three young children. Mark was the other dentist there. He has a great heart for helping those in the rural areas away from the ship. We chatted about the logistics of organising this, whilst working within the limitations of *Mercy Ships* protocol. Mark had worked in the US Army for a time, and had experienced field service in places like Afganistan.

Chapter 21

Jane and I went down to the wards again with Rosie, to explain the Gospel. That evening, four hernia patients and two thyroid cases gave their lives to Jesus. We sang *When the Storm Rolls* and *Our God Is a Great Big God* and prayed. The interesting thing was that other nursing staff, and the ward doctor who visited the ward after we had left, wanted to know what had been going on - the patients were so happy and relaxed and cheerful. They had never seen this before.

We had four hundred and fifty new patients lined up for the screening, but were able to take only one hundred and thirty for that day. However, that still meant we had a very busy day. At lunchtime, we looked out of our clinic to see the President of Guinea walking past, having decided to visit the port on foot. He was surrounded by fifty security men in suits and dark glasses, two hundred gun-wielding troops, and countless others. There was much African agitation as he progressed down the half-mile route to the port. He was off to visit a French Naval aircraft carrier that had arrived early that morning.

After finishing our day, we had great difficulty getting back to the port, since it had been sealed off by the Army. Military vehicles everywhere, brandishing heavy-calibre machine-guns on the back. Large clusters of troops standing on every corner. Roads were closed, and spiky stinger-bars were spread across the tarmac to prevent cars from entering areas. Despite all this, we slowly persuaded and asked and prayed our way back to the port and to the ship, to find total pandemonium on board - the President had given two hours' notice that he would like to visit, and was coming at any moment.

Our good old dental team, hot and sweaty, and lugging water drums and bags of sharps for incineration, were met at the top of the gangway by **all** the *Mercy Ships* bigwigs, all in suits, posh frocks and marine uniforms, ready to greet the President and his entourage.

He arrived late, accompanied by his elite royal troopers and security detail, who spread themselves along the dockside - the *Africa Mercy* did not allow any guns on board.

It was his first visit, and he was visibly touched by what he saw when going round the wards and seeing the patients there. He shook everyone's hand that he could, and thanked the crew for helping his people.

We were just sitting down and having a cup of tea, following a quick supper, when Barbara, one of the ship's security officers, found us and said that we had some visitors, and that she had been searching the ship for us for the past thirty minutes.

They were two men, Fabian and Graham, with whom Jane had travelled out to Conakry on the *Air France* flight, and had chatted about *Mercy Ships*.

They worked for *De La Rue*, the company that prints the currencies for about one hundred and eighty countries.

We gave them a tour of the ship and explained what it did, and how and why. They, too, were visibly moved. They departed in a great big, chauffeur-driven, black limousine. Returning to their world of high finance, banking and international currency. Had God touched their hearts, bringing them to see the *Africa Mercy*? We hoped so.

Later that evening, once things had calmed down a bit, Don Stephens, the Managing Director of *Mercy Ships*, disclosed that they were hoping and praying to build a second ship, finances permitting, and that work had started on the design process. This ship would also be deployed along western Africa. When the ship would be built depended on God, finances and many other variables, but they were praying for four to six years (As I write this, the new Global Mercy ship has been built. Jane and I had the privilege to visit it in Rotterdam in March 2022 just before it sailed off to Senegal. It has six operating theatres and beds for 191 patients. Accommodation for 680 crew. It's spacious and modern and when talking with Don Stephens, he told us he hoped and prayed it would be in operation for the next fifty years.)

The weekend found people heading in all directions: ladies visited the prison, others went off to the orphanage, and some ventured to one of the local islands in small, local fishing boats. A group of the ship's medical staff, surgeons, anaesthetists, nurses and I, went to help clean up the sterilisation area of the local hospital in Conakry. It was not a reassuring sight.

Instruments were being washed in cold water in a cracked basin, and then dipped in antiseptic before being used for operations. No autoclave (bear in mind that Guinea had very high rates of AIDS, hepatitis and TB). The general operating theatres were covered in grime.

Our cleaning team returned to the ship, a silent, rather stunned bunch.

Tim Brown, the fiddle-playing anaesthetist, left the ship and headed back to Dorset. We had spent a couple of evenings playing Irish jigs and sea shanties, to the amusement of people round the ship's town square. We first met on the *Anastasis* in 2006, whilst in Liberia. I'm glad to report that Jane's luggage did arrive at last. Which meant she could wear something else besides surgical scrubs.

We returned to the wards that evening, to tell the wordless book story and to sing songs with Jane, Rosie, Diana and some translators. About thirty people, mums, children, nurses, day-care helpers and translators all crammed into D Ward. We were making so much noise that we had to go and repeat the performance for the C Ward next door, who felt they were missing out.

That afternoon an enormous, tropical rainstorm arrived, slowly making its way across the Atlantic Ocean, exactly like a scene from Stephen Speilberg's *Twister* movie. As it approached, the wind began to howl and, when the rain came, there were simply tons of it, accompanied by multiple lightning flashes. All very dramatic. So much so, it drew a lot of the ship's company from indoors, standing on the deck-side watching the spectacle.

We went down to Deck Three, and sang songs and told the Gospel message to a new batch of hernia patients in A Ward. Jane and I then spent some time with Comfort and Ebenezer, a married couple on board, who were off to Ghana that day. Both had lost their mothers suddenly, and were returning home to organise the funerals. We talked and prayed with them.

Monday was a very hot day. The line-up was packed with four hundred and sixty potential patients. It was a day of large swellings and large infections. We were all working hard to treat very, very, sick people. A few we had to admit and put on drips of intravenous antibiotics. There were four or five tumours and numerous external draining sinuses. We returned to the ship quite tired, but pleased we were making a difference.

Down to the wards again after supper, to do the wordless book and the Gospel with the hernia patients and to sing songs with them.

We went and had a meal with Barry and Cheryl from the Hope Centre, plus Peter, a friend of theirs who was acting crew doctor for a couple of weeks. They attend an evangelical church called *The Woodlands*, in Bristol, named after the road it is on. It has a membership of 1200 people.

Rosie Timms was informed by Clementine, the ward pastor, that she was to stop telling the Gospel to the patients in the evenings. Clementine, an African lady, had been with *Mercy Ships* for a continuous twelve years. She lived on the ship and, therefore, had a different perspective from us "short-termers", and probably operated under different directives from higher management. It was a shame, and Rosie was very sad - proclaiming the Gospel was her whole reason for living. We spent the remainder of the evening praying for wisdom in this matter and sang some praise songs. Romans 10 tells us that sharing the Gospel is our job.

We all trooped out to the clinic and performed a record number of extractions, fillings, etc. One sad case I had to see was a young lady of thirty, who attended with her mother. She had had a growth in her mouth for one year but, in the last month, the tumour had grown below her chin to the size of a small melon. It really looked nasty and was almost certainly malignant. I asked the Muslim pair if it would be all right to pray for them. This she agreed to. I got a group of us together, and we laid hands on her and prayed for her. The mother was in tears. The daughter I sent off for an histology test, on the ship.

In the evening, Jane and I had arranged for all the dental team of twenty-five to come out for a Chinese meal. The restaurant was situated on top of one of the few hotels in Conakry. We sang songs between courses; we had a private room, so there were African worship songs, guitar music being played, and photos being taken. It was good to get the team together away from the clinic. It was a good way to say goodbye, before heading home.

Leaving the ship is always a poignant moment. Close friendships had been made. Many were long-termers and so found it hard to keep having to say goodbye to the short-termers.

Jane and I had checked out as ship's crew and had taken our bags down the long gangway to the dockside. We were saying our farewells when Rosie Timms appeared at the top, calling down from the deck, "Hang on, Nigel and Jane; wait a moment." She was leading a patient by the hand.

Slowly, one hospital patient appeared in their hospital gown, followed by another and then another, carefully shuffling down the gangway, some with limbs in plaster and others with bandages, and one or two carrying their IV drip bottles. Until there were twenty to thirty in a long, descending line. They were some of the patients we had been singing and praying to on the wards each evening.

Somehow Rosie, all seventy-four years of her, had got them out of their beds and up two decks to the exit. Gradually, gently, and with increasing gusto, they sang *When the Storm Rolls* and waved us goodbye. It still brings tears to my eyes, as I think on it now.

Matthew Ch 8 v 23-27: *"Then Jesus got into the boat and his disciples followed him. Suddenly a furious storm came up on the lake, so that the waves swept over the boat. But Jesus was sleeping. The disciples went and woke him, saying, 'Lord, save us! We're going to drown!'*
"He replied, 'You of little faith, why are you so afraid?' Then he got up and rebuked the winds and the waves, and it was completely calm.
"The men were amazed and asked, 'What kind of man is this? Even the winds and the waves obey him!'"

Chapter 21

Our dental team

Open wide? Maybe not!

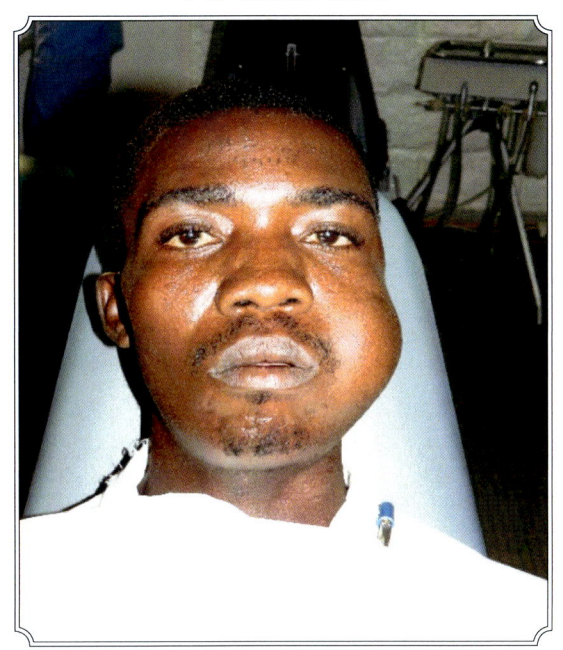

Morning Queue outside our dental unit (off ship)

Swollen faces were seen daily

https://youtu.be/Iaf2HTh-jH8
Conakry 2012 video

Nigel on Piano with Tim Brown the violinist and Anaesthetist

153

Chapter 22

Burma January 2013 – Our fifth Trip – Burnt Monks and God's timing.

Each time we set off for Burma it was in a step of Faith. People would ask us, "Whereabouts are you travelling to this time?"

We would have to say that we were not sure. This time, the districts suggested were the Katchin area in the north-east, a principally-Christian area. But this had a longstanding friction with the military junta. They had been having problems with electrical supplies, and there were tensions over a proposed hydro-electric dam that the Chinese wished to build.

Plan B was to again try and go to Hpa An in the south-east, but reports had been coming out of more troubles, so that was doubtful, too. Jane and I prayed a lot about the trip; we trusted that God would put us where he wanted us to be and would place us next to those he wanted the fragrance of Jesus to permeate. Our son, James, was joining us on this trip. It was to be his first time in Burma.

His participation had resulted from a chance remark he had made whilst having a meal with Dr Ko and ourselves. He was progressing through his reconstructive plastic surgery training and had just spent a year at Derriford Hospital in Plymouth, treating burns patients.

His original plan had been to travel out with us to spend some time with Professor Albert De Mey, helping with cleft-lip repairs but, since that chance meal, there had been a big incident in northern Myanmar over a proposed copper mine. Demonstrations had taken place against the compulsory land requisition and a few hundred monks had been burnt with phosphorus flares, fired into their gathering by the military junta.

The established medical hospitals and staff refused to treat those injured due to the fact that, in the past, those being seen to help "law-breaking demonstrators" would also be arrested and punished. Nobody in the country of Myanmar was prepared to see and treat the burnt men.

As James was already booked to travel to Myanmar, he was asked, through Dr Ko, if he would be prepared to see and treat these two hundred or so injured monks. We communicated back to Ko's contacts

Chapter 22

that James was not yet a fully-fledged consultant, and there were many limitations to what he could do, depending on the severity of the injuries. We prayed about it and entrusted the enterprise to the Lord.

This offer was grasped with open arms by the authorities and, when we went to pick him up from the airport at Yangon, we were a bit surprised to find a few reporters and a TV camera crew there to record his arrival.

We located a supplier of plastic surgery instruments in Yangon, right in the centre of a large, medical supplies market similar in appearance to an indoor Petticoat Lane. There were lots of small kiosks crammed, cheek-by-jowl, into a covered area and selling every medical and pharmaceutical product. There were probably about two hundred stalls, with groups of customers getting tablets, medicines and healthcare products for surgeries, for patients and for hospitals. It made you realise how fortunate we are to have a Health Service.

We managed to source a dermatome (a bit of kit for taking skin grafts), and also procured an assortment of post-op dressing materials. I managed to purchase a complete set of twelve dental forceps for the same price as one item would have cost us in the UK, and some disposable gloves.

It became clear that there were high levels of anxiety regarding the incident that led to the people getting burnt. With political sensitivities and professional pride to be negotiated, we realised we were going to have to tread carefully to obtain a successful outcome.

We again prayed that God would lead us along a good path and would equip us all for the task ahead, and that He would be glorified in all that took place. We also prayed for great wisdom and that, like Daniel (in the bible), we could show anything we did to help others would be by God's hand, not just our own.

We all travelled up to the Sagaing hospital to find frantic preparations going on to make three wards ready for the influx of injured monks being bussed down from the region north of Mandalay. We were met by Dr Zaw in his trusty, brown jacket, as usual.

The hospital was full to the brim with cleft-lip repair cases and the burns cases, not to mention the normal, day-to-day patients, so all the corridors were also filled on one side with beds plus patients.

Jane and I walked up to the orphanage school to set up a screening for the Monday morning. The headmaster was very welcoming and arranged everything. We wanted to review the hundred or so children we had treated the year before.

We dropped into the hospital dental clinic and were very pleased to see it humming with patients and four dentists. The surgery was in operation four days a week, offering free treatment to the community. This was all we could have hoped and prayed for.

At 5pm, we went on the burns assessment ward round with James, Jane, Dr Ko, Patrick (a doctor who helped us the previous year with translation), and approximately fourteen other doctors, nurses, etc.

Praise God, the process went very well.

Of the eighty-seven that we saw, only six required surgery. This was planned for the Monday afternoon. The other patients needed only a structured care programme of dressings and skincare. There were a further eighty burns patients due to travel to the hospital that coming Tuesday.

We had some supper, and chatted with Prof. Albert De Mey and his anaesthetist, who were sorting out the cleft-lip patients.

That Monday, after breakfast at 7am, we were just planning our day when the Burmese government's lady Health Minister arrived, along with the local media and fifty other assorted officials. They advanced through the hospital like a tidal wave, casting all before them. James and I were sorting through instruments in the operating theatre and were asked to join the melée. It was rather like stepping into a swollen river in full flood. The burns patients were seen, James was introduced, and bags of goodies were handed to each patient by the minister as a sign of care and apology.

It was good to witness an openness and a willingness to say sorry, albeit with half an eye on the media coverage. But a first for the people of Burma.

Jane had taken her team up to screen the orphanage children and, once again, hoped to treat some of the most urgent cases that afternoon. I helped James, really to facilitate any request he had. It was always tricky working in a new place - things one needs are not always there, and it was hard to pre-plan for all eventualities. We all prayed together that morning, for God to be with us, and especially with James as he operated.

As a father, I was so happy and proud to work with my son and assist in the treatments, and to watch him work, something that hospital protocols, legal indemnities and patient consent would make impossible to do in the UK.

We managed to do all six of James' burns cases. The skin grafting dermatome we purchased in Yangon worked very well. The large wounds were covered, following cleaning and debridement; some needed full-thickness skin grafts.

Chapter 22

The operating list took us through to 7pm. We then had to see a further eighty burns patients who had been sent up for assessment.

Supper was had in the hospital, with our little group rather lost in the large refectory area. Seating for about eighty people, and just the nine of us sharing a meal together! Quite a few mosquitos about in the evening, which led to us dividing our attention between conversation, eating and watching out for the flying pests.

After an early breakfast of some Burmese noodles and curry we set off, at 7.30, for a large town called Monwya, which was a two-and-a half-hour road trip from our hospital. This town had grown considerably over recent years, since it was the main trading town with India and on the through road leading to the Assam region.

We were introduced to the director of the hospital and proceeded on to the dental department. This was a five-roomed, single-storey building built in colonial times. No running water, no suction, but good staff and three working dental chairs. The patients attending were very varied. On our visit, there were two traffic accident patients with broken jaws, one man with a huge, infected cyst in his jaw, two cancer cases, children with gross decay and adults needing extractions and fillings. Jane and I saw about twenty-five patients.

Dr Kokolay was the resident dentist; his wife was a Christian. He was very welcoming, although a bit suspicious of us to start with. We arranged to send him an autoclave that was donated to us by some friends, Andy and Heather, who live in west Scotland. This was shipped out and was sitting in the corner of the surgery in Sagaing, awaiting a good home.

James had had a good day, doing the last big skin graft and assisting Professor De Mey with some cleft-lip repairs. We left him to it, and travelled into Mandalay to visit the orphanage, which had over six thousand pupils. We spent the day seeing a wide variety of young people amongst the hustle and bustle of the school day.

One of Jane's patients invited us to have some food with them, which was very enjoyable. All seated round a low table and trying to make ourselves understood, with Burmese and English languages all mixed up.

It had been a busy few days, but God had been with us, working in so many ways. Our little bubble of activity had been spreading out like when a stone is thrown into a pond, the ripples spreading across as far as Yangon.

It was frustratingly hard to bring the Gospel into conversations with the Buddhist people. But, with crosses sewn on to our scrubs, prayers being said before all meals, morning prayers, Bible-reading and wishing God's blessing on everyone, plus handing out our gospel pens and *CrossCheck* booklets to everyone we met, we endeavoured to shine a light for Jesus.

We returned to the large Mandalay Orphanage to continue treating the children and teachers there, working on the ethnic minority group from the border regions. They were quite delightful to treat; a lot were Christian, and all were cheerful and quite cheeky, dancing about after finishing their turn, joking and winding up their friends, and, as usual, we had to work surrounded by a crowd of onlookers.

There were no formal classes that day, so the 6223 pupils were entertaining themselves, playing football, chatting and sitting in groups, buying snacks from the street vendors, chasing about, playing tag. Interspersed with all this were announcements on the school Tannoy and a very loud clock that chimed and pinged every quarter.

After completing our treatment list, we emerged into the school high street, eyes half closed, unaccustomed to the bright daylight, watching all the hundreds of feet charging about. A miasma of dust swirled around and softened the scene in the warm sunshine, similar to a late UK August afternoon, the sun somehow magnified in the Mandalay sky by the sheer volume of particles floating about in the air. All the sounds of delight and laughter resembled a busy day at the seaside, rather than the Mandalay metropolis.

With all the travelling to different clinics, our bones began to ache from the constant jarring and vibration of the poor road surfaces. The van we commuted in had lost its shock-absorbers long ago, so the vehicle transmitted every bump, hole, crack, jolt, etc. that we drove over. It probably explained why we were asleep by 8pm most nights.

We returned to the Sagaing Baptist church we had visited during the last four times we had worked in the local hospital. That year, they were celebrating their centenary, the church being founded on 2nd November, 1913. Their youth choir were very good, singing three worship songs on their own. Regrettably, the message was in Burmese, so we could not follow the narrative. At the end of the service, everyone came and greeted us; we were made to feel so welcome.

On the way back from the church, both Jane and I came out with the same comment - how wonderful it was to spend time with fellow Christians wor-

Chapter 22

shipping our Lord, yet so far from home. Especially after being surrounded by all the Buddhist superstitions and rituals.

After lunch, we went the short distance to the Sagaing town centre, which was about a mile from the hospital. A bustling centre of trade with a thriving market place. We were walking about and discovered a pre-war dental shop, equipped with a Victorian chair and a Chinese gentleman, aged seventy-seven, who was the proud proprietor. I do not think sterilisation was at the top of his agenda, but we took some photos and had a good chat (see photo on page 162).

Our walk took us along dusty, tree-lined lanes, past rattan-covered kiosks and tiny cafés, until we reached the road that bordered the massive Irrawaddy River. It floods for three months of the year, covering large areas of land, then shrinks down to allow the farmers to swarm over the newly-enriched fields to grow crops of watermelons, tomatoes, rice, sweetcorn and many types of bean. In January it was at its lowest, so everywhere we looked there were teams of people working the land.

We returned to the hospital by tuk tuk, a motorcycle with a little cabin welded to the rear that allows for six passengers to be bounced and jarred along the dusty road to their destination.

After lunch, we took some dental equipment to the Mandalay Orphanage and explained to them how to use it. It included an amalgamator, a machine for mixing the metal amalgam filling material. There were exactly three such machines in the whole of Burma.

All brought over by us.

Without these, the filling has to be mixed by hand (even in the teaching hospitals of Yangon and Mandalay), leading to low-grade mercury poisoning of the dental staff.

James' surgery efforts had been reported on the Radio Free Asia programme and in a number of newspapers around the country. He became known as "Dr James", since the Burmese people carry only one name. We prayed that the Christian message of Hope and Healing would also be seen to have taken place with all that he did.

We also gave thanks to God for all His help; without His Holy Spirit guiding us, we could have fallen into numerous pitfalls along the way, leading to a totally different outcome.

We were off to Monwya again. The hospital was in full swing by the time we arrived. We joined in the business of seeing the patients.

My first lady was eighty-one years old and had a chronic jaw infection. The next man had a huge, squamous cell carcinoma of the jaw on his left side. Cutting it out would not lead to a cure but, in Burma, cancer treatment is expensive and there was a three-month waiting-list for radiotherapy. All I was able to do was pray for him and send him off to Mandalay General Hospital. I was told he would be unlikely to go, since the cost would be beyond his means. Meanwhile, Jane was removing a large mucocele from a six-year-old's lip. The day continued in that way.

It was good to see the Scottish autoclave in action, which had replaced the old, rusty, hot-water boiler they had been using.

We wended our way home in the warm afternoon sunshine, the shadows of the roadside trees getting steadily longer as we journeyed back to Sagaing. After an hour of travelling, we stopped at a small village café. It was obviously a popular stopping-point, as there were three old buses carrying locals, and also a selection of motorcycles. Mixed amongst these were women selling snacks from large trays on their heads, weaving their way cheerfully between the vehicles and calling out their wares and prices. Stalls by the side added to a general hubbub of community life.

We squeezed our way through to a small, wooden table amongst about thirty others, all filled with what, to some, might appear appealing morsels. But roasted sparrows on a stick, or crunchy fish and deep-fried grasshoppers, were not really what we felt like, so we just had a three-in-one *Nescafé* drink.

As we were nearing our hospital, we had to cross the old railway line. Trains were fairly infrequent there, the rail track was rather overgrown and the lines worn. So, to our surprise, there on the line stood a young girl, waving a flag to warn us to stop. As soon as we did, the level-crossing gates were shut.

The only problem was that we were inside the gates, next to the railway track, rather than on the safe side. We could see the huge, old, diesel locomotive approaching and managed to squeeze ourselves a few yards away from the line. It was quite a hairy moment. Despite the gates, mopeds and cycles were crossing both ways with feet to spare before the train slowly rumbled past. At least we got a good, close-up view of the train and its 1950's rolling stock!

We met a married Christian couple at the Holy Trinity Church, Anna and Andrew Hay. He was a retired engineer from UK and she was from Norway, both in their seventies. They were on their way to China, where they had been working for a number of years in the south-west region, explaining and spreading the Gospel. They had two sons, one of whom, Robert, at that time lived in Bristol, next door to our daughter, Sophia, and Tom! (our son in law). We spent the evening together, exchanging notes and praying. They lived in a rented house in Kunming and would be there until the spring.

A week later, we had a chance to see all the patients James had operated on. Wonderfully, praise God, they had all healed very well. All the grafts had taken and all the sutured wounds were fine, too. I took some photos as a record. Dr Zaw said he would keep the patients in the hospital for another week or so, just to make sure all was OK.

This trip to Myanmar had been quite varied. We had to react and adjust to different events as they happened. It was only through God's Grace, and through prayers, that things went so well. We managed to see and treat three different schools/orphanages, and visit and help in three dental clinics. We were able, as a team, to help with the "burns crisis".

But had we been able to promote Jesus in all this?

The community here knew that we are Christian and that this was our fifth year of coming to aid and treat people. We were invited to a meal at a nunnery and were able to sing the whole of *Amazing Grace* to the nuns. We were seen to be praying before every meal and at the start of each day. As we prepared to leave, one of the women who supported this hospital had given us three small crosses. She said that because we were Christian, she knew we would not want any of the Buddhist symbols.

Where just about everything for sale in Burma related to Buddha, it was touching to find someone going to the trouble of locating and choosing something that meant a lot to us.

Psalm 115 v 3-8: *"Our God is in the heavens, and he does as he wishes. Their idols are merely things of silver and gold, shaped by human hands. They have mouths but cannot speak, and eyes but cannot see.*
They have ears but cannot hear, and noses but cannot smell.
They have hands but cannot feel, and feet but cannot walk, and throats but cannot make a sound and those who make idols are just like them, as are all who trust in them."

A Step or Two of Faith

Hla Myint, a local Sagaing dentist

Hla Myint's surgery

Monwa dental team

Roadside fruit-seller

Dr Kokolay's horrendous, rusty hot water steriliser.

And the autoclave we provided three years later via Andy and Heather, our good friends from Scotland

162

Chapter 23

Manila, October 2013

A MISSIONARY COUPLE, Gareth and Malou, had been supported by, and had visited, our home church for the previous twenty-five years or so. They spent forty-five weeks of the year travelling to different countries to run teaching courses, and also travelled with OM's ship, the *Logos Hope*.

Gareth started *Amen Ministries* a number of years ago, and this charity supports developing churches around the world.

Hearing about our dental ministry, they asked if we might be able to help with a small, formative church in Manila, run by Joe and Beth Gonzalez. They were hoping to put a dental surgery into their church to provide a free service for the people of Tondo.

So it was, that we found ourselves on a flight to Manila in October 2013.

We had been in constant e-mail contact with Joe Gonzales over the past month or two and now it was going to be interesting to actually meet up in person.

Joe was the founder and leader of a group called the "SIbikong Kabataang Taga-Tundo", or "SI KRISTO Ang Tagapagligtas ng Tundo" (SIKATT), which means "JESUS CHRIST is the Saviour of Tondo". This group shared the Gospel with students, teachers, school staff and parents at the high schools in the Tondo area.

Joe used to be a gang leader in the Tondo district of Manila, until he had an encounter with Christ.

The dental surgery was to treat the very deprived areas in Tondo, where either no dental treatment was available, or it was just too expensive for them to afford.

We had been praying for guidance, and Joe had responded to say that a Christian dentist, living in Manila, was interested in helping with the clinic, should it be possible to set up. We asked to meet her, to see where we might establish a clinic, and to also visit some dental companies to arrange for some equipment.

On arrival at Manila Airport, we fought our way out of the building (Manila Airport has been voted by international travellers as the worst airport in the world! Having been to some strange airports in the past, I think this label was a bit unfair. Joe and his son, Gilbert, were there to meet us. His daughter-in-law had lent her car to Joe for the week we were staying, since he did not own one himself.

Joe was about five feet four inches tall, having a wiry build, and bustling with energy. He spoke English in a fast stream of phrases, interspersed with letter abbreviations - BBC, SIKAT, FDA, DCC - leaving us quite confused at the start.

We headed through the gridlocked streets of Manila, Joe expertly pushing, squeezing and honking his way along, waving his arms, quoting Bible verses and explaining his Tondo ministry. As our vehicle jostled with jeepneys, pedal taxis and street-sellers, it all seemed very confusing in the hot, humid, dust-filled environment.

The Tondo district ran adjacent to the port and continued until it engaged Manila city. There were over ten million people living in this overcrowded, desperately poor region.

Joe and his wife, Beth, had five children, one son living and working in the UK, a daughter living in Singapore, and the other three living either with them, or at the sister's flat. They had grandchildren as well.

Their centre was made out of two adjacent shops that sat at the base of an old, eight-storey tower block situated in the Tondo district. The shops had very high ceilings and had a couple of rooms at the back, which Joe and his family stayed in.

The school they ran was very small and quite basic (eight or nine pre-school children).

The church was in the shop site next door. The rental was 30,000 pesos a month - about £500.

Joe was a lively, extroverted person and, for the first few hours, it was hard for Jane and I to follow what he was talking about. We looked at the concept of a dental clinic, but the space available and the condition of the place were depressing to say the least. Joe and Beth really had no idea what it took to run a clinic - licences, permits, patient care, etc.

Joe took us to the small *Pearl Hotel* we were staying in, with cold and cold running water, live music from an adjacent lot, and armed guards on the door. But it had good, clean sheets.

We prayed for wisdom, discernment and energy.

Once again, we were well and truly outside our comfort zone. In this fast-moving, survival environment, we

Chapter 23

were like babes in the woods. We had to simply trust that God would walk alongside us with Joe and his family.

Both of us woke up with severe headaches, due to the dodgy air con recycling the air. We tried to locate some breakfast but, apparently, we were too early. Eventually we got an egg each and Joe picked us up.

On Sundays, they started their service with a Sunday school study for the toddlers and kids primary school groups. This flowed into their 10am service.

Both were well attended (around ninety souls). I was asked to preach, with Joe translating where necessary. It was heartening to see Joe in action with his flock; he was vibrant and related well. He knew his Bible, quoting verses left, right and centre.

We had some lunch and met up with Imelda. She was forty-seven years old and a qualified dentist, working six days a week in two different practices. She had heard about us coming and felt called to offer her help. She was prepared to do one day a week free of charge, offering her services to the Lord! She qualified in 1989 and was experienced. What an answer to prayer. With Imelda on board, the project might have a chance. We spent an hour talking and planning, and agreed to meet up for the whole of Tuesday to plan some more.

Without a dentist on the ground, Jane and I had felt it was not going to be possible to install a surgery and then manage it, maintain it and keep it from being misused. We had felt really depressed on Saturday evening, wondering what to do but, after spending time with Imelda, our hearts began to cheer. She loved the Lord and wanted to help.

At 4pm, the church filled again with another group of young people, some who had come in the morning, some new faces. After the worship, I was again asked to preach, so I decided on Exodus for a bit of drama. We got everyone to sing some songs.

After the service, we chatted to the music team about their very old electric organ. It was rather like the ones you find at a car boot sale, or advertised, or on eBay for £6. We wanted to see what we could do.

Jane had a very good time with the children and with Beth (Joe's wife), who was calm and loving to all the women and children who attended the church. Very much the mother hen. Somewhere along the way, we both were asked to give our testimonies.

The following day we helped in the school, singing songs, and Jane gave the children a lesson in looking after their teeth.

After lunch at midday, we set up some instrument tables with all our dental kit we had brought along, and made a long, flat, examination table on which to treat patients. The room was small and airless, but it was as private as we could get. At least it had a door.

By one o'clock, people started to arrive; and they kept coming. We stopped at 7pm, mainly through weariness. In the heat, we seemed to quickly tire, coupled with the poor air quality. The general dental health was poor, principally due to their poor diet - lots of sweets and energy drinks. We were able to remove bad and broken teeth, and do some simple fillings but, until we had a proper surgery installed, there was a limit to what we could achieve.

As the evening progressed and the word of our presence spread, the place filled up with people. Joe and his team were busy explaining the Gospel, we prayed with and treated all our patients, and Beth helped to interpret and generally assisted. The schoolteachers were all involved. It was a good day. There was certainly a huge need for dental care, coupled with a great opportunity for Gospel outreach.

On Tuesday we set off with Imelda, the Christian dentist, for the downtown area of Manila, where all the medical, optical and dental traders were situated. It was an area of narrow streets, filled with street-traders, hawkers, rickshaws, jeepneys and thousands of people. A veritable marketplace, apparently renowned for pickpockets. As we followed Imelda through the crush of people, we clutched pockets and bags tightly, and tried not to lose her, as she expertly wove her way through the throng of activity. It was hot, humid and a little unnerving, but we found the street which housed all the dental companies and thrust our way into the store.

There were plenty of staff, but all looked a bit cautious or dazed. We came to the conclusion, after being in the shop for three hours, that it was due to the extremely loud music being relayed from a local radio station, through ceiling speakers situated every five feet, at a volume that caused staff and customers to have to shout at each other in order to be heard. We escaped to a local *KFC* for some lunch and then resumed battle for another two hours.

We had negotiated a complete surgery package, plus hand instruments, hand-pieces, autoclave, delivery, installation, servicing and guarantee with paperwork in triplicate. We emerged, ears ringing, on to the bustling street and took a taxi, travelling the one-hour journey to Imelda's studio flat (which she shared with four other people), where we spent another hour talking and praying with her. We prayed that the project would

Chapter 23

go ahead smoothly, in an honest and open way.

Joe asked me to do two more talks to the youth, so I set about preparing for that, before getting to bed at one am.

The following morning was interesting since, at breakfast, we were surrounded by fifty to sixty Benedictine monks and nuns! They were all there for a Global Benedictine conference. Austrian, African, Brazilian and Asian. We had a good time, talking and laughing. The whole place resounded with chatter and with a good-natured courtesy to one another.

Jane gave a dental talk to the parents of the children at the school, and I taught everyone the song, *Prayer is Like a Telephone.*

We had been asking Joe to take us right into the heart of the Tondo district so, today, that is what he did. All personal belongings - wallets, watches, bags, etc. - were removed, and old clothes were worn. With ten million people living in such a small space, murders and robberies were, apparently, a daily occurrence.

Joe, Jane, Joe's son, Gilbert and I, set off along the narrow, teeming streets towards Smokey Mountain. This was a 150ft-high, three-quarter-mile-long refuse tip that sat between Tondo and the sea. Gilbert took our camera, not wishing it to be grabbed by passers-by. The area had a large drug, gambling and vice problem. Rooms housed four to five families, and finding work was extremely difficult. One household member usually had to support eight others with his wage of, on average, £95 a month.

Gangs ran protection rackets and vied for territorial control. They had tattoos, such as dragons or serpents, on their upper arms to show which group they were a member of.

This was where Joe's parishioners lived.

As we walked along, people would greet him, tease him and call out. He took us on to the Smokey Mountain, where people had built their packing-case homes. We chatted and talked with people he knew, saw their homes and how they lived. Their dwellings were constructed from anything found on the refuse area - pallets, old metal windows, plastic sheeting, boxes and metal drums.

Water had to be carried and stored, or collected from the rainfall. Cooking was done with wood or charcoal. All homes were illegal, but the police never entered the Tondo region, as it was controlled by the gangs.

A regeneration project had encouraged them to plant vegetables and banana trees right over the surface of the tip. Amazingly, they grew! But everything was polluted, and smoke from charcoal-burning, copper-wire-burning and constant digging for scrap metals, caused the place to be unstable, especially when it rained. Old scrap wire cabling was valuable for its copper, but the plastic or rubber outer coating was not wanted, so it would be burnt off, creating plumes of acrid, eye-stinging, cough-inducing smoke.

We returned to the centre very hot and sticky. But we had a group of patients waiting, so Jane and I set about seeing them whilst Joe and his wife explained the Gospel. Imelda arrived and helped. By 6pm we were done, just in time for the mid-week prayer evening. There were about sixteen of us, and time was spent sharing what God had been doing in our lives, and singing some songs. I was asked to give a Bible talk and Joe translated where required. We then had a good time of prayer, finishing at about 8.30.

Having seen where these people lived, and their daily hardships, it really showed what an oasis Beth and Joe had started here in Tondo.

We met with a carpenter to construct the walls, floor and cupboards for the new surgery, and also an electrician, a plumber and an air-conditioning engineer. We also had to get a compressor from a hardware store. Floor plans, wiring diagrams and plumbing routes were written out on any available pieces of paper.

On Friday, I preached at the youth service. I had prepared something on Joshua but, with Halloween approaching, Joe asked me to do something on spiritual battles, horoscopes, tarot cards, etc. - apparently quite a problem there.

The days flew by. As things progressed, we began to understand each other and felt a common goal of simply serving the Lord, using our different gifts. We managed to buy a better keyboard for their worship.

Life in this Tondo region was incredibly tough. We were to find out a lot more on our return trips to Manila, and how the phrase "Leaning on the Lord" was really put into practice.

Psalm 46 v1: *"God is our refuge and strength, always ready to help in times of trouble."*

Chapter 23

Jane and I with Joe Gonzales by Smokey Mountain, Tondo

Jane, Beth and Imelda

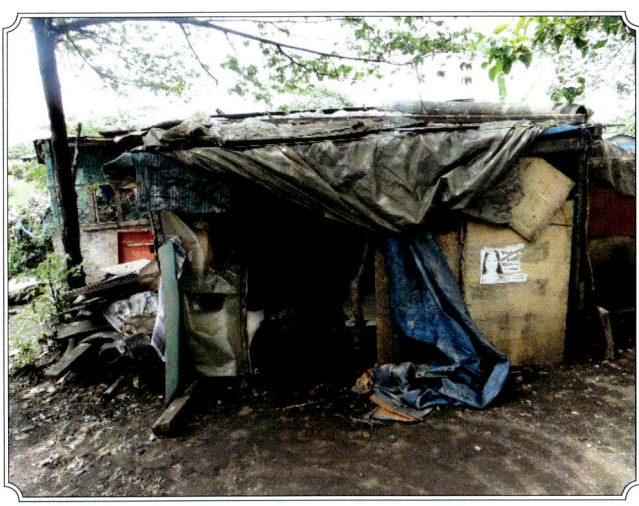

A typical home on Smokey Mountain

The noisy dental store in Manila

Jane with The Ramos family on Smokey Mountain

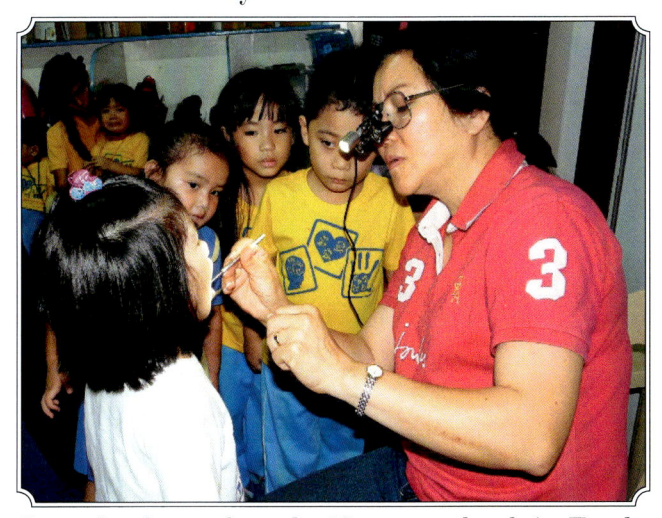

Jane checks teeth at the Nursery school, in Tondo

Chapter 24

Burma, January 2014
Simply an Amazing trip

Travelling to Burma in 2014 we were, by now, pretty adjusted to certain aspects of Burmese life. We had learnt Burmese phrases for Hello, goodbye, how can I help you? Where does it hurt? etc. We had begun to know what we could and couldn't eat safely.

We were also good at locating hidden churches.

But this trip we were about to embark on was on a different level altogether.

During our previous visits, we had heard about a group of Belgian surgeons and colleagues doing plastic surgery, eyes and cleft-lip operations. There were three or four regions where it had not been possible for any medico-dental teams to reach, due to impassable roads or their remote position. We therefore arranged to be in Burma at the same time and to travel as a medical/dental team.

Only God knew what He had planned for us to do. We prayed we could listen to His voice above all the cheerful clutter and hustle and bustle that seemed to be part of life there.

After meeting the twenty Belgian team members, we worked out our plan for the next few weeks. We arranged to fly to Homalin, see and treat patients there for four days, and then split into groups to travel by helicopter to the regional areas in the Naga Hills territory. Our dental team would end up in La He and then, perhaps, travel to the outlying regions, like Layshi and Nanyun.

We made our way to the airport, where our chartered plane was waiting for us. Whilst at the reception centre, Jane and I found a group of Christians attending a conference. It was good to talk with them and also have a chance to pray together just before we set off. The total team was about thirty in number, including four assistants and administrators, who were there to sort out luggage, food, accommodation, communications, health issues, local communication with patients, etc.

Two sixteen-seat helicopters had been lent by the President to facilitate our

Chapter 24

transport between the regions, the roads being criss-crossed by a network of rivers which made overland transport time-consuming and difficult. This was the first time a military bit of kit, plus pilots, had ever been loaned, so it was felt, at the time, as though a bit of a breakthrough had occurred in the provision of compassionate care for the tribal areas. Morale was high; this region was very rarely reached, and none of the team had been there before.

The flight up to Homalin, via Mandalay, went well.

What no one had expected was the reception we were to get. As the plane landed and we were taxiing towards the little airport building, all we could see was a teeming mass of people. As we stepped from the plane, there was cheering, dancing, flags and drums. Many were in traditional dress, all smiling, laughing and wishing us welcome. Probably a thousand or more.

We worked our way through the throng of arm-waving people, were loaded into vans and then driven towards the town; the whole route was lined by the town community, schoolchildren, government employees, townsfolk, the fire and police services and local army, all waving and singing as our convoy navigated slowly through the colourful sea of local humanity.

Arriving at the hospital, there was yet another crowd waiting to greet us. We disembarked, blinking in the dusty sunlight, all looking a bit self-conscious, waving and saying hello to people. After a brief greeting, we moved on to locate our accommodation, the one and only little guest house, adjacent to the Chindwin River.

Homalin town appeared to be in a bit of a time warp; dusty, earthen roads, wooden, open-fronted shops, lots of people sitting and walking about, and very little evidence of motorised transport, almost like some nineteenth-century film set.

Our residence had a generator, but this was turned off at 9pm, so we were thankful for the torches we had brought along. Power was not reconnected until 6am, so getting about at night was tricky. There was no hot water so, mornings and evenings, screams and groans of anguish could be heard along the hostel corridors, as brave team members eased themselves into their ice-cold showers. The other challenge was that any towels provided were usually the size of a handkerchief.

Our dental clinic presented itself as one room, with a broken chair, no instruments and a leaking sink! This could have been viewed as a setback but, by now, this seemed normal for dental provision in this part of the world.

Jane and I prayed for guidance, energy, health and wisdom.

We got the plumbing fixed, and sent people out to borrow and find benches, chairs, bowls, tables, towels and tissues.

Word had been sent round the area, and we had a hundred people coming that day. The main worry was for an adequate supply of materials, enough to last us the whole trip, not just one or two days. The hospital had none of its own, so we had only what we had brought with us.

In the end, we saw one hundred and fifty patients that day. All from the local area; very gentle, very cheerful people. Our team began to pull together, our helpers increased to ten with a number of nurses and patient marshals. By the end of the day, all had gone well, praise God.

Jane and I had time every evening to read and study our Bible (Romans at that moment).

It got dark by 6pm and there was no TV, cinema, theatre, pub, restaurant, or sporting event to go to, or watch.

As the sun set, the region took on a hazy, dusty appearance, people walking about wearing woolly hats and scarves - a sort of UK "October atmosphere", with the smell of woodsmoke drifting around. Food was cooked on wood or charcoal fires, the air filled with a mix of smoke, plus a moist mist drifting in from the adjacent, wide river.

Locals crouched on the ground in small groups, chatting, watching, or playing games. Others plodded through the dusty streets; fortunate ones sped along on bicycles, sometimes with three precariously sharing, resting on handlebars and luggage rack.

As night set in, this being a rural, agricultural community, growing rice, tea and nuts, all went quiet by 7pm.

For the next few days, we were up at 6am; the morning temperature was around the 3 to 4°C mark. Many of us had not expected such chilly weather, so we walked through the town of Homalin, arms folded, hugging our jumpers and coats to ourselves.

The route took us past past wooden, open-fronted shops, owners carrying their wares out on to their store-fronts to display, traders offloading market goods from ancient-looking river boats and running their wares up the river bank, often slung between bamboo poles on their shoulders.

We shared breakfast in a small, wooden café. The ceiling was low and the interior dark, with school benches to sit on and chilly, worn, gnarled boards underfoot. Breakfast was rice or noodles, with some

Chapter 24

chicken-stock soup, some local bananas and jasmine tea.

We packed ourselves into vans, or open trailers attached to a motorbike, and bumped and weaved our way to the hospital building.

We opened for business at 8am. The morning temperature was cool, so patients were wearing woolly hats, coats and scarves. We treated about eighty patients a day and saw another twenty or so for advice. The hospital was abuzz with people, lunch being provided by the local women's guild, and transport by a group of car- and motorbike-owners.

The Belgian team were busy repairing cleft lips, the eye team were removing cataracts, and the plastic team were repairing burns and trauma. The result - a lot of patients, relatives and helpers all over the place.

We completed our last day at Homalin Hospital, boxed up all our instruments and prepared for the trip to La He.

The following morning chaos ensued, since the Deputy Prime Minister and some of his staff wished to travel, too. This caused some of us to be bumped off the flight. Carefully-allocated luggage went adrift, organisers were rushing around with walkie-talkies, military personnel appeared in truckloads.

We were told differing places and times. Eventually, we were deposited at an air force hangar belonging to 82 Helicopter Squadron. We had been briefed at some length that talking with the military personnel was forbidden and the taking of photos could lead to arrest and imprisonment.

Since this was a first, everyone disembarked from our transport and sauntered here and there, trying to look well-behaved. However, after an hour of sitting about, our rather maverick team was to be found all over the military heliport. Photos were being taken and groups clustered round the old Russian helicopters. Military hats had been borrowed, medical masks donated, laughter began to spill out. Only the minister retained his air of detachment. He was there for national publicity, to get his photos and film shots into the Myanmar media.

We were eventually packed into the functional, dull-green helicopters. Each took sixteen, at a squeeze, and both had seen quite a few flying hours, judging by the state of the interiors and the paintwork.

The noisy flight took an hour; it was deafening inside and we could only converse in raised shouts so, after a few excited minutes, we all settled down, engrossed in our own thoughts, our very teeth being rattled by the vibration.

We flew over forest and river, slowly climbing above tree-covered mountain peaks, across untouched tracts of land; undulating, twisting and turning, we travelled northwards, eventually arriving at La He.

This town was very remote, spreading itself across the side of a hill. The Naga people were darker, more cautious and just stood and stared as we arrived. There were few smiles, just acute, undisguised interest in our arrival and the business of setting up our equipment.

The Naga people speak eighty-seven different dialects. Villages adjacent to each other, but in different valleys, could often speak totally different languages.

The hospital was "cottage" in size, serving an area much more rural and widespread than Homalin.

Because there were about four hundred people standing about waiting in the hospital grounds, it seemed sensible to start seeing some of them. Communication was difficult due to the huge number of local dialects, Burmese coming a poor second and English, well, not at all, really. Our interpreter turned out to be the assistant pastor of the church, and our two allocated nurses were Christian, too! How wonderful was that? Often we would need to translate twice to find out what the patient wanted - English to Burmese, Burmese to Naga Dialect.

Our accommodation was ultra-basic: sleeping bags, mosquito nets, wooden slabs to sleep on, and buckets of water (cold) for washing. One toilet for all of us to share. Food was organised and seemed good.

La He town woke at sunrise, with the sound of cock-crows and the smell of hundreds of fires being lit to cook the morning meal. There was a penetrating cold in the air, coupled with a mountain breeze that carried the smoke over the town of stilted, bamboo-and-rattan houses. Locals wrapped themselves in colourful blankets and hats, looking almost Peruvian in their dress. There was very little flat land, so the dwellings were perched on hillsides, connected by threadlike, earthen pathways. People walked about in twos, and the odd motorbike picked its way along the footpaths, there being only a couple of true "roads" in the entire district.

Today being a Sunday, Jane and I got up early to read some Bible, had breakfast and then walked down a narrow track between some thatched houses to start work.

We were first at the hospital. Two large tables had been made for us overnight, so we carried them into the dental clinic and rearranged everything, ready for the day. By 8am, patients and staff had arrived, so we began treating patients. Gradually, the area outside our clinic filled with people until there were about one hundred and forty standing or crouching, waiting their turn.

We had arranged to attend the church in La He with the assistant minister (our interpreter). At 10.30, he arrived at the rear of the clinic to collect us. We each rode pillion on the back of a motorbike for the ride up the hillside, winding between houses, following a muddy, rocky and pitted pathway for about a mile to the church. This was quite a large, wooden building, with a capacity of around two hundred and fifty. It was good to see so many Christians worshipping in such a remote area. We were introduced and interviewed, and offered to return in the evening to teach some songs with actions.

Although we had left a lot of patients waiting back at the La He hospital, we wanted to show, publicly, that our faith in Christ was important.

Following the service, we were returned by the bouncy, dodgy motorbikes to our clinic, and continued through the rest of the day, treating about eighty-five people.

After some supper, we had a quick turnaround and were, once again, biked up the hill track to the church. In La He there was no mains electricity so, at night-time, the only light was by generator, battery or flame. The church was dimly-lit, but there were over a hundred and fifty young people sitting waiting for us.

English was taught at their schools but, even so, song words in a foreign language can seem complex. We taught them *My God is a Great Big God* and *The Name of the Lord is a Strong Tower*, but the real hit was *When the Storm Rolls*, especially effective when all the power failed us, so we sang it in the dark! We had an interpreter, so it was possible to talk about Jesus, Sin and Repentance, finishing with a prayer of invitation of Jesus into their lives. The young people had an amazing ability to repeat and remember in a new language.

On returning to our accommodation, there was time for an ice-cold wash (bucket and scoop) before climbing into our mosquito-netted sleeping bags.

Gradually, as we all worked together and treated the local people, their initial suspicions began to fade away (we later discovered it was a fear of the military helicopters and their previous experiences with the armed forces), to be replaced by a wonderful cheerfulness. Groups of locals returned our smiles and gifts were brought to say "thank you"; patients were so happy to get their longstanding problems treated.

Life there was tough; it rained heavily from June to October and, when the rains came, food became scarce, the road out of La He turned into a muddy quagmire. It became impossible to grow crops easily, hunting was treacherous, and so food supplies were insufficient. The whole town often went hungry, so this paradise had a sting in its tail. A lot of the people wore no shoes, their feet being as tough as leather.

On clear days, when the sun shone, it was wonderfully warm by midday but, by four in the afternoon, the colourful blankets and hats were back on again.

Amongst the many people whom we saw and treated, there was a man who had travelled three days to reach us. He looked very sick and frail. On examining him, I found that he had a severe case of osteomyelitis in his lower right jaw. Removing his brokendown and bad teeth on that side, I realised that a lot of his jawbone was black and rotten. After taking away great chunks of this necrotic material, I was getting worried that his mandibular dental artery could get damaged in the process and, without any access to electrocautery, he could bleed to death.

This is where having the Belgian team with us was so good. Wilfred, the Maxillofacial surgeon, came and gave me a hand and we slowly but surely removed chunks of black, necrotic bone. Stitching him all back together, we kept him in the hospital on intravenous antibiotics and, by the time we had to leave, he was looking a lot better. Praise God.

We continued to work in the clinic; occasional worries over running out of local anaesthetic, gloves, needles, energy, etc. were sorted. Our prayers for help were, thankfully, answered.

Gradually, the time approached for us to finish. Our last patient was treated using our last pair of gloves. We packed up our equipment and prepared to leave these open and hardy people, many of whom we had found to be Christians.

Our next journey was up to Nun Yun, a small border town right in the north of Sagaing State and only thirty-two miles from the Indian border.

Once again there was the complex dynamic of waiting on the Burma health minister (a paediatrician), plus the state president of Sagaing and their team, so we hung about, all forty of us, until all was ready and then off we went, from the hilltop pad, rushing like a noisy bird, flying over upturned faces, thatched houses and barking dogs. We followed the valleys for about an hour, landing at a small village called Doh He. Perched on a hilltop, miles and miles from any other sign of habitation, the village consisted of a small cluster of houses and a new school, built to serve the surrounding district.

Chapter 24

The minister and his minions went off to have a talk with the local village leaders, so Jane and I wandered down to the school, past large groups of very dusty local people, all there to watch the helicopter land and take off. The building was not quite finished yet (no windows or doors), but the children and teachers had occupied the place. We tiptoed into the sixth form, and ended up teaching some basic English, such as "Hello, how nice to meet you," which they learnt quickly, proceeding on to the next five forms, doing the same and ending up with the largest form, of five-to-seven-year-olds, with about fifty in the class.

The "Hello, how nice to meet you, repeat after me," went very well, with lots of the locals peering in through the unframed windows.

We then discovered that most of the pupils were Christian, so proceeded to teach *When the Storm Rolls*, with the Bible story of Matthew Ch 8 v 23. This got so noisy, and there was so much laughter, that the minister and his entourage decided to walk down the hill to investigate.

Jane and I had returned to the helicopter by this time, thinking that we might be heading off again. As the minister wandered about the school we could hear the distant sound of "Hello, nice to meet you," being chanted out!

Once reloaded, the helicopter took us over the hills and trees to Nun Yun, a town on the old Silk Road route, and right on the Indian border.

Once a year, the Naga people have a New Year festival and, this time, it was being held in Nun Yun. This town, which had a resident population of one thousand, was full of surrounding tribal groups, so accommodation was at a premium. We ended up sleeping six to a room on the floor, again, with one shared, flooded bathroom, no hot water, a broken toilet, and occasional generated power.

The hospital was the most basic yet, the sterilisation hut (see photo page 181) primitive. Our dental room had a family living in it, so we ended up treating patients in the outside corridor!

A wonderful thing happened. A lady who had been praying for help with her painful wisdom tooth arrived just as we were there. This I managed to remove, using a borrowed syringe and local anaesthetic. It turned out she was working as a missionary, with her husband, in one of the villages. Her name was Esther (see photo). It had taken her five days to walk to the hospital.

An example of God's timing.

The festival took place down on a flat piece of land next to a broad area of forest. There were games, such as climbing a slippery, greased pole, rattan-ball and tribal dancing. Shades of Scottish Highland Games came to mind. I could not help wondering if some long-past, colonial Scotts regiment had somehow left a legacy in this distant land.

We found a very simple church just above the festival ground, serving a cluster of stilted huts, run by a young minister who was keen to chat and explain his evangelical outreach.

This had to be the most primitive area we had worked in/visited yet.

Having run out of everything, including clean clothes, batteries, dental supplies, etc., we once again waited for the helicopter to take us over a 9000ft mountain range and on to a town called Khamti. We had to wait for the morning clouds to clear so that visibility, especially over the mountain range, would be OK. The alternative was a fourteen-hour road trip along unmade, potholed roads.

As we sat in clusters on top of our luggage and medical kit, next to the two green helicopters, their massive rotor-blades bending down at the tips, everything was shrouded in a dense mist. The thick morning cloud was gradually burnt off by the sun, to reveal a series of tree-topped mountain peaks, sitting like islands in a sea of fluffy cloud. The sun broke through, and all was slowly revealed.

The two pilots eventually received radio confirmation that visibility was fine, so we crammed ourselves, plus all our gear, into the machines and, with a roar, the mountain tranquillity was broken as we slowly rose and floated across the cotton-wool clouds passing by the floating island peaks. On arriving at Khamti, a plane took us, via Mandalay and Naypyidaw, to Yangon.

The circular trip we had taken, and the many people we had met and helped in small ways, as I write this, are still as fresh to us today, eight years on, as they were then. We prayed that we had been good ambassadors for Christ in all that had taken place on our trip.

Each year, as we returned to Burma, new things happened. The **Trust** that was built, through our intention to help in this small way here in Burma, seemed to result in a greater acceptance of the **Faith** that we stood for.

Molly, Ko's wife, who professes to be a Buddhist, attended a missionary school as a child, in a town called Mogot, in Northern Burma. She had travelled with us on all our trips, helping to translate and acting as a receptionist. She told Jane:- "We like travelling with you and Nigel. We feel safe. When things go wrong and difficulties arise, we know that your God will watch over you both, and keep us all in safe hands, too."

Chapter 24

Which is what he did.

Deuteronomy Ch31 v 8: *"The Lord himself goes before you and will be with you; He will never leave you nor forsake you. Do not be afraid; do not be discouraged."*

The Homalin team

Usual dental chaos on arrival

A Step or Two of Faith

Our helicopter pilot, Soe Myint

Dental team at La He

La He patients keen to be seen

Gifts from patients adorning our reception

Jane arriving at the church in La He on the rather dodgy motorbike

La He house

180

Chapter 24

All firewood was delivered by hand

Dental team, La He

Esther, a missionary in Nun Yun

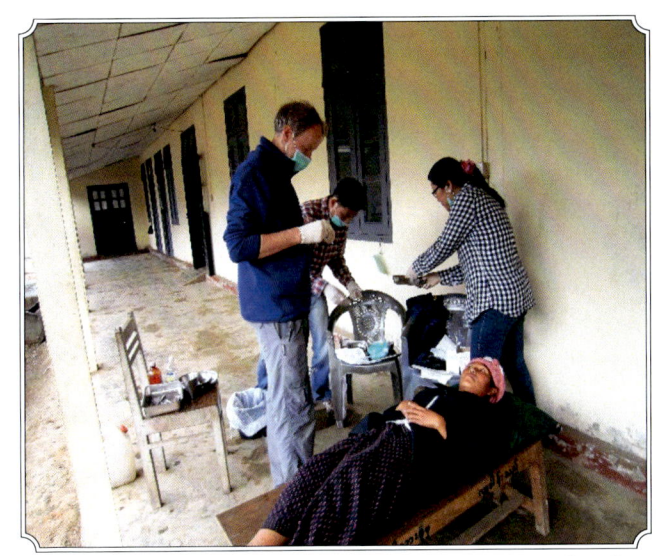

Not so deluxe surgery in the hospital corridor for Esther's wisdom tooth

https://youtu.be/m5Ua8kcwfeA
Homalin and La He, Burma, 2014

https://youtu.be/mzN6TKviOzY
Teaching *When the Storm Rolls* in Do Ha school

Chapter 25

Africa Mercy, Pointe Noire, Congo, 2014 – Our last trip with Mercy ships. God blesses our prison visit.

OUR FLIGHT TO THE CONGO was full to the brim with assorted rough-looking, seasoned oil-workers, all returning after their three- or four-week home-break. Most of them worked one month on and then one month off, commuting back and forth to their home countries.

Pointe Noire is on the Equator, so it was humid and 30°C. There was a lot of tropical monsoon rain there, too. The Republic of the Congo, or Congo-Brazzaville, has a total land area of 132,047 square miles - that's slightly larger than Italy. Its population was 5.25 million in 2018.

The airport was welcoming, small and calm, for an African state. We were met by a friendly Mercy Ships Land Rover driver and made our way through the traffic to the port.

The city appeared to be in a better state than any other West African port that the Africa Mercy had visited. Roads were metalled, with few potholes and even pavements present. Ex-patriots lived here, so some of the houses looked quite smart.

Whilst chatting with Alison, our driver, I asked how the Mercy Ship had been faring on its first visit to Pointe Noire. Due to oil and iron ore reserves, trade was good and the city was comparatively better off. But there was **No** health care provision and **No** dental school so, not surprisingly, since August, the dental section had been having queues of five hundred people, twice a week, for assessment. The numbers waiting to be seen were actually going up, rather than down.

The demand for eye and plastic surgery was constant, but there had been a lot of facial swellings and Ludwig's angina (swelling in the neck due to dental infection) requiring admission to the ship's hospital. After installing our luggage in our cabin, we had to sign on as crew and attend the usual regulation "tour of the ship." We had seven pieces of paper each, to get ticked off and signed, as part of "new crew" induction. I am convinced that an extra form is added each year we come out to the ship.

Chapter 25

It was good to meet up with some familiar faces. Gary Parker, the maxillo-facial surgeon and chief medical officer, came round to say hello and we had a long chat regarding the dental problems in Congo, ship morale, families and education. Gary had been on the ship, with his family, for over twenty-eight years.

Saturday being a rest day, Jane and I set off to explore the city. The port was huge, it was one and a quarter miles from the ship to the port gates! No taxis were allowed in the dock area, so a shuttle service operated, shank's pony being the other option. The risk in walking was due to the volume of large lorries, trucks, tankers, etc., charging about the place and leaving very little room for pedestrians.

We located the town market, which was teeming with people, all spread out along roads and alleys over a two-mile grid area. Here we found the real community, anxious to make a trade, jostling and shouting, amongst muddy puddles and rubbish under foot. Dried fish, vegetables, fruit, clothing, electrical items, there was an abundance of goods for sale and thousands of sellers and buyers. Although there were some people living in Pointe Noire with a high income, the majority were poor and had to work hard to survive.

We found our way to the sea front, which extended for miles and miles either side of Pointe Noire. The Atlantic Ocean, warm and murky, threw its rolling waves on to the steeply-banked beaches. It being Saturday, hundreds of young people walked and collected in groups in the soft sand. A few brave ones went in for a swim but, by the look of the sea, there were treacherous currents lurking beneath the waves, so most contented themselves by dipping a toe or two. There was a salty mist over the shore area, creating a softness about this maritime scene. Nobody wore standard beachwear, everything was improvised. Pointe Noire is 90% Catholic. When asked, people told us they were Christian. We did spot one large mosque on the outskirts of the city, though Muslims were in the minority there. Average wages were £1 to £2.50 a day. Those connected with the oil business did considerably better than that.

Total number of registered dentists – fewer than twelve (World Health Organisation). Most were employed by the oil companies to treat the expatriates and as a result, come our first Monday, there were five hundred or so lined up to be assessed for dental care; two hundred and twenty were given tickets for that day, Tuesday and Wednesday, the next line up being Thursday

The dental clinic we worked at was five miles from the ship and was attached to the Hope Centre, where patients waited before and after surgery on the Africa Mercy. Whilst we were there, it was full of women waiting for VVF surgery for bladder repair. Our dental team of twenty-five were quite keen, but rather fatigued after working continuously for five months. We would daily ask God to provide safety and energy for the team.

The number of large infections presenting themselves was always very high following a weekend. Patients with swollen faces, due to infections, looked very sorry for themselves, and were really quite ill. It was fairly usual to find that they required seven or eight adult teeth removing. The Congolese jawbone is very strong and dense. This resulted in very difficult extractions and long, prolonged struggles, by ourselves, trying to carry out any treatment.

Returning to the ship, the first requirement was a cup of tea, the second was a shower. Working on so many patients each day was physically exhausting, and required a high level of concentration to avoid any slip-ups. Dinner was served from 4.30 to 5.30. We'd usually be asleep by 7.30.

On Tuesday, I was asked to do the morning devotions for the engineers on board ship. This was a surprise, and a great joy, to read some Bible (Exodus - Moses by the burning bush) and share with the twenty-five men and one woman on the team.

Life on board ship was, in some ways, simple:- Eat, work, pray, sleep... repeat. But it was also quite complex and varied. There were, on average, thirty-five nationalities on board, so there were a lot of differing cultures, habits, expectations, etc. We were all living in close proximity to one another, so the potential for friction was greater. Even in a Christian community, small mannerisms and habits could become magnified when there were six sharing a cabin, and some of those could be on a night duty roster. Providing medical and pastoral care to the Congolese people was often draining over extended periods of time, even with prayer, worship and rest. It was important, therefore, to have some stress-breaking activities to allow people to unwind and relax.

Saturday was Team Race Day.

There were eighteen teams, each of four or more people, sent all over Pointe Noire on a kind of treasure hunt/task challenge, with prizes being awarded to teams with the most points collected and the shortest time to complete the cross-town circuit.

What the locals made of it all, I have no idea. It was 32°C and very humid; there were some very hot, tired teams staggering up to the finish line by the end of the afternoon.

Chapter 25

Jane and I set off to the prison in the morning, joining the prison ministry team.

The building was situated near the coast, about a mile from the port, in a quiet part of Pointe Noire. It was about the size of a small primary school, and set in a cell-lined quadrangle with high, red walls topped with razor-wire. There were about one hundred and forty prisoners, mainly men. They were all sat down in rows on the ground in the hot sun, awaiting our arrival.

The mood was not good when we first arrived.

We sang African worship songs and were able to mingle and talk. French was required, and my school day French, mangling my tenses, seemed enough to get by. Life in the African prisons was very tough, and justice was corrupt and arbitrary.

We took turns to tell a Bible story so, when my turn came, I asked thirteen men to represent the disciples and Jesus in a boat. We then acted out Matthew Ch 8 v 23. This seemed to cause a great amount of fun and laughter, the message that Jesus will help us in the storms of our lives, striking a chord that seemed to touch some of the prisoners.

Jane and Serenity, a girl from mainland China, had come to see a seaman who had been abandoned by his Chinese fishing vessel. He stood accused of murder and had been left there in the prison. He spoke only Mandarin, no English, no French. Let Jane continue from here:

Jane:

Serenity and I entered this prison, passing through a series of gates, and came into a hot, dusty courtyard full of men. After a short time, we found Wong An. He was in his fifties, a fisherman with a strong and open face. Serenity had met him two weeks before, when she first visited the prison. She told me about him and asked if I would accompany her to visit him that week. We prayed that God would be able to use us to tell him the gospel. God was amazing; he softened Wong An's heart in answer to our prayers. That day, in the prison yard, this man said the prayer for forgiveness and asked the Lord Jesus into his heart. I went through CrossCheck with him. Although he could not read English, he loved the pictorial aspect of the message. He pointed to the man lying on the ground and asked if that was him, and I told him, "Yes, it represents all of us."

Then he pointed to the fire and asked if that was where he was going to go.

I said, "Yes, if you do not believe that Jesus, God's son, has died for you."

He said, "But I killed a man in the fight."

I gently told him of the two men who were crucified with Jesus, and that they had probably killed someone in their time. Yet one did not believe, and the other did. The one who asked Jesus to remember him was promised by Jesus that he would be with him in Paradise.

"That could be you," I said.

I explained that he had to invite our Lord into his heart to live with him, even in this terrible prison. He told me that he might face a death sentence. I explained that, whatever the consequences of this earthly life, would he like to be restored to God?

His fear of Hell was palpable so, when we invited him to pray to be forgiven of his sins through Jesus, it was like taking a thirsty man to the well and giving him living water.

The hot, Congolese sun shone upon us and we knew that the Lord had forgiven this man. Serenity had brought a Chinese Bible and Wong An read the first three chapters of Genesis avidly to us.

Then we brought him to John 3: 16, and explained how the Lord our God sent His own Son for us. His face was one of such delight. We left him the Chinese Bible.

We discovered that his eldest sister was a committed Christian. We explained to him that she had probably been praying for him and The Lord had moved our hearts to come and visit him. We serve a living God, and this was no accident that we were there together in the Mercy Ship and visiting him that day.

I had saved my hard-boiled eggs from breakfast, plus a slice of bread for him. Nigel also had a bar of chocolate for him. The prison was such a bleak place. The rooms were overcrowded and they had to do hard labour each day, like building roads and doing repairs for the Government. Each day they received a bowl of rice and, occasionally, some lentils. Mercy Ships had been trying to get some filtration for their drinking water to remove the usual parasites.

Three weeks later saw Wong An being publicly baptised in a bath brought into the prison by the Mercy Ships team.

Nigel:

Sunday found us down in the wards, attending the ward service. All the patients who were able, the African day-workers, the nurses and people living on the ship can come to this service.

It was held in one of the empty wards.

We managed to shoehorn about one hundred people into the room, patients wrapped in bandages, ten VVF (vesico-vaginal fistulas) ladies carrying their catheter bags, and nurses and crew. Clementine, the ship's Ward Pastor, had asked if I could give the message so, following a very African, noisy, cheerful, clapping, drumming and singing worship session, I told a Bible story and got a group of patients to act out the story.

A lot of our free time was spent talking and sharing with other crew on board. All had a story to tell. The current Captain, Dainis Briedis, came from Latvia. He was a strong, square-shaped man, with hands like shovels, a ready smile and an infectious laugh, speaking English with a heavy accent. He had two children, a daughter living in Birmingham and a son living in Latvia. His wife was a schoolteacher. He had served on ninety-five ships and felt God calling him to serve. But how? One day he spotted a small article about Mercy Ships in a maritime newspaper.

He wrote to Mercy Ships head office and sent his credentials in. At the time, he was working for a German shipping company and was sailing across the Pacific Ocean.

When he asked his employers if he could have three months away from work, they initially replied no. However, he prayed about it and the company came back within a week to say he could have the time off. Not only that, the German company also said they would continue to pay his salary whilst he was serving with Mercy Ships. So he was now on the ship, meeting and working with the Christian community. The first person to serve from Latvia. He told me, "I am so happy to be able to use my lifetime's shipping experience for God's service."

On Monday it was back to our dental clinic. We had a new dentist, Bob Russell, come to join us. A sixty-seven-year-old man with a wonderful Christian heart (see photo page 191). Full of energy and a desire to serve. It was the first time our paths had crossed, although he had been serving for the past eleven years as well, coming out to the ship for three or four weeks at a time. We all had a good day seeing and treating about seventy-seven patients. Tuesday and Wednesday went on in a similar vein.

As a postscript to the prison story, Serenity, the Chinese girl, managed to phone Wong An's sister in China and tell her the good news. They asked what they could do to help. They said he was a good, hard-working man, and they were shocked to learn of his plight.

With the arrival of Bob Russell, we managed to up the number of patients treated, from seventy to ninety-five a day. This added an extra hustle, bustle and energy to the place.

The African day-care workers were excellent at translating and helping to assist chairside. With three dentists, sixteen chairside assistants/translators and eight patients all working together in one room, there was never a cross word; time was taken, where necessary, and extra help was given, if required. Prayers were spoken and shared, and difficult dental work completed. Each Monday and Thursday, the line-up held a thousand hopeful patients, of whom we could see and treat four hundred and seventy-five a week.

Thursday saw the arrival of a small, fact-finding delegation from Burma (Myanmar) arranged by Jane and me.

Mercy Ships were very good, providing their senior management team to guide the delegation round the ship, and discuss the functions, purposes and challenges of working in a third-world country. They were taken round the off-ship centres on the next day - eye clinic, the Hope Centre and dental clinic, plus surgery observation on board ship in the afternoon. Eight of us set off in torrential rain to collect the Burmese group for lunch: Gary Parker and his wife, Susan, Pierre Christ, Brenda Van Stratten, Keith Brinkman, Paula Kirby, Jane and I.

The conversation flowed, speeches were made and concepts agreed. Mercy Ships was building a new ship in China, the Global Mercy. The possible concept being discussed was for this new vessel to provide an outreach to Burma on its way over to Africa. (Despite great hopes, it did not materialise.)

One evening, the ship's catering staff provided a barbecue on the dockside for all the ship's crew, plus the African day-care workers. It was a warm, humid evening, the sun slowing sinking in a dusty haze, lines of people chatting and laughing together, waiting for their turn to collect bread, beefburgers, salad and ginger cake. One of the ship's worship team groups played live music, people danced about and, into all of this celebration, at the top of the ship's gangway, appeared the patients! Slowly, they descended the steps, most wrapped in bandages, all smiling and waving. As they reached the dock, they were greeted and cheered. Some had been operated on only that day. They were hugged and clasped and seated amongst the throng of crew members. More songs were sung and time shared and, as the sun slowly disappeared below the horizon, the warm, dark evening enveloped us all.

On Sunday, we attended the ward service with a message on the ten lepers and only one returning to thank Jesus. (Luke Ch.17 v12-19)

We had a repeat of When the Storm Rolls at the end, by popular request.

When it rained in the Congo, well, it really rained. During the night, we had been woken by the regular flashing and crashing of lightning and thunder. Pointe Noire was built on sand - lorries driving into and out of the port spread this sand about, and teams of sweepers brush sand to the sides of the roads and into the drains. The result - city flooding; total gridlock, chaos, shouting, traffic jams, horns, arm-waving, and lorries disappearing into holes filled with water, leaving only their rear ends showing.

One area, which we normally travelled through on our way to work, became a river about one hundred yards wide, washing away furniture stores, houses, and livelihoods. Very few people carried umbrellas or wore raincoats, simply walking in the warm deluge, getting soaked, avoiding deep areas of water and making their way through the logjam of submerged cars, sometimes having to wade through the chest-high, muddy water.

We had to take a long detour to get to our clinic, arriving about and hour and a half late. The day-care team had also had difficulties, so we were a depleted group for most of the day. We still managed to treat around ninety-five patients. One of our German dental nurses received a needle stick injury and had to return, with the patient, to have a blood test in case of AIDS or hepatitis.

This was always a risk working in Africa though, with God's grace, problems were very rare.

One afternoon, Jane attended the VVF ladies' leaving ceremony, where they were each given a wonderful new dress and gifts, and there was much dancing and singing.

Jane:

Eight ladies, from the ages of eighteen to fifty, had the operation to repair their bladders and wombs. Each of them had a testimony to give about their life before arriving on to the Mercy Ship. The women were called the untouchables. They had usually given birth to dead babies and the treatment, or lack of treatment, they had received left them with damaged bladders and wombs. They could not control their water-works, so they smelled bad all the time. If married, their husbands abandoned them and they were not welcomed anywhere, because of the puddles they made wherever they went.

Life was very miserable for all these ladies.

At any one time, there are over one million such ladies all over Africa.

When the operation had been done and the women healed, Mercy Ships held a great celebration of thanksgiving for them. A team of nurses dressed them in brand-new dresses. For the ceremony, sixty of us were crammed into one ward for worship and praise, to thank the Lord for their healing. Each of them received a symbolic gift from kind donors.

It consisted of a soap to symbolise the cleansing of our souls by Jesus, body cream to symbolise the anointing of the body and a Bible each to guide them in their new life. Their testimonies reduced us to tears.

Some were victims of rape when they were very young, and their bodies were not mature enough to conceive a baby. One was aged only eight when it happened. The celebration was like a baptism for most of them, as they realised how much the Lord must have loved them, to have sent a medical team to help them and lift them out of their sorrow. Praise God.

Nigel:

On our last evening, we took all twenty-five of the dental team out for a Chinese meal, in a restaurant vetted by Jane. This was a good opportunity to sing songs, talk, eat and have some fellowship together. They had not been out for a meal since the beginning of the outreach in Pointe Noire.

Congo had been a little different from many of the other West African countries that the Africa Mercy had helped. It had a huge need, with a vast number of poor. At the same time, Congo was sitting on six billion dollars of foreign reserves; the President and his family were amongst the Forbes top one hundred wealthiest in the world. The port was enormous and had a huge turnover; oil was being pumped out of the ground. Its population was around 4 million, not too large by African standards. The wealth was held by less than 1%, with the remainder fighting for the scraps.

Psalm 103 v 10-12: *"He does not treat us as our sins deserve or repay us according to our iniquities. For as high as the heavens are above the earth, so great is His love for those who fear him; as far as the east is from the west, so far has He removed our transgressions from us."*

Chapter 25

Pointe Noire clinic

Bob Russell

Dental queue

Regular flooding

Dickensian prison conditions

Barry and Cheryl at the Hope Centre

Chapter 26

Burma - Delta Region and Mawgyun Town 2015 - Seventh Visit

THE CATHEDRAL OF THE HOLY TRINITY was full to the brim and was well cared for by Rev. Reginald Bennett. He was still continuing with his post-service Bible study.

We chatted with an English girl, Sarah, who was teaching music at the International School. She said she attended a Gospel outreach meeting by the church, where forty people gave their lives to Jesus.

The massive Irrawaddy River finishes its bisecting journey through Myanmar, having travelled down from the Himalayas, ending in a huge, flat delta region (see maps).

The district, or, to use the English term, county, is called Irrawaddy and its capital is Patbein.

We managed to commission a local metal workshop to construct two portable dental chairs, and also obtained a simple, sixty-litre compressor for an air supply. These, together with twenty boxes of gloves, portable control-boxes, a pressure cooker for sterilisation, 50kg of dental tools, towels, tissues, bowls, masks, lights, packs, filling materials, antibiotics and medicines, two hundred *CrossCheck* books and a Bible or two, meant that we were, at last, ready for the delta region. All this created quite a collection to be transported the one hundred miles from Yangon to Mawgyun town, where we were headed.

Our team, such as it was, consisted of Dr Ko and his wife, Molly, two general doctors, one from King's, London and and Patrick, who had travelled with us for the past seven years, acting as helpers, assistants and translators, and Jane and me. We were also allocated three local nurses to help marshal the patients, sterilise the instruments and generally help.

The method of transport was by boat - a nine-hour trip.

As usual, Jane and I prayed for health, safety and opportunities.

It being 5am and very dark and with none of us knowing where to find the

Chapter 26

river vessel, there was a fair amount of searching up and down various wharves before the craft was located.

Carrying our equipment across a slippery, oily jetty, my first thoughts were: *African Queen*! Humphrey Bogart! But perhaps that was a bit too flattering.

Our craft for the next nine hours was sixty feet long by fifteen feet wide. Set very low in the water, it resembled a wide barge with a wooden roof; it supposedly took ninety passengers. It was a muddy, yellow colour, with a huge engine at the stern of the vessel providing a cheerfully noisy forward propulsion. So much so, that a loud shout was necessary to talk with one's neighbour.

Hawkers were set up on the jetty, to sell us food and water for our journey. The boat was pretty much full to the brim, locals taking goods back from Yangon to their homes, which were set along the route the ferry was due to take. Despite the early hour, there was a cheerful banter going on, people finding their seats, passing babies and children about, bottles of water and food.

Our large parcels were stowed on the roof.

With a few blasts on the boat's hooter, the engine roared into life and we set off at a merry five knots into the pre-dawn night.

Our little dental team were fairly sleepy and jet-lagged, so the initial shock of our travelling conditions only slowly began to sink in, as the sun gradually rose above the river banks on our port side. Bedbugs and mosquitoes were a concern, due to the well-travelled nature of our seats.

The steady clatter of the engine seemed to vibrate right through our bodies and, somehow, into our heads as well. Every now and again, the craft would give a tired shudder, as though seeking sympathy from its crew and passengers, for all the endless trips it had done.

We gradually slipped into a sort of dazed, hypnotic coma, occasionally sleeping, but awakening with a start when the claxon was sounded to warn off other boats in the morning mist that hung about over the river. Now and then, small craft would come bumping and crashing alongside, dropping people, plus possessions, on to and off the ferry as we continued on our way.

The delta region consists of a massive network of rivers and channels, all spreading out from the Irrawaddy River. The collected silt from this great river continuously adds land to the area. This is so fertile, that two or three crops of rice can be grown each year. That, plus the fish that can be caught, means that there is an abundant food supply and the area is well-populated. All along the river banks, wooden houses could be seen, and fishing boats and other craft are everywhere.

We stop off here and there. At each brief pause, groups of people flood on to the craft with great trays on their heads loaded with local delicacies, bottles of water, or fruit, all yelling out their prices and bargains. As they mingle about us all, the boat's captain gives a blast on his whistle and there is a mad charge as they all try to get off before we cast off. Total turnaround time four minutes.

As the sun rises, the temperature builds up, too, and our limited ventilation, through cracked and opaque windows, becomes a precious commodity. Windcheaters, hats and jumpers are removed, hand-held fans appear, water is drunk.

There is one toilet at the very stern of the ship, next to the engine. The cubicle hangs over the stern, just above the propeller and the wash of the ship.

It is a truly terrifying experience. Once perched inside, everything is shaking, and water is blasting up through the giant hole in the floor. Knuckles turn white, knees are shaking. Nine hours is a long time to wait. Some have cast-iron control; for the rest of us, it was shut your eyes, hold on tight and pray.

At last we arrived at Mawgyun town. Surviving the gangplank disembarkation was the final challenge. A springy, twelve-inch-wide piece of old, worn wood, linking the boat to the local jetty. Hands that seemed always well out of reach were offered to help. Crowds watched; perhaps someone would slip? Not this time.

The town was quite extensive, but fairly basic. Cars were few; motorbikes, bicycles and carts were most common. The houses were mainly wooden; the market was very extended and bustling with vibrancy, colour and life.

We were taken, in a variety of transports, to the hospital and given some water. Still in a daze, the boat engine still ringing in our ears, all we could think of was food and sleep. One apple over ten hours since we had woken, was a little meagre, but the on-board snacks had looked way too risky to try.

The building we had been offered was excellent for our purposes. A twenty feet by eleven room, clean and tiled, just nice for our two portable chairs and tables for all our kit. Other, smaller, rooms lay adjacent to a connecting corridor for compressor, sterilisation area and tea-making. All tiled and clean in appearance.

We established a reception area with room for fifty to sixty people to wait, and were all set to have a wash and rest, when twenty patients appeared from the

Chapter 26

throng outside, so, to test everything out, we saw and treated them.

Because an ophthalmic team was at the hospital, as well as us, accommodation was in short supply, so we were taken, tired and travel-worn, through the winding and dusty streets, honking our way through cyclists, scooters, and people pushing cartloads of produce to sell, arriving at the one and only hotel in town.

The building looked quite impressive from the outside. The only three-storey building in town, it stood with tiger statues guarding the entrance. It was squeezed on to a piece of land adjacent to a large rubbish dump; the edge of the town market and the hotel were connected to a very large saloon bar. This latter feature had modelled itself on wild west films, with a long drinks bar and beer for thirsty farm-workers; music was playing, and there were a couple of TV screens. It even had twin swing doors at its entrance.

Our $4 rooms were just a bit larger than a broom cupboard. The two floors had shared washing and toilet facilities. The beds were solid wood. We shuffled into the small entrance, dragging our oversized luggage, trying to establish where our respective rooms were, and yelling to the fifteen-year-old receptionist above the noise from the bar. Guys were wandering about through the swing doors, roll-up cigarettes hanging from the corners of their mouths. All that were missing were the guns in side holsters.

Keys were tossed in our direction and we located our respective cupboards for the night. On the first floor, six rather heavy-looking characters were watching a martial arts film, smoking and drinking beer. Our rooms lay adjacent to this area, so it was a great relief when there was a power cut at 12.30am and the TV at last fell silent.

The temperature being 28°C and no fan, we had the choice of sweating it out, or opening the window and allowing the swarm of mosquitoes to come and feast. Our tested bladders, already strained from the boat journey, were again expected to hold out, as the toilet facilities were flooded, unlit and hazardous. What kept us going was the knowledge that this was for one night only, as we were due to stay at the hospital from the next day.

The night was long, with much noise, door-banging, laughter, etc., mostly calming down by 3am. Our window overlooked the generator and the rubbish dump, so fighting dogs and the diesel motor starting up and turning off, all added to the night's sleep, or the lack of it. Come the morning, we endeavoured to clean up a little, amongst some interesting ladies dotted about the corridors, and we returned to the hospital for breakfast.

The first treatment day went well, one hundred and seven patients seen and treated, all from the surrounding community areas. Patients from two to eighty-eight in years. What a joy to see all these people and to be able to help.

For the next day or so we continued along this path, our team gradually being added to, and the patient flow, instrument sterilisation, reception and corridor management all becoming streamlined.

I was chatting with one patient, a man in his thirties, and the subject of the tsunami came up. The delta region had been very severely hit by the tidal wave and many had lost their lives on 26th December 2004. Swe had been walking near the coast with his wife and three children when the wave hit. All he could remember was holding on to one of his children and then being totally engulfed by the seawater. He was forced up against a coconut tree and clung to the trunk for an hour or more, losing all his clothes in the process. He was the only one of his family to survive. He opened up his shirt to reveal his chest. Marked in deep dark scars was the imprint of the coconut-tree trunk, right across his front. Hundreds of his friends and relatives had perished that night. Help arrived weeks later, and was totally inadequate.

Our new accommodation was upstairs, in a room adjacent to six hundred other local people staying in a large, upstairs open conference room. They were all patients who had received, or were about to receive, treatment for cataracts or lens replacements. They had to stay for a few days or so.

Our room opened out on to this hive of humanity, all curious, chatty, excited, sleeping, or walking about. Also, families were visiting, preparing food, washing, queuing for the toilet, etc. Once again, bladders were tested, as we had to tiptoe through this throng of sleeping, one-eyed patients on our way to the three toilets available.

Regrettably, on day four my rather sensitive gut decided to react to the local flora and fauna and I was completely knocked for six, having to sleep most of the day; with the help of seven Imodium tablets, calm was restored. This left Jane to do the clinic on her own for most of that day, though I was able to help a bit in the afternoon. We were still treating about one hundred people a day, which was good.

The word had got out that two Christian dentists were in town, so two groups came to the hospital to find us: one from the Mawgyun Baptist Church and the other from the Kayin district Baptist Church.

Chapter 26

A couple of evenings later, we got a lift in a van to visit the Mawgyun Baptist Church, set down a small side-path, adjacent to one of the river deltas. We were given a really warm welcome by about thirty members of the church and, with the help of an interpreter, we were able to have a good talk. They sang some songs for us and, using a keyboard that was there, we all sang *Amazing Grace* and *Holy, Holy, Holy*, which I could play from memory.

After a Bible verse and a couple of rounds of *When the Storm Rolls*, which they threw themselves into, we all sat down for tea, snacks and more talk together. They were such a friendly, warm group of fellow brothers and sisters, and it was very special to share time with them and to pray together. It also appeared that many had received treatment at our dental clinic over the past few days. We handed out *CrossChecks* and pens.

The surrounding communities, both local and from across the extended waterways, seemed to have passed the word around that the two dentists working in town, provided free treatment and, more importantly, they didn't hurt.

One of my patients was tiny, about four feet five inches in height, but with the energy and personality of a giant. She was a grandmother of twelve grandchildren, and ran her own market business.

Following our trip to the local Baptist church, the evening arrived for us to go to the Kayin District Baptist church. The Kayin people are a close community and they live mainly in a rural suburb of Mawgyun town. We left at 5pm, a little earlier than expected, after seeing a day's worth of patients; this was because we were warned that the paths leading to the church were quite narrow and crossed a lot of single, bamboo walkways. So our quick turnaround allowed us one and a half hours of daylight.

When being invited to a church, you never know quite what to expect, what to prepare for, or what you might have to do. All we knew was that church members had been back to the clinic a number of times to check that we were still OK for the visit. The church was located amongst a large number of rattan-covered houses on bamboo stilts. The land was pretty waterlogged, so there were numerous banks and pools of water, with vegetables and rice planted. The district was also thickly wooded, so it was hard for us to grasp the extent of the community. We were walked along the winding, earthen paths, crossing this ditch, that stream, all the time accompanied by an increasing number of children and families, everyone giving us a warm welcome.

By the time we reached the church, there were about a hundred people, of all ages. We were introduced to the

Minister, the Assistant Minister, the five Sunday school teachers, the deacons and elders; photos were taken. We then sort of flowed into the church in a giant, cheerful buzz of kindness, where we were seated right at the front of a raised dais.

For the next hour and a bit we were entertained by all the age groups, performing Christian songs, dance routines, plays about Jesus' life set to music, the full, sixty-strong church choir performing their competition song, and then more musical items. It was quite amazing and wonderful to witness. Costumes were worn. The church became packed, with everyone clapping and encouraging the performers. Additional families were clustered at the open windows and doors.

What, I wondered, did God want from Jane and myself here at this church? What could we offer, what could we say?

Before we knew it, microphones were thrust into our hands and we were up on stage. We managed to keep them interested and engaged with a mixture of grateful thank-yous for all their preparation and performing, Gospel messages, songs with actions, Bible story enactments, prayer and last of all, a duet of *Holy, Holy, Holy*. This latter was under duress, but was kindly received.

Please remember that this was at the end of a day of treating seventy patients, and with a wobbly tummy. These things happen only with the help of the Holy Spirit.

On leaving, everyone wanted to shake our hand. Two hundred and fifty handshakes later, we threaded our way, in the dark, through the maze of paths back to the town, and returned to the hospital It was wonderful to find such a joyous, vibrant church in the depths of the delta region. We pray it continues to flourish. They had never had any foreign Christian visitors before.

We continued to see patients over the remaining days. A constant flow appeared each morning and were happy to wait the entire day to be seen. It was hot there in the delta, reaching 32°C at midday. We had fans, but no air con in the clinic so, by the hundredth patient, Jane and I were pretty bushed. We just gave thanks for the opportunity to be there to help.

Our team had now swollen to about twenty-four so, for our last day, we took them all out for a meal to the restaurant they recommended. We were flabbergasted, when arriving, to find that it was booked at our first day's wild west hotel! This time on the roof, not in the saloon with the eighty guys and girls. The roof afforded a night-time view over the town and a private dining area seated around separate picnic tables. Still we all had a good time.

Chapter 26

We packed up our kit, re-boxed it all and caught the "delightful nine-hour ferry" back to Yangon. A lasting memory was as our craft eased away from the simple bamboo jetty, we were waved off by a cluster of fourteen of our new-found friends and team helpers, calling out their goodbyes.

"Come again, please," one called.

"Thank you and bless you," another added.

"Don't forget us, please," drifted across the water.

They stood and watched, a small group gathered together, waving slowly with outstretched arms, until we rounded a corner in the river.

John Ch 14 v 27: *"Peace I leave with you; my peace I give you. I do not give to you as the world gives. Do not let your hearts be troubled and do not be afraid."*

Our trusty vessel to Mawgyun

Precarious exit gangway

Plenty of patients

Not so private sleeping arrangements

Walking to the Mawgyun church

What a welcome we had

Chapter 27

Burma, Nov 2015 – A fascinating town called Kalay, north west of Mandalay.

THIS WAS OUR EIGHTH VISIT to Burma. We had groups dotted all over the world, praying for our trip.

Yangon, the capital colonial city, was buzzing with post-election euphoria. A new government had been elected for the first time since 1952.

Cars had been allowed to be imported for a year and the result was that the traffic was gridlocked from 8am to 8pm; hotels were being built everywhere, the streets all covered with a dusty haze. It was a humid 34°C.

On our arrival from the U.K. we had one day to pre-check our equipment, and buy gloves, tissues, towels, disinfectant, cottonwool rolls, tooth brushes and, last but not least, tins of sardines, corned beef, etc. for myself, in an attempt to avoid the need for an Imodium onslaught.

We joined up again with the Belgian team. They was still a group of three plastic surgeons, three anesthetists, three nurses, two eye-surgeons and an equipment technician. To this we added our dental team of six, plus some coordinators, arranging accommodation, liaising with the local town and getting the word out to the surrounding community that we were coming to town.

We had a small plane to take us from Yangon up to Kalay provided by the government. Assembling at the small, internal flight terminal, we met up with the Belgian team, all looking a bit travel-worn after flying from Brussels to Paris to Bangkok to Yangon. All our gear was loaded on to the twin-prop plane and forty of us squeezed in through the back door, with our hand luggage on our laps.

With a loud, rattling roar, we were aloft and away, heading off to north-west Myanmar.

We were the only flight in to Kalay that day, so the one-room terminal building was not overloaded. Everyone's luggage and all the hospital kit were loaded on to a queue of waiting vehicles, and we set off through the bustling town centre to the hospital.

Kalay is set on a large flood plain, with mountains along its western border. The area grows a lot of rice and lentils. The large town is spread far and wide, with all the buildings being one or two storeys. There was the usual throng of motorcycles, pushbikes, farm trucks and people going about their daily lives.

Awaiting us were about six hundred locals, some prospective patients, some just curious.

There ensued a chaotic and enthusiastic unloading of baggage and possessions; photos were taken and everyone set off to locate operating theatres, wards, etc.

Our small dental unit were kind of left standing in the receding dust storm as the Belgian group disappeared.

One of the common traits we have noticed about hospitals in general, and especially in Burma, was that the dental unit, if there was one, was often the last item added on to any planning, and it was usually under-funded, old, under-staffed and an embarrassment to be seen in.

So, having been assured, prior to our arrival, that there were two working, modern, dental chairs, compressor, autoclave steriliser, etc., our expectations had been subdued, if not sceptical.

What we found, when we tracked down the dental building, was that it was an un-modernised, decrepit, wooden, 1930s colonial backwater. The chairs were old and the two tiny rooms small, dark and depressing; the place felt unused and its main job seemed to be housing junk and old medical bits of kit.

Oh yes, one other minor point; there was no electricity and no water.

After coming all this way, our team morale was, I have to admit, at a bit of a low point.

We prayed for help.

So, why had God brought us here?

Well, the first bit of good news was that the town's inhabitants numbered 300,000, 75% of whom were Christian (actually members of a church)!

The place was full of churches. That was great news.

The next bit of encouragement was that a dentist turned up (nothing to do with the hospital). He was very happy to help and, what's more, he worshipped at a local church and offered to take us there on the Sunday.

His name was Tan.

Despite a bevy of hospital administrators in denial, we managed to explore the hospital and found a Christian doctor in charge of all the operating theatres.

She kindly found us a room next to the intensive care unit which we felt we could transform into a surgery. It had been used as a general dumping-ground for old furniture, tables, chairs, trolleys and boxes of junk. But it was a good size, and nice and light, so we set about clearing the room of its accumulated junk, washing and cleaning the walls and floor, and arranging water and electrical supplies.

Not only that, two ladies turned up from I know not where, again asking if they could help in any way. Both Christians from a Baptist church, and both nurses.

Come Sunday, Tan came and collected Jane and me and we endeavoured to clamber into his Burmese-made jeep, a vehicle that had seen better days. There was no floor-well in the passenger area, so you sat with your knees at the same height as your head. Fortunately, the journey to the Kalay Brethren Baptist Church was not too long.

We were warmly greeted by the equivalent of the church oversight team, and I was handed a phone so that I could talk to the church minister, who happened to be in the USA doing a theology exam! He, too, was effusive with his welcome. The church seated about two hundred and thirty people and was full. They were in the process of building a new church right next door, big enough to seat about nine hundred and fifty people!

The service was lively and Bible-based, the worship sung in harmony.

Jane and I were introduced and asked to give a short talk. There was so much joy in the Lord, and we shared in a post-service meal provided by their hospitality team.

The visiting minister, who spoke excellent English, explained that there were thirty-two Baptist churches in the district, many growing.

It was so uplifting to find God's work going on six thousand miles from Wallington.

The same enthusiasm, the same joy in the Lord as we found in our home church.

Tan squeezed us back into his jeep and took us round the town, bumping and rattling about. It was dusty and hot (34°C) but, whilst we sweated and bounced, he earnestly asked us our thoughts on sections of the Bible, the Gospel, about gifting, tax and Christian responsibility. With the swerving to avoid the myriad of bikers, perspiration trickling into our eyes, the constant sounding of car horns and our backs stuck to the plastic seats, it was hard to concentrate fully but, between us, we had an excellent time sharing a kind of Bible study on the hoof.

We ended up back at the hospital and started setting up our kit in the new room given to us. It was not that well decorated, but it was a huge improvement on the original dental site. People gradually dropped by as the afternoon progressed, all lending a hand, connecting the compressor, trying to locate an electrical power source, moving tables about, setting up the autoclave, running extension cables (there were plenty of electrical sockets about, but most had no power). Nurses and doctors made packs for us.

A lot, if not most, were Christian, so the working atmosphere was a joy. Almost like being back on the *Mercy Ship*.

By 6pm we had got most of the place set and ready.

Apparently we had a few hundred patients, all down on a waiting list.

One other blessing: our accommodation had to be the best we had ever stayed in whilst out and about in Myanmar. Hot water to bathe, an actual mattress on the bed, and clean towels. Marvellous.

All in remote, deepest, darkest Kalay.

For our first clinical day, Jane and I were keen to check things over, knowing how hard it was to do any adjustments and mending once the place was full of patients. So, we were there by 7.15am, only to find that there were still problems with some of the dental kit. Airlines were blowing off, there was no electricity for the autoclave and no staff to start with.

Our first collection of patients was all the hospital staff - nurses, doctors and administrators. All wanted to be seen and advised and/or treated. Next arrived about fifty from the Brethren Baptist Church we had visited the day before, all cheerfully sitting about and waving at us.

A posse of schoolchildren arrived, and so the day continued.

We handed out *CrossCheck* booklets and pens, with the message **The Lord is my Strength and Shield - Psalm 28 v 7**, on them.

By 5.30pm, Jane and I could hardly stand. The working environment was challenging, the help, when it arrived, willing but untrained. The Chin people spoke their own dialect, which then needed translating into Burmese and then into English, so getting the communication right took a lot of effort.

With myself, a nurse or two, a patient and two interpreters, a common conversation would go as follows:

"Which tooth do you want removing?" Translation, translation.

Answer in Chin language. Translation, translation.

Chapter 27

"He's not sure," comes the reply.

"This one?" I'd ask, pointing to a suspect tooth, wanting to be absolutely sure.

Translation, translation.

Answer, translation, translation.

"All of them."

"That can't be right!" I'd exclaim.

Long inter-discussion takes place for five minutes.

Then, they all turn to me and nod in agreement.

By God's grace, we would usually get to the actual problem.

One of the things in Burma and, indeed, in Africa and Mongolia, was that the patients were not used to being asked what they wanted. Usually, when visiting a local doctor or dentist, the patient was told the problem he had and what was to be done.

So our normal process of obtaining "informed consent" was very foreign to them.

All that being said, the Lord's hand was evident in so many ways that first day, seeing us through a potential minefield of difficulties. We had patients declaring His goodness and saying, "Alleluia", when treatment was completed. We had a lot of laughter, and moments of despair.

We were taken to another hospital site that evening and I was asked to design a dental clinic on its first floor. The roof was on, but no partitioning walls were there yet. So, after supper, time was spent drawing out floor plans for the new clinic, showing electrical, water, air con, dental fittings, etc.

They promised to have it completed the following year, which they did.

Over the next day or two, a lot of our patients came from local churches. The Mother Superior of the local Roman Catholic convent came with some of her nuns, and the Bishop came the next day!

In all that took place, God was good. Our new team had now gelled.

We continued for a few more days, before preparing to set off to Mandalay and on to Monwah.

At the end of our dental mission in Kalay, we took the team out for a meal to say thank you. The group had now stabilised at eighteen, including ourselves. They recommended a restaurant near the hospital.

Eating-places in these rural towns were spread out along the road networks. The fronts were open, with a few tables and chairs out on the pavement/street. Their wooden construction seemed to be painted a universal bluey-green colour. Large signs were fixed to the

A Step or Two of Faith

Tan's Burmese-made car

Bethel Baptist church, Kalay

Deacons and Elders by their new church

The Abbess and her nuns came for treatment

Kalay dental team

Monywa dental clinic, post-earthquake

Chapter 28

Tondo, Manila, May 2015
School and Graveyard ministry.

ON OUR THIRD VISIT to Tondo, we pondered what difference our little grain of sand might make to this veritable "Sahara Desert" of poverty.

Everyone had trials and tribulations, and desperate individual survival struggles in Tondo, but how might we promote Christ amongst this community of souls?

There were 79,297 persons per square mile in Tondo, all living cheek-by-jowl, up to fourteen per room, in tenement blocks, shanty towns or, often, trying to shelter beneath the road overpasses.

One dual carriageway near the seaport had lost one of its roads through house-creep. This happened where the locals spread themselves on to the pavement, setting up stalls and selling items. They then needed to guard their pitch, so slept there. This then spread on to the road, packing-case-and-tarpaulin-style; relatives moved in and, a couple of years later, the whole roadway was missing! Covered in wooden, DIY-built shacks, forming haphazard communities. Wires everywhere, no drains, no mains water, unpoliced.

Life was extremely precarious, particularly for the children.

Amongst all this bustle was Joe's small community church, housed in two old shops, set side by side, and now with a dental surgery.

Its funding was haphazard, and reliant on donations from *Amen Trust* (https://www.amentrust.co.uk), and members of its church and family. They had to trust entirely in the Lord.

We looked on and, in reality, our own lives were running in a different dimension from theirs. We probably never could completely understand the difficulties they had faced over the years, their total reliance on the Lord, living from day to day, never sure if they could pay the rental on their church building, or have enough to buy food.

We hoped and prayed that our visit would encourage and be beneficial to their ongoing mission work.

Joe Gonzales met us at Manila Airport and took us to the hostel where we were staying. He had a lot of rheumatism and also had progressive kidney failure. We are the same age chronologically, but he has had a much harder road to travel than ourselves. He said it was only by the Grace of God that he was still alive. (as I write this he was on full time dialysis for a year and went to be with the Lord in March 2021).

We were up at 6am, had some breakfast and were picked up by Joe.

The Manila traffic was much lighter early on, so progress through the crowded streets to our first destination was good.

This was a school called *Jose Abad Santos*, a high school with 4500 pupils!

We spent some time with Mrs Laura Macarinao, the head teacher, who was a Christian, and had an opportunity to pray with her.

The school was set out in a large quadrangle, with high-rise buildings totally surrounding it. The pupils wore everyday clothes and swarmed about the facility. Laura sailed along, with us in tow, a serene aura of calmness about her.

She took us to a large room filled with about eighty pupils, and introduced us.

Jane and I then spent the morning talking about health issues, teeth, *CrossCheck* gospel, and *Mercy Ships*, together with Bible stories and songs with actions.

Their ages ranged from eleven to fifteen and they were very disciplined, considering that the school was free and state-run, and that most of the young people came from Tondo, with its ramshackle housing and social problems.

At the end of the talk, I asked them what they might fancy doing as a career or job.

Some hands quickly shot up. Hoping that our talk might have inspired some to strive for greater things, I asked one girl, "How about you? What do you want to be?"

"A gangster moll," came the quick reply. "You just have to look pretty and you get lots of money."

"What about you?" I indicated to a fourteen-year-old boy sitting nearby.

"A policeman," he replied.

"Well, that's good," I said. "Why's that?"

"They get plenty of bribes and earn a good living."

The heat in the classroom was over 32°C. We were seriously overheated by the end of the morning.

From there we travelled, through the nightmare traffic, to the SIKAT centre.

Chapter 28

Since the previous year, they had completely redecorated and redesigned many sections. It looked a lot better and far more presentable. About eight young people (aged eighteen to twenty-four) were there. They helped with the school, the dental surgery and with the ministry. We did a Bible study on Acts Ch 2 with them, sang some new songs, ate ice cream, took photos, and chatted and listened to their worries.

At about 6pm, Joe took us back to our hostel. With the heat peaking at 35°C, coupled with the dense traffic and volume of people, we crashed out at 8.30.

We visited the main Tondo school the next day.

Tondo High had 5,500 pupils, one hundred and sixty-four teachers and staff, and one head teacher, called Joy. She was calm, loved the Lord, and seemed in total control of the establishment.

It was situated right in the heart of the tough Tondo district, amongst the stalls, motorbikes, rickshaws and total street chaos.

The buildings were functional and grim-looking, with heavy, steel bars separating zones of the school; to my mind, almost like a prison. However, the place was so full of young people that their cheerfulness and energy masked the brutal environment.

I was flagging as soon as we stepped out of the car. The temperature was a sticky 37°C, and the area in which we had to do our presentation and talk was just an outside space surrounded by bars and metal gates. We did have a roof to keep the sun out, but little else.

After meeting up with Joy, we set about trying to locate chairs, tables, sound system, etc.

After a while, it was discovered that both projectors were broken, so no pictures could be shown. It helps to be adaptable in this mission work.

Young people started to assemble, chatting and jostling one another. Many lived on, or beside the streets, and all studied at the school then went home to help with the family business.

Once again, we were introduced by the principal, Joy, and chatted away to the hundred or so children there. Health, teeth, sleep and work were all talked about, and then the Gospel message, using *CrossCheck* in a simplified form.

We looked at all their teeth, and gave out toothbrushes and toothpaste.

We ran again with Matthew Ch 8 v 23, enacted the story and sang some songs.

By now, I had lost about two pints of fluid and I was soaked! Jane was feeling dizzy and we were both a bit light-headed.

One of the hardest things, we found, was getting used to the terrible air quality in and around Tondo. It was the worst we have every experienced anywhere. It got into your eyes, your mouth and throat, and your lungs. When we showered at night, the water running off us was dark grey.

To add to the heat, someone had decided to light a bonfire, burning plastic and general rubbish, just the other side of the open area where we were all gathered. The smoke flooded across, causing our eyes to sting. The students appeared not to notice, and I realised that they were quite used to living in such a polluted environment.

Despite these difficulties, our efforts were well-received and nobody fell asleep, or wandered off.

We had a chance to meet some of the teachers and to cool down in Joy's air-conditioned office. However, we were so hot, that it took three to four hours to settle down.

We left the school and had a lunch at a *Jolly Bean* with the two dentists who worked voluntarily in the dental clinic. They were Nessi and April. We chatted and prayed with them, and discussed problems they encountered. Wonderfully, they had a great heart to serve.

On from there, it was back to the SIKAT centre to meet up with the young people, play music and chat.

In the evening, we had a Bible study.

Earlier on, we had spent a lot of time with connectors and wiring to try and get the soundtrack of *My God is a Great Big God* to play from my laptop into the church sound system. Jackplugs were the wrong size, and everything was humming and crackling but, after some prayer, joy of joys - it worked!

So we started the evening with the full version of *My God...*, with actions and jumping about.

The study on idols went well. We had a time of prayer and then prayed about personal problems. Each one of the group, of about twenty-four people, had chosen a Bible passage, with an interpretation and application to their life. We raced back and forth through the Bible pages, investigating those verses.

Getting back to our hostel by 10pm, we were pretty tired, but it had been a good day.

Many young people there had a heart to serve and love the Lord. Life was very difficult in Tondo. Jane and I were privileged to spend some time with them.

Chapter 28

Graveyard Ministry in Manila

We read about many different life situations in the newspapers, books, magazines, etc. We see documentaries of slum areas around India and Brazil, but this was new to us.

We went and distributed food to families living in the city's huge, Catholic graveyard.

Joe Gonzalez's daughter, Gloria, was a teacher at a local school in Tondo. She taught classes of sixty to seventy children, five days a week, and then returned home to help at the church nursery school. All her earnings were pooled into the church ministry funds.

Some of her children were missing on the odd school day, and they were not getting their work done, so she asked them where they lived.

"At the city cemetery," was the reply.

So she investigated, and discovered a whole community of people living there.

We went to the supermarket, bought five sacks of food, and set off to visit just five of the hundreds of families living amongst the mausoleums. As we entered the final resting-place of the Manila community, we followed two funeral cortèges, with their grieving relatives in tow. Many dressed in white. A variety of transports, from jeepneys, to tuk tuk bikes, and the odd smart SUV, and with colourful umbrellas, raised to protect individuals from the strong sunshine.

Amongst these transient, mournful visitors lived a permanent community of residents. They had strung up tarpaulins and set up small kitchen areas, and often slept on the smooth, marble resting-places. Children ran about, weaving their way between the stones.

We drove around the area, in the intense heat, trying to locate the various families. The cemetery covered several square miles. It was hard to find them, since a lot of the memorials were one or two storeys high and everything was packed closely together.

To see the tears well up in their eyes when told that this food was from God was unforgettable.

Their existence at the cemetery was very precarious - no toilets, no running water, small charcoal stoves, and very little food or money. They exuded a palpable fear of the night, when they had no security. Children were napping during the day, sprawled out on the cool marble slabs of the sarcophagi dotted about the graveyard.

Their cheerful adaptation to this surreal environment was quite amazing.

We sat and prayed with each family, and listened to some of their problems.

Gloria had a special ministry there. She held Bible studies in a large, two-storey crypt once a week, attended by about twenty-five young people. She had a special gift.

Once again, the hot sun wore Jane and myself down; after four hours or so, we returned to the SIKAT centre to cool down and discuss future plans for the centre.

The number of volunteer dentists had now grown to four, sharing the days between them.

Patients who showed an interest in the Gospel were visited by members of the church team, on occasion six or seven times.

The newly-decorated centre looked fresh and presentable. Joe had a team of young helpers dedicated to the Lord. God willing, we were to return in a year to see what had happened.

Nahum Ch 1 v 7: *"The Lord is good, a strong refuge when trouble comes. He is close to those who trust in him."*

Chapter 28

Surgery shoehorned at the back of the church meeting room

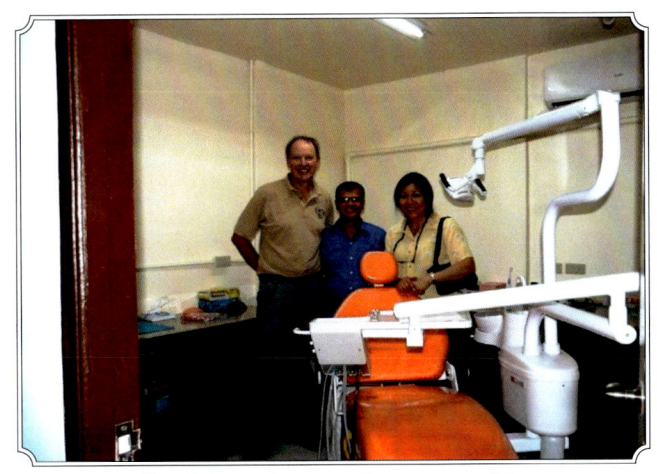

Looking clean and presentable

Tondo school

School talk

The SIKAT centre from the street

Graveyard ministry. Mum, Divina and her four children living in the graveyard

Chapter 29

Burma Kalay, November 2016. Ninth visit. Hard work and much Joy

Jane, Dr Ko, Molly, Patrick and I took a small plane to fly us from Yangon up to Kalay; it was a twin-engine turboprop that seated about thirty people.

No Belgian medics this time.

We had assembled at the small, internal flight terminal that morning, following some considerable consternation by the ground staff regarding our compressor and dental chair, and the fact that we were 160kg overweight.

Eventually, after some prayer, all our gear was loaded on to the plane and we squeezed in through the back door, with our hand luggage on our laps.

We exchanged greetings and smiles with our fellow-travellers and, with a loud, rattling roar, we were aloft and away, heading off to north-west Myanmar.

Our flight was the only one in to Kalay that day, so the one-room terminal building was not overloaded. We were greeted very warmly by a team of doctors from the hospital and some other organisers.

Everyone's luggage, plus all our dental kit, was loaded on to a couple of waiting vehicles and we set off through the bustling town to the hospital.

Kalay was busy, as usual. Its roads were almost all lined with giant, shade-providing trees, and there was the usual throng of motorcycles, pushbikes, farm trucks and people going about their daily lives. November through to January was the dry season so, along all the roads and paths, the mud that had built up during the wet months dried out and got dispersed like an aerosol, literally everywhere; it covered the trees, the houses, the cars, the shops, the people. The town, therefore, had a hazy appearance; it was as though we were looking at the world through a net curtain. Sunlight was streamed into focal pools, highlighting zones of activity, in the same way that a spotlight picks out areas on a stage.

Earlier on that year, the town suffered one of its worst floodings for a long time,

Chapter 29

some areas being swamped to a depth of fifteen feet of muddy river water.

So, as we travelled through the town, weaving amongst the bustling community, great plumes of dust were hanging like gentle, dirty, cotton-wool clouds, suddenly to be shattered by a truck, or motorcycle, bursting through their midst, their drivers often wearing colourful hospital facemasks, or scarves and goggles.

The new dental clinic we had designed last year had now been built and, much to our amazement, it was fit for purpose.

We had an enthusiastic team of about twenty helpers to set everything up, assemble the chairs, connect up the compressors, scalers and lights, organise and find five tables to lay out all our kit, and set up a sterilisation area, waiting and recovery zone, plus reception area.

A cheerful group of eight young dentists arrived to say hello, as well as a few sceptical, gnarled, old characters we had come up against last year.

Before we knew it, there were about forty people crammed into the new premises, all picking up things and taking photos. So, to try and regain a bit of order, we gently eased the visitors out into the rest of the unfinished hospital building and finished setting things up, ready for the morrow.

We had seven hundred patients signed up. Our last year's efforts had somehow percolated through the city, and many did not want to miss out this time.

We had supper, kindly prepared by the women's support group.

The morning found me a bit unsettled in the tummy department, but a couple of Imodium tablets seemed to stabilise things. (With my reliance on Imodium over the years I was, by now, seriously considering buying shares in the company that supplied the tablets.)

We saw eighty-nine patients between the two of us, requiring a variety of treatments. Jane coped brilliantly, doing nearly all the children who came, plus adults; I saw teenagers through to eighty-six-year-olds.

Perhaps my finest hour was successfully cutting out a 4cm-diameter benign tumour from a sixty-four-year-old lady, Chewa (meaning "She who is great"). It had been steadily growing on the floor of her mouth for fifteen years and had pushed her tongue way back, so she could hardly eat or breathe.

A good number we saw were Christian.

Friday was another fruitful day, ninety-five patients being seen and treated. The trouble was that Jane and I were a bit exhausted, despite having an excellent team looking after us. So, straight after supper at 6pm, it was bed.

On Saturday, we saw one hundred and six patients, starting at 7.45am and finishing around 6.30pm. There was a lot of need there, and many were very poor.

Come the Sunday, Tan (the local Christian dentist we had met the year before) came and collected Jane and me and we clambered into his Toyota pick-up, a vast improvement on the jeep he had used last year. The journey to the Kalay Brethren Baptist church was not too long.

We were warmly greeted by the equivalent of the church oversight team. The church seated about two hundred and eighty people and was full. They were still building the new church right next door, big enough now to seat about one thousand people! Last year we had visited this same church, and it was good to see the progress they had made. They hoped to have the new building working by 2018. This was truly putting Faith into practice. It was such an ambitious project.

The service was lively and Bible-based, the worship often being sung in harmony.

Jane and I were introduced and asked to give a short talk, which we did, on Romans 10, coupled with the use of the *CrossCheck* booklet. There was so much joy in the Lord. We then shared in a post-service meal provided by their hospitality team.

The minister, who spoke excellent English, explained that there were thirty-two Baptist churches in the district, many growing.

Tan squeezed us back into his pick-up and took us around the town, bumping and rattling about. It was dusty and hot (34°C) but, whilst we sweated and bounced about, with lots of swerving to avoid the myriad of bikers, and with perspiration trickling into our eyes, we had a good chat about Christian life here in Kalay.

In the afternoon, we were taken for a drive out to the surrounding hills, and then to a school which was number four in Burma for its results.

Jane and I were both asked to give a talk to the classes (one hundred and forty in a class), which seemed to be received well.

Straight after that, it was off to visit some families in their homes. We had requested to see where and how the locals lived so, kindly, they took us to six homes. All were basic, some rudimentary, and some not much more than a shack with earthen floors. However, they all welcomed us with tea, fruit and warm, cheerful hospitality.

Monday saw us busy again, seeing one hundred and fourteen patients and not

Chapter 29

finishing until 6.45pm. The team were beginning to gel well and were exceptionally willing to help in every way possible. The patients laughed easily, offering words of encouragement to each other. Often, there were eight people surrounding a treatment chair, all keen to enlighten the child or aged patient about what would happen next.

Jane was most impressed with a little four-year-old, who sat quietly through an extraction of his fractured front tooth plus the removal of a large lump from the inside of his lip. His reward, promised by the parents, was ice cream for the next two days. What a hero!

Our last patient for the day came from the Methodist community nearby. This poor lady could open her mouth only 3mm, due to acute stress. We prayed with her for fifteen minutes, and it turned out that she had been a victim of regular physical assaults from her husband, who was an alcoholic. The people who brought her to see us were very shocked to discover this, and promised to help her. There appeared to be a lot of shame and stigma attached to such a thing. It was probably the first time she had ever spoken about it to anyone. God is so gracious to have answered her prayer for help. Praise God.

The lady, Chewa, returned for review after some days of healing. She looked so much better and so happy, now that she no longer had to cope with the huge tumour in her mouth (see photo page 224). All had healed up well. After I had helped her back on her feet, she took me by the hand and led me outside the hospital building, where thirty people were patiently standing. It turned out that she was the head villager of a community living three to four hours' journey away. They had all come to say thank you, and to ask if we could join them for a meal at their village.

I was overwhelmed by their kindness.

Over the next four days, we saw four hundred and fifty patients. Each day we prayed for steady hands, opportunities to speak about Jesus, strength and stamina, compassion and kindness.

Our final day was meant to finish by 4pm, to give us time to pack our equipment, but a school party of twenty-five fourteen- to fifteen-year-olds turned up at 4.30. They were from a local boarding school, and all required one or two teeth removing.

So we finished at 7.30 instead.

Nine hundred and sixty-five patients seen and treated.

The catering committee had arranged a farewell gala dinner, which was most enjoyable. Speeches were made, songs were sung, and many photos taken.

The following day, we'd packed our stuff into cases and boxes and had a few hours to explore Kalay itself.

Going round the local market, we kept meeting-up with patients we had seen.

All looking very happy, I am glad to say.

We discovered that we'd underestimated the number of churches there. The correct number was seven hundred. How amazing was that?

It is only through God's grace that we had no problems. No needle stick injuries, no infections, and no dry sockets, despite removing over eighteen hundred teeth and doing around five hundred fillings. Not to mention cyst excisions and surgicals.

Last, but not least: no tummy upset.

We'd made good friends with a young Christian couple, both dentists, who were married six months before, Geoffrey and Mei Mei. They offered to man the dental surgery one Saturday a week, to provide free care.

Their father was a minister in a local church, and had a recording studio for Christian music, which we visited.

The initially-untrained staff all worked well, and became a well-oiled machine towards the end of our dental mission.

With a few tears, we bade farewell and loaded our stuff on to the plane, heading back to Yangon and then home to the UK.

Psalm 147 v 3: *"He heals the brokenhearted and bandages their wounds."*

Chapter 29

Holy Trinity Cathedral, Yangon

Holy Trinity

Orphanage with 6000 children in Mandalay

Jane in Kalay with her helpers

Giving a talk at Kalay Baptist church

Shoes that spread the Gospel?
(Ephesians chapter 6 v. 15)

223

A Step or Two of Faith

Dr Jar Lou(left) joined our team in Kalay

Kalay Baptist church

Patient waiting area

Chewa (meaning "She who is great")

Our travelling luggage

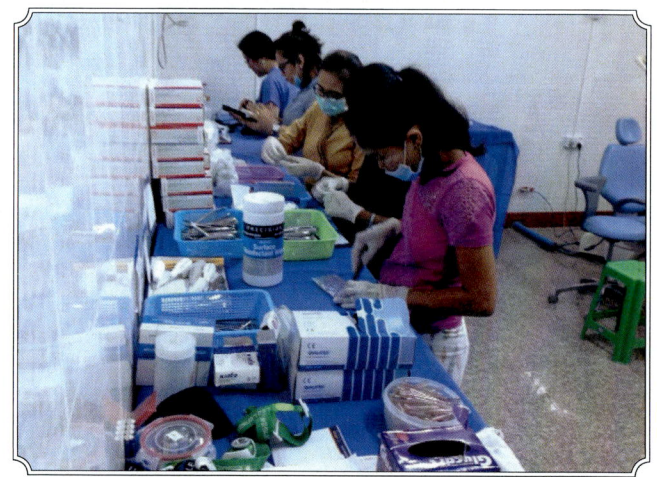

Setting out our kit

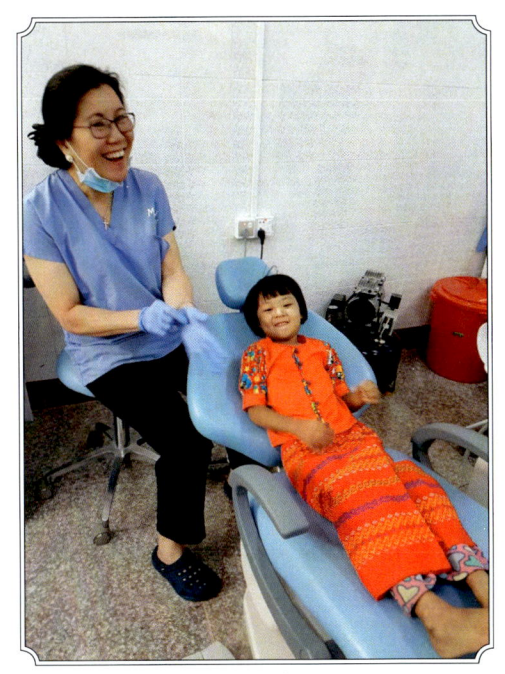

Chapter 29

Jane, the child supremo

Typical lunch

The Kalay Baptist minister and family

Our Kalay dental team

https://youtu.be/aXUe9-LOTSI
Film of Kalay, 2016

There was a lot of joy in Kalay

225

Chapter 30

Brunei and Lawas, 2017
A new venture for Jane and I.

Brunei is a fascinating country; positioned like a small thumbprint on the Northern coast of Borneo, it sits on the Equator, basking in a steady 30°C. all year round. It has a mind-numbing 95% humidity that saps all energy. It is an absolute monarchy, fortunately ruled by a benevolent, benign dictator: His Majesty Sultan Haji Hassanal Bolkiah of Brunei.

It is a Muslim state, Islam being the national religion. There is, technically, freedom of worship here, there being around ten thousand Christians (mainly Chinese) out of a population of five hundred thousand (mainly Malay). It is, however, illegal to convert a Muslim to the Christian faith, and Christmas and its festivities have been recently banned in the shops and public places, with a two-year prison sentence and ten thousand dollar fine for offenders.

So, it was interesting to watch about a quarter of the population, including the Sultan himself, leave the country each December to celebrate Christmas elsewhere.

Gareth and Malou Bolton, from OM (Operation Mobilisation), joined us in Brunei and Gareth preached for the two morning services at St Andrew's Church, his topic being "Salt and Light."

This small church is sited in the capital, Bandar Seri Begawan, and was built in 1908. In the early 1990s it was demolished, an agreement having been struck with the planning authorities that it could be rebuilt to the same size and shape, but with modern materials and a modern interior.

Once it was knocked down, the government and Muslim religious authorities refused to sign the permits to allow the rebuild. In response, the congregation set up a 24-hour vigil, praying to allow their church to be rebuilt.

After six months, the permits were forthcoming and St Andrew's now stands in the centre of the capital, providing five services every Sunday.

Thus Gareth was able to give his message, without censorship, a couple of times that Sunday.

Johnny, the minister at St Andrew's, was very welcoming and both services were full to the brim. This was a testimony to perseverance and determination on

Chapter 30

the part of the congregation in actually **getting** to the service.

For the past few Sundays, the authorities had declared the centre of Bandar a "traffic-free zone" so as to allow the streets to be used for exercise.

This resulted, rather conveniently (for those opposed to Christian worship), in the Catholic and Anglican churches being cordoned off by cones and duty police, preventing access by car. The first Sunday morning it occurred, only seven made it to church! And thirty for the second service. The nearest places to park were about half a mile away, all the usual parking slots in the side streets next to the churches being shut off.

If it was raining, and here I mean torrential, tropical downpour, then access was even more tricky.

Nobody knew how long this Sunday morning run-a-round was going to go on for. There was no doubt that it made life difficult for the churches, and they were praying for wisdom and patience.

Meanwhile, everyone adapted, and worked at just attending the services.

We had established a supportive relationship with an evangelical church in Lawas over the previous three years. It had been run on a shoestring and existed in a second-floor converted office, having a few side rooms and a meeting area for about fifty people.

On one of our earlier visits, we had managed to arrange for their square footage to be doubled by renting the vacant office area below and getting it decorated. So Margaret and David now had two floors of space, with a new meeting area that could seat three hundred people. They named it *The Sanctuary*. It was right in the centre of town, so it was a good location for their ministry.

Gareth, Malou, Jane and I arranged to travel up to Lawas to spend a few days with David and Margaret at their Agape church. This involved a boat ferry and a road trip across the border into Sarawak. Estimated journey time about 4 hours, in the 32°C, 95% humidity.

We boarded our little craft at 8am. It sat low in the water and had a roof running bow to stern to keep the baking sun and the tropical rain away. You therefore had to enter through a hatch at the front, carefully passing your luggage through, before descending the stairs. It held about fourteen of us sitting on long benches, so we all faced each other. The engine was powerful and our captain for the day had an air of bored experience; having lived and worked around the water village and its maze of waterways all his life.

The boat trip was quite enjoyable, wending our way through the mangrove-covered banks of the river, following its twists and turns, our boat heeling over as we avoided floating logs and debris. Our fellow-passengers, dozing, or checking their mobile phones in the early morning sunshine and enjoying the humid wind generated by the speed across the water, were mostly local; they seemed to be regular commuters.

We carefully manhandled our luggage off the bow of the vessel and wobbled along the connecting walkway to shore. We were met by Margaret and David, who drove us for the remainder of the journey into Sarawak and on to Lawas.

This town was surprisingly tidy and organised. Colonnades of trees along the roadways provided shade from the strong sunlight, and great swathes of bougainvillea were dotted about the town, creating colourful splashes of purple everywhere. It is about the size of our local Sutton central town, but its buildings are only two storeys high. The town is adjacent to the wide, muddy Lawas River, which was rather too full, so the locals told us, with crocodiles at that time.

The most common vehicle was the SUV pickup, preferably covered in mud spray, and even better if loaded with a cluster of hardened lumbermen in the open rear section. There were many cafés and eating-places; it had the reputation of a frontier town. On the other side of the river, as far as the eye could see, stretched the endless jungle covering distant hills and valleys.

Margaret and David had started the church in 2005 as a fresh plant with the help of Agape. It had grown and prospered in that time. It was situated on first and second floors above some shops, and provided a large meeting area, office, children's room, youth area, kitchen and accommodation for them both.

We were invited for lunch, cooked by two local ladies in their wooden, two-room house, tucked a few hundred yards off the road and nestling in the luxuriant jungle. A few pre-school children played outside, amongst chickens and a couple of tired dogs. Piles of wood and odd scraps of machinery lay about amongst water-filled potholes.

As we stepped out of our van, the heat of the sun felt like a weight pressing on our heads and shoulders. The effect on us visitors, especially me, being unaccustomed to the solar intensity, was to somehow scramble one's thought processes. I found myself slurring words, forgetting names, places, time of day, and struggling to stand without a slight sway from right to left. Somehow, the very ground seemed to sway and pitch.

Meanwhile, we were being introduced so, with friendly smiles and words of encouragement, we were guided indoors to a simple, one-room area. One table and a few chairs had been borrowed for us to sit and share in their meal (their houses had very little furniture, the floor being used for all activities).

They had prepared a veritable feast for us. Embarrassingly, it filtered out, that it was what they would normally eat in one week.

Chapter 30

From there, we visited the church premises, and had time to catch up and to plan for the evening meeting.

After checking into our hotel (one of only two in the area) and having had a rest, we were taken to a food hall situated beside the river. It had a very high, arched-metal roof with open sides, the borders being lined with hawker stalls; the rest of the area was filled with clusters of plastic chairs and tables. A couple of stalls were grilling satay sticks, creating huge clouds of smoke and steam that permeated the area. As evening approached, with the shadows getting longer, the muted sounds of people chatting and eating were mixed with the sounds of croaking frogs, crickets and multiple other insects. A TV screen mounted in one corner of this hangar-sized building relayed some South Korean soap opera.

We ate, chatted, prayed and laughed together, then squeezed into a car and set off for the church.

The service went well, with lively worship and a dance performance; Gareth spoke well on Luke Ch 18 v 35-42 (the blind beggar). It was an evangelical message, smoothly translated by Margaret into Bahasa Malay.

Following his talk, about forty people came forward for prayer, so we spent time simply praying and being with them.

Everyone went home with a noodle "takeaway", since it was now 10.30 in the evening and people had to get home and be ready for work or school the next day.

The following evening's service also went well, ending with an enthusiastic, all embracing rendition of *When the Storm Rolls*.

Gareth and Malou left us to fly off to their next mission trip, and we stayed on in Lawas.

The next four days were really a maelstrom of activity. We were invited into many homes, and asked to speak in prayer centres, churches and meeting-places.

We shared a lunch with Pastor Bian, who was head of Borneo Evangelical Mission (BEM) on day three. He offered to set up a conference, the following May, for Jane and me to launch and teach the *CrossCheck* booklet in Bahasa to around two hundred ministers and their two- or three-man teams.

This was exciting, since we would get to spend two days with a large section of the evangelical movement in Sarawak. You'll read about it in a chapter or two.

One evening, we visited a branch church that held its Sunday meeting in an old, wooden room with a rusty, corrugated roof. This was accessed along a bumpy, jungle track; the village, a cluster of ramshackle, wooden huts, resembled some remote, wild, forgotten town. We were told it was due for demolition at some stage (it was still there in 2022).

There were about sixty people in this ramshakle meeting place, including some children. After preaching a simple message of Jesus and sharing my testimony, I encouraged them to give their lives to Him and, wonderfully, seven stepped forward to accept Jesus into their lives.

We all celebrated with a shared meal at the end of the service.

The following evening we were taken to two prayer centres, which turned out to be a bit of a challenge, since they were both in remote areas of jungle, one up a steep, very rutted, muddy path with a rather alarming steep drop to one side.

We bumped and swayed along the trail, negotiating our way at a steady 1 mph, grinding gears and clutching door handles, at last reaching sanctuary number one.

Perched on a hill, the small building was shrouded in great clumps of dense greenery.

The night before, Jane and I had been rather savaged by swarms of hungry mosquitoes whilst visiting some remote household so, this time, rather than dwell outside, we hot-footed it indoors, to find a simple prayer room.

A small group of thirty awaited us, so we conducted a short service with a long period of prayer afterwards. These people thought nothing of spending a few days just praying and waiting upon the Lord.

Margaret and David took us around their town during spare moments, so as to meet their flock whilst they were in their workplaces in cafés and market stalls, retail and hardware, hairdressers and printing shops. Many worked outside the town itself. Most could not read or write.

We prayed that we had provided some help and encouragement to these people, here in remote Lawas.

This was a town that served the logging industry, and a lot of the men spent months away at a time, working in remote jungle areas. This often led to difficulties and tensions in family lives. The small cottage hospital of forty beds had no full-time doctor. The wages, in general, were pretty low. There were also many problems with alcohol and drugs.

As a result, the ministry there was huge. Jesus was needed in so many lives. Yet, although we were seven thousand miles from London, the problems people faced were similar to those in the UK.

Psalm 103 v 2-6: *"Let all that I am praise the Lord; may I never forget the good things he does for me.*
"He forgives all my sins and heals all my diseases.
"He redeems me from death and crowns me with love and tender mercies.
"He fills my life with good things. My youth is renewed like the eagle's!
"The Lord gives righteousness and justice to all who are treated unfairly."

Chapter 30

St Andrews Church, Brunei

Gareth preaching

David and Margaret, Lawas

Ferry through the mangroves

A service in the Sanctuary church in Lawas

No tables or chairs in most homes

Chapter 31

Myanmar 2017. Tenth Trip
A return to Kalay

A YEAR HAD FLOWN BY, and so Jane and I were heading once again to Myanmar.

The country had been very much in the news over the past few months, because of the clashes between the Rohingya people and the military junta forces. The press coverage had been patchy, due to the difficulty in obtaining journalistic access from the Burmese side. The previous military regime had been in total control for sixty years, and they still had their hands on the country's governing tiller, which Aung San Suu Kyi was gently trying to prise free from their clutches. But, at the time of writing (2021), everything has reverted to military control once again.

After staying a couple of days with some of Jane's family and visiting their church on Sunday in Singapore, we returned again to Kalay, which was about two hundred miles from the troubled border area.

Kalay, being a mainly Christian area, was not really affected by the troubles. The plan was to go back to the clinic we had started the year before. The local staff had added on a waiting room, sterilisation area and reception zone whilst we had been away, so we were excited to see how things had progressed.

In Kalay, life carried on as normal. The rainy season had just about finished and the fields, spreading as far as the eye could see, were all filled with ripening rice and vegetable crops. The population of this city and surrounding countryside bustled about the streets, carrying their goods, their families, or even their livestock. Slow-moving trucks, heavy with their burdens, groaning and belching smoke, carried trade goods to and from the Indian border, which was only seventy miles away.

Jane and I were installed in some accommodation adjacent to the newly-built dental clinic in the hospital. It was the usual wooden bed, with the super-bouncy pillow and the occasional dribble of hot water.

Resuming where we had left off a year before, the expanded clinic worked well. We had seen about six hundred patients after five days. They had come from far and wide, ranging from two and a half to ninety-five years old!

A lot of the staff who were there last year had volunteered to help again, resulting in the treatment and patient flow being very smooth from the outset.

We used to enjoy watching them all arrive early in the morning on a variety of Motorbikes, scooters and pushbikes. Often their handlebars had a collection of plastic bags, with spare shoes, satsumas, noodles, phone chargers, etc. Frequently two would arrive on one bike, the passenger sitting side saddle, swaying and adjusting automatically to any bumps, twists and turns whilst checking their mobiles or doing their hair. Some with huge helmets, others with ones bought cheap from the market. Many travelled fifteen miles or more from outlying villages.

We always had to get used to the Burmese approach to healthcare. Everyone liked to be involved in the process. Health issues were a shared, community problem. At any one time, there were usually twenty-seven people in the treatment room. No place for patient confidentiality here; photos were being taken, people offering words of advice and encouragement, post-treatment patients sitting in the ten chairs provided (so we could keep an eye on them), eight nurses, three patients being treated and a relative or two to provide moral support, three translators, a "patient-bringing-inner" person and a "patient-taking-outer" person, two dentists (Jane and I), and two instrument-steriliser persons. Everyone was chatting and offering words of encouragement and advice, leading to quite a hubbub at times.

We had a Christian doctor who joined us on this trip, called Jar-Lou. She was Burmese, and acted as a translator as well as being a great help to us with the patients. She was trained in obstetrics, but wanted to give her holiday time to help others, and she had heard about our annual trips. At the time of writing this book, Jane speaks to her on WhatsApp almost daily.

Many of the patients were Christian, this being a predominantly Christian area, so it was good that we could offer free dental care for them. Countless patients had quite gross decay, requiring five or more teeth to be removed, as well as fillings. Lots had been in pain for a year or more. Some had tumours, others straightforward, traumatic injuries.

Jane was a fountain of patience and saw ALL the children! On average, about eighteen each day were mixed in with the adults. Many required supernumerary teeth to be extracted. How she successfully managed to do it on such young children, I really don't know.

Our day finished at 6.30pm. We'd have a quick wash, and then supper was at 7pm, following which we normally went to sleep.

We both had sore backs by the end of each day, not to mention eyes, neck, feet, legs and arms. But God is good; he watched over what we did, and there were no mishaps, despite the high volume of patients seen.

We attended a different church in Kalay this time. It was called The Kalaymyo Baptist Church. Our welcome was extensive and warm. It was really good to share in their worship. We arranged to spend the next Friday evening with them, to share in some songs and some Bible study.

On Sunday afternoon, we were taken to the Indian border and had a chance to see the huge number of churches in villages along the route. It was good to see such an active Christian fellowship everywhere.

From Monday through to Friday morning, we continued seeing patients. There seemed to be an endless number of people needing dental care. We were amazed they kept coming, despite the rain and the distance some had to travel to get to us.

We revisited the Kalay Baptist church on the Friday evening and there were about eighty to ninety folk there, which was a pleasant surprise, so I taught them two songs. One with the passage from Matthew Ch 8 v 23. We acted out the boat scene with twelve men from the congregation and one boy, who acted the part of Jesus.

Then we sang *When the Storm Rolls*, which went really well. Following that we sang *Our God is a Great Big God*, with all the actions, downloading the music and lyrics from *YouTube*. They so enjoyed that song that they planned to sing it on the following Sunday.

The church had about five hundred members. They had three services and three Bible-study sessions on Sundays.

On Saturday we flew, with our fifteen bags and boxes, back to Yangon. We sorted kit and belongings out that day, after attending the service at Holy Trinity Yangon church. Rev. Bennett was full of life and energy, and very warm in his greeting to us.

That was our last visit to Kalay. We had a great yearning to return to see the people there once again. What with Covid 19 and the breakdown of democracy, we would have to wait upon the Lord.

1 Corinthians Ch 10 v 31: *"Whatever you do, do it all for the glory of God."*

Chapter 32

Our relationship with the church in Lawas, Sarawak had initially developed from one of Jane's relatives, Dong, who had visited David and Margaret back in 2008-9. She told us how their ministry with the local people was so touching and how many lost souls had been turning to Christ. But they were very under-resourced and this was limiting their outreach.

Margaret and David had started the church in 2007 as a fresh plant. It had grown and prospered since that time . David used to be a very committed Buddhist; he had been seeking other gods and spirits to follow, whom he hoped would give him peace, but he found none, until he accepted Jesus as his Lord and Saviour. He had been a businessman as well as a head chef, until he left everything to serve in full-time ministry. His calling, he felt, was to serve the indigenous jungle people in Sarawak – the widows, orphans, single parents and broken families.

Margaret had been a true atheist earlier on in her life, and her family had hated Christians. Jesus had come into her life after she had been completely healed from a bad illness. After accepting Christ, she was persecuted by her own family, who disowned her. She was working as a bank manager, but left because of God's calling. When she was twelve, she dreamed of looking after orphans and elderly people. She was English-educated, but taught herself to speak Bahasa since starting full-time ministry.

She and her husband, David, worked full-time in Lawas, teaching children English, visiting, praying, providing meals for the elderly and running their church. This was situated on the second floor above some shops, and provided a large meeting-area, office, children's room and kitchen, plus accommodation for them both

Jane had been to visit them whilst she was on one of her many trips to visit her mother in Brunei, who had been getting quite frail during her latter years.

Following that visit, we had arranged to give them some support and tried to visit them once a year.

It was a new venture for us, as it did not involve any dentistry, just ministry. We were each, therefore, required to do a step change in our skill levels, so as to be able to give Bible talks, lead prayer sessions and preach whenever requested, often with little or no notice.

We gave thanks for Paul Adams' teaching programme, for our experience in giving *Mercy Ships* talks, and for my training and instruction received whilst learning to preach at a small church in Reigate, called SandCross. At the time, we did not realise that we were being prepared for Lawas and other places.

Lawas, Sarawak, May 2018. Sharing Jesus Conference

During the previous year, I had managed to keep in touch with Pastor Bian (BEM) via Margaret. Regrettably, his English was limited and my Bahasa Malay was even worse, so we needed Margaret as our go-between interpreter.

He was a bundle of energy and had a very good relationship with the Lun Bawan people, who lived in the longhouses in Sarawak. As head of Borneo Evangelical Mission (BEM) in Sarawak, he was in charge of about two hundred and nineteen churches.

When I had shown him the *CrossCheck* booklet, he had been very excited about its prospective use for evangelism and wanted it to be translated into Bahasa Malay.

This we managed to achieve with the help of *BeaconLight Trust*. A process that is far more involved and time-consuming than you might imagine (It is worth noting that we now have *CrossCheck* in many languages – Chinese, Tagalog, Japanese, Nepalese, Bahasa Malay).

We also wanted to introduce a teaching book called *Truth Unlocked*, which covers the main Bible verses which one needs to know and understand when becoming a new Christian.

We had managed to get ten thousand Bahasa *CrossCheck* booklets printed in Sarawak, but the *Truth Unlocked* translation was completed only a week before our visit, so we had to just photocopy about one hundred books.

Bian was as good as his word, and he had arranged for ministers and their church leaders to come to a two-day conference in Sarawak. It was almost disrupted, due to Malaysia having a general election. This apparently always shut everything down for three weeks, due to security issues. The knock-on effect was to compress other planned church events. The result was that there were two other conferences taking place at the same time as ours so, instead of the predicted five hundred delegates, we just had to pray and try to guess how many would attend.

It was a good thing, therefore, that we managed to arrive in Lawas a few days early, since there was a lot of organising to do. We wanted everyone to have a folder containing all the Bible verses, a *CrossCheck* booklet in English and Bahasa, *Truth Unlocked* details and various *Sharing Jesus* notes.

We also wanted every delegate to receive one hundred booklets each to take back to their churches.

Locating a photocopying shop that was prepared to copy thirty-four thousand pieces of paper, clip them together and arrange into booklets, all within two days, was a challenge, but the one we found was an answer to prayer.

We also needed to get the Sanctuary's presentation equipment upgraded, a new 52in TV, computer cables, radio mics, aircon working, cooling fans and seating. A manned welcome desk, posters and all the catering arrangements had to be sorted. All this in 33°C heat and 95% humidity!

On the day itself, we still had no idea how many would be able to attend. In that part of the world, people have time for each other, for meals together, for simply talking over a cup of coffee. However, there is a consequence, in that arriving at a given time is not habitual.

We had built this known fact into our day plan, to allow for latecomers, so the morning started with soft drinks, coffee and then a time of worship, to give time for everyone to turn up. By 10.45, we had about a hundred people out of an expected three hundred and fifty. This was a blessing, as it gave us more time to spend with each person attending.

The *Sharing Jesus* conference went really well, I am glad to report. The ministers really liked the *CrossCheck* and the *Truth Unlocked* material. It was well-understood and, apparently, the best they had ever experienced, principally because of its simplicity.

We prayed the grain of seed would bear much fruit.

The food produced by the local caterers whom we found through Margaret was delicious. The tea breaks were much appreciated, and the lunches provided a good time to chat and share together. The vegetables, fish and chicken were freshly-sourced and the spices were subtly used. Master chefs came and cooked in the upstairs kitchen of the missionary pair, David and Margaret.

God held off all the storms predicted till after the two-day conference had ended. This was an answer to prayer and was crucial, since many ministers were based in jungle backwood areas only reachable along rough tracks. When the storms came, these routes become muddy quagmires. So nobody travels.

We spent a lot of time practising how to use the CrossCheck booklet. On the last day, we had some ministers taking it in turns to present the Gospel story from the *CrossCheck* pictures alone, having memorised the booklet! They were universally thrilled with the content, and stated that it was an answer to prayer.

Of the one hundred who attended, most had congregations of two to three hundred. They each left equipped with one hundred *CrossCheck* and eight Bahasa *Truth Unlocked* study books, plus one English version.

The workshops were really enjoyed, all saying that they intended to use them in their churches.

The 100 pastors also went home with a pen-drive each, with the *PowerPoint Sharing Jesus* notes attached, and other resource material. We hoped they would have the confidence to conduct the same conference in their own churches. The possible outreach was to about sixteen thousand people when they taught their own congregations.

Some of the post-conference comments from the ministers:-

1. "Praise God. I have been praying that there was a simpler way of telling the Gospel. Instead of an hour, by which time my listener has gone to sleep, this will take me ten minutes. Thank God."

   Pastor Bian. Head of BEM Lawas.

2. "God has answered my prayers. I prayed that I would be able to find all the answers to the crucial questions about our faith with the correct references in the Bible, and here it is. Praise God."

   Pastor Lipang.

3. "What an amazing tool the Lord God has given us today. We can teach the youngsters and older ones alike at different levels.

   We have forty children almost each month coming from all over Malaysia for three to four days of camping trip with Bible study in our jungle sanctuary.

   We can teach them and their teachers this *CrossCheck*."

   The pastor from Bethsaida Christian retreat.

4 "Thank you, thank you for coming to share the Gospel with us. It is so simple and clear. Praise God."

   Pastor David.

5. "Not many of us read the Bible properly, or know our way round it. We use the popular verses, but we do not know the context or sequences from where they came. We are not well-educated, but principally too lazy to read the Bible from cover to cover.These verses and references

have encouraged us to read the rest of the letters, or Gospels from where they came. Thank you."

A deaconess from Gunong Hosana retreat.

6. "Thank you for the pen drive and all the material. We want to share the seminars with our churches to enable our staff and leaders of home groups to use them."

Pastor from The Bible School in Johore, W. Malaysia.

7. "You have convicted our spirit. We have to do more to spread the Gospel with this simple and illuminating method. The urgency is what we are experiencing."

Pastor Balang of Lawas.

8. With tears in her eyes she said, "I could hardly say the words as we practised *CrossCheck* with each other. I discovered that I should have been using these words from the Bible to tell my husband about Jesus. I have been trying to do it in my own strength. That was where I failed for twenty years. I now feel equipped to work with the help of *CrossCheck* to tell him about Jesus. I am so ashamed that I failed in my own strength, but now I know that I have the full armour of God as a very sharp, double-edged sword of the Spirit. Thank you for coming to share this with us."

9. "Would you mind if we use this material for our tired pastors who come for refreshment in Gunong Hosanna? (Hosanna mountain). Will you come and share it with them? They are all so thirsty and hungry for God's word. This is a feast. Praise God!"

This elderly lady in her eighties was a deaconess at the Gunong Hosanna retreat, providing spiritual refreshments for pastors from Brunei, Sarawak, Sabah, West Malaysia and Indonesia.

10. "I am returning to the Bible school in Perak, West Malaysia, today. I thought that before I go I could just stop by for an hour to hear what you are doing. I have never heard of *CrossCheck*. I came to visit my family. It is so different to anything I have ever heard. Such clarity with such brevity. What a blessing! I cannot wait to share what I have learnt today (She had delayed her travel to hear the rest of *CrossCheck*). Thank God for all this material - I am glad I came to Lawas."

A lecturer from a Bible college in W. Malaysia.

A Step or Two of Faith

Lawas town adjacent to the Lawas River

Practising *CrossCheck* on each other

CrossCheck booklets going out to the churches

Conference meal

Conference team photo

Lawas baptism. Crocodile-free

Chapter 33

Myanmar, January 2019. Eleventh and Last Trip

PAKUKKU IS A SPRAWLING, TREE-COVERED town, lying adjacent to the main artery of Burma: the Irrawaddy River. The region is two hundred miles south-west of Mandalay. It is reached by crossing Myamar's longest road/rail bridge, a Chinese-built, square box-shaped affair that spans the waterway for over a mile and a half. Prior to its construction, everything had to cross the river by ferry.

Jane and I flew into Pagan Airport early on Monday morning, walked through the tiny, three-room terminal where we were met by the chairman, treasurer and secretary of the hospital, three solid-looking, cheerful characters in their late fifties. The chairman owns the local bus company ferrying people to and from Yangon, the secretary owns the local hardware store, and the treasurer used to do geological surveys for oil companies around Burma. Their "can-do" approach to helping us set up was so good - we had five chairs, plus all the dental technical kit and the sterilisation room, all sorted by the evening.

The hospital was built in 2016, and had never had a dental unit. It looked smart in its blue-and-white livery and the room we were allocated was a really good size.

Our accommodation was nearby and was a period, wood-lined affair, spacious, and with HOT water. Wonderful.

The town population of sixty thousand was predominantly Buddhist, but we had located four churches - two Methodist, one Baptist and one Roman Catholic. We prayed that we would have a chance to visit and meet fellow-Christians.

The first day (Tuesday) was about team-building and patient-flow management. There were ten young helpers, plus two trained nurses, to whom we explained our ethos and expectations. They were split into sterilisation, chair assist and reception teams. Next came five young dentists, all with two to five years' experience. Again, we tried to impress on them the importance of compassionate care, gentleness and kindness to the patients.

Mixed amongst these were one hundred waiting patients, the catering team and the hospital management personnel.

It was a little bit like herding cats, but gradually, as the day progressed, a sense of order began to develop.

We treated one hundred and seventy-eight patients that first day. A record for us.

By Thursday evening we had seen six hundred and forty-nine patients.

During the day, Dr Ko and I had a private meeting with a husband and wife who wanted to see if anything could be done for her, since she had an extensive Squamous cell carcinoma of the mouth and throat (a common Malignant cancer often caused by chewing Beetle nut). I think they were hoping for a Western miracle, but we had to very gently explain that there was nothing that could be done. I prayed for her, since she probably had only a few months to live. Betel-nut-chewing is very common in Myanmar, and it causes a lot of mouth and throat cancer.

On Friday, another two hundred were seen and treated. Our dental team was featured by a local TV station. Neither Jane nor I was aware that a team had visited and taken film, so it was a bit of a surprise when it was released on one of the national channels. As a result, visitors started dropping in to see what was going on.

By the end of Saturday, we had seen just over a thousand patients! All ages, with about 80% never having had any dental treatment before.

Come the Sunday, we managed to find a church at which to worship. It was Pakokku Baptist Church, established in 1901.

The church was set in a white-walled compound in about one acre of land. When originally built, it was probably situated on the outskirts of the town. One hundred and eighteen years on, the trees had grown large, bushy and tall, and the area was surrounded by little gravel lanes with multiple wooden houses, all closely packed together. The church and vicarage looked in need of a total refurbishment. The compound was covered with packed mud and cluttered with assorted items.

When we arrived on the Sunday morning, in the warm sunshine, the place was a buzz of activity; the church had a serving membership of one hundred and fifty, with an additional eighty or so new or occasional attendees. The two-hour service was filled with worship and we witnessed the new oversight team being sworn in for their next three-year term.

They had just been given permission (after a wait of six years) to build a new church to replace the existing one.

After the service, we had a chance to meet and chat with the minister and his senior team. They seemed very happy to have some foreign visitors. Their new build was expected to cost $300,000 US.

They were prepared to take a step of faith. They started the rebuild three months after we met them. They had only had one tenth of the money so far.

Chapter 33

We have stayed in touch with the church after returning to the U.K. and Ro, the minister's wife sent us regular updates. As I write this (April 2022) life is very tough with the Military Coup continuing in Myanmar.

The building works started with knocking the church walls down, but leaving the roof so that services could continue. Foundations were dug around the perimeter of the church, to double its size. Reinforced concrete was poured into the foundation trenches and some pillars were constructed. At this point, the builders asked for a one-third payment. This seemed to catch the church elders by surprise, since they had only $30,000 saved.

The builders then downed tools and threatened to take the church to court to receive their money. Two of the church members mortgaged their homes to raise funds, but they were still short.

At this point, Ro contacted us to see if we could help in any way and, through God's grace, we were able to send them some funds, via UK, Singapore, Yangon and Mandalay to help. But the church was still only half-finished as I wrote this, which was a shame.

Returning to our clinic the next week, it was just as busy, with queues every day.

Our health was good; some of our party had mild stomach upsets, but no major issues. This was a real answer to prayer.

The final number of patients treated was one thousand seven hundred and ninety-six.

A record for us.

We finished on the Thursday and spent the end of that day packing away all our equipment and dental materials.

The people of Pakokku were incredibly hospitable, looking after us so well and organising all our transport, accommodation and food. A short walk from our hospital, we were taken around the town market. Set up over an area of five acres, it sold just about everything you might ever need, with most of the produce coming from the fertile surrounding farmland.

We asked what a typical farm was like and, in answer, one of our helpers and interpreters offered to drive us to his family farm, about twenty-five miles north of Pakukku.

We arrived at his farm that afternoon, to be greeted by his seventy-six-year-old mum and some other family members.

Try and picture a fifteenth-century English rural village during midsummer. The house was a wooden, rambling, two-storey building, made from weathered planks and logs. Attached to it were outhouses and sheds full of old farm equipment, plus a few livestock. The entrance courtyard was lined by a wooden, rather haphazard, rough, stake fence. The mud enclosure was filled with various piles of produce - peanuts, cashew nuts, straw, palm leaves, wood and dried fruit. A few dusty trees provided some shade.

We were ushered inside for some fruit, nuts and tea. His mum spoke excellent English. She had lived in the village all her life. The farm had been her father's. The rooms were quite dark, and filled with old, wooden furniture, plus an assortment of household items acquired over the years - a wonderful valve radio, a tape deck, and graduation pictures quietly fading on the wall.

She insisted on showing us round her farm and village, so we spent an enjoyable hour as she slowly and gently guided us along mud lanes lined by wooden homesteads. We looked at her Tanaka tree plantation, the neighbour's betel-nut plants, the local smithy working from a thatched, wooden hut near the furniture maker, the wood carver and other farm holdings. It seemed a step back in time. Yet they were well-placed to survive any political upheavals, and they kept below the parapet as far as the junta was concerned.

We returned for a gala meal and celebration for our last evening there, with ninety people attending. Tables had been set up in long rows outside the hospital front. Speeches were given, photos taken and e-mail addresses exchanged.

It was always poignant and ironic that, just as we got everything running like clockwork and everyone became skilled in assisting, sterilising, reception work, patient aftercare, antibiotic distribution, etc., that was when we had to stop.

We prayed that everyone was happy with the treatment they had received and that we had displayed Jesus' love in all that took place.

With the junta taking over the country in February 2021, it would be unlikely that we will be able to visit until things settle down. Only God knows if we would ever be able to return to this very special place.

Romans Ch 8 v 38: *"And I am convinced that nothing can ever separate us from God's love. Neither death nor life, neither angels nor demons, neither our fears for today nor our worries about tomorrow, not even the powers of hell can separate us from God's love."*

Chapter 33

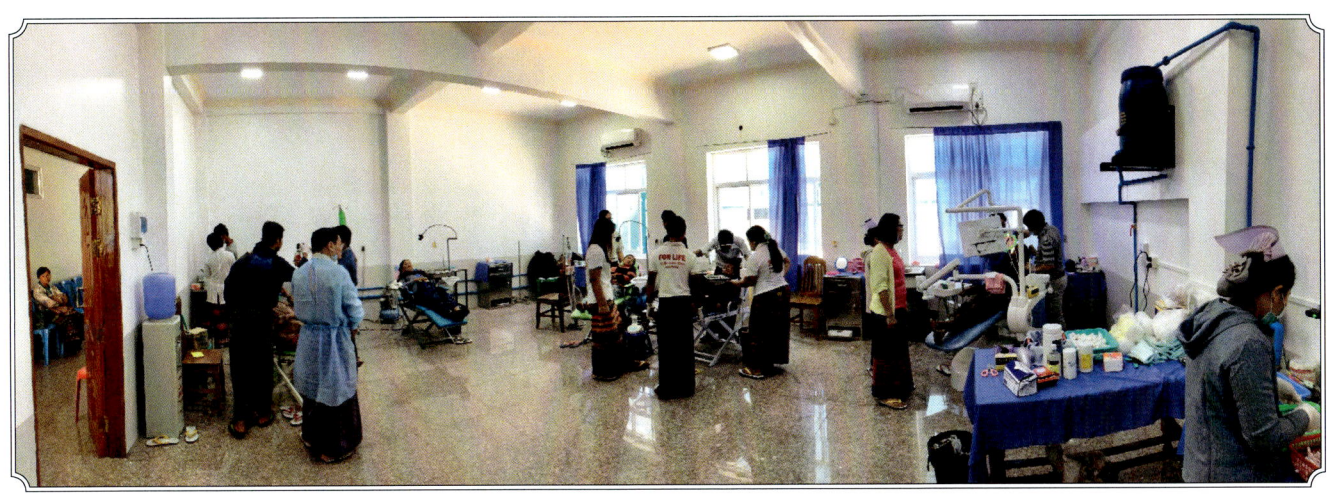

Pakokku was the largest surgery we ever had in Burma

The Town's elders who were responsible for the Pakokku hospital and our stay

Local produce

Pakokku Hospital

245

Pakokku Baptist church

https://youtu.be/REcAEgW-6LO

Pakokku, January 2019

Our team of young local dentists

Chapter 34

Years 2010-2020

THIS TEN-YEAR PERIOD SAW BOTH our children get married.

It was also the busiest time for our mission trips abroad.

Sophia married Tom in June 2012. It was an amazing, Christian wedding, with three hundred and fifty-seven friends and family attending. A truly special moment. Tom became a GP in Crawley and Sophia a dermatologist. They had two children, Amelia and Henry. They lived five minutes away from us, in Carshalton Beeches

James met Alli, his wife-to-be, at St Marks Church, Battersea Rise. They got married in September 2017. We had a great wedding in Cornwall, with people travelling from the USA to join the occasion (Alli is American).

They were living in Glasgow as I wrote this, where James continued with his Reconstructive Plastic Surgery training. Alli worked at the university. They had a son, Charlie and another child expected in November 2022

We feel very fortunate to have such wonderful, Christian children and, now, grandchildren.

Whilst serving on the *Mercy Ship* in 2007, Jane had a needle stick injury, which meant she had to have a blood test to check that she had not contracted AIDS or hepatitis. When the results came back, the haematologist suggested it would be a good idea to have her liver checked on our return to the UK, as the test had revealed a problem.

This we arranged, and she ended up under the care of a Professor Foster, up in Whitechapel, North London. It transpired that she had only a functional ten per cent of her liver working. At the rate it was deteriorating, she would have needed a liver transplant in a few years. Jane was really struck by the fact that she might not see her son and daughter graduate or get married, or have a chance to see any grandchildren.

Suddenly faced with her mortality, she made her peace with the Lord and entrusted herself into Jesus' hands.

Amazingly, when we returned to see Prof. Foster, he explained that a new trial drug had just been released and asked whether she would be prepared to be part of the testing group.

She has been on the medicine now for fourteen years and her liver is still working OK. She feels so blessed to have seen so much and done such a lot over these past years.

It was also during these latter years that we have been on most of our trips, as described.

Quite amazing really.

In September 2016, my mother passed away. She had spent the first few years after my dad died staying at the homes of myself and my three sisters. But, as she got more frail, she tended to stay with my sister, Helen, more, eventually living her last year in a nursing home in Perranporth, Cornwall. She then had a massive stroke so, knowing there was a limited time, we were all able to share her last two weeks together as a family.

In February 2018, I was baptised at our church in Banstead.

Yes, I know what you are thinking; what took him so long?

After Billy Graham in 1989, I wanted to make a public statement and, being in the Church of England at that time, I was confirmed by the Bishop of Croydon at St Patrick's Church.

I had been baptised as a baby, as was the tradition in those days.

Jane and our friend, Bob Hedderly, were baptised at Banstead church in 2001, having a desire to declare their faith, but I felt quite content to stay on the sidelines, encouraging and giving witness to their testimonies.

Gradually, over the years, passages from The Bible kept leaping out at me about "Repenting and being publicly baptised."

The deciding factor came when I was leading the worship in Lawas, in one of the very rural areas. After giving my testimony and preaching, seven people gave their lives to Jesus.

I had instructed them to repent, ask Jesus into their lives and get baptised.

As I was saying that, a loud voice in my head said, "But Nigel, you too need to be baptised."

Which gave me a shock, and kept me awake most of that night.

There are over sixty verses about baptism in The Bible. For the next few months, every time I opened my copy, a verse about baptism would stand out, as though in illuminated lights.

So, that February, I felt totally at peace in being baptised.

Dental practice memories

Having a dental practice which is open to the public can lead to a variety of signature incidents taking place. Managing late-night callers knocking on our door, with severe toothache, very much the worse for wear from the pub, was a regular problem. It was a common misconception that alcohol would deaden the pain of toothache. Regrettably, it has no analgesic effect until the patient is virtually comatose.

So, a ding-dong at our door, late in the evening, was often approached with caution.

Sometimes, I'd open the front door on a Saturday or Sunday morning, often still in my pyjamas, to grab the milk and there, on the doorstep, would be someone clutching their jaw in pain.

"How long have you been here?" I'd exclaim.

"Half the night," they'd reply.

"Why didn't you ring, or knock?"

"Didn't want to wake you."

My eyes were opened to the vagaries of dental practice during my early days working in Teddington. One of the dentists was using a technique called "relative analgesia". It was popular in the 1970's and involved an apprehensive patient breathing a mix of nitrous oxide and air to relax them during their treatment. From downstairs, we heard a huge crash and a bang; suddenly, the surgery door opened and out rushed the patient, wearing blue bib and protective glasses, making a dash for the front door. She was hotly pursued by her dentist, who caught up with her halfway down the garden path, whereupon he performed a fine rugby tackle and brought her crashing to the ground. She was yelling to the outside world, "HELP! HELP!"

The dentist held on grimly to the patient's legs.

Peter, our laid-back New Zealand principal, went out to see what all the commotion was about.

"Help! Help!" screamed the patient.

"What's going on?" Peter asked, above the yells.

"I can't let her go; she's too far under with the sedation gas," our colleague muttered through gritted teeth, still holding on to her ankles.

Peter went over to the patient and knelt down in front of her, to try and gently wake her up.

After a few minutes, she recovered and was then super-embarrassed at the scene she had created. The waiting room was full at the time, with open-mouthed patients watching this escape attempt with obvious horror. It wasn't the most confidence-building event to witness.

I am not sure what the practice image was like for a while, as people walking by had also witnessed a patient trying to escape and then being fly-tackled by her dentist.

In our own practice, we had a similar event when one of my associates was quietly treating a man in the upstairs surgery. Suddenly, two police cars screeched to a halt outside our building.

Hearing their arrival, the patient leapt out of the dental chair and dashed out of the upstairs rear window and into the garden, hotly pursued by four policemen and two huge dogs. They caught up with him, and he was handcuffed and marched back through the surgery.

Apparently, he'd skipped bail.

The other patients loved that event.

A potentially more serious episode took place early one morning. I was downstairs, in my own surgery, when I heard quite a commotion coming from an upstairs surgery.

I rushed up there, two steps at a time, to meet David, the dentist, dragging a dental aspirator machine out of his room. It was belching flames and thick, black smoke.

We both grabbed fire extinguishers and proceeded to spray the machine, each other and most of the corridor with foam. Eric, the other dentist had, meanwhile, locked himself in the toilet.

The insulating foam surrounding the motor had overheated and caught fire.

But the flames were soon extinguished. David and I were so relieved that we clung to each other for a bit, laughing at the mess we had created. We then proceeded to open windows, to let all the thick, black smoke out, which took five or six minutes or so.

His surgery was still thick with acrid fumes, so we opened the windows in there as well.

To reveal his patient, still lying in the dental chair!

"What are you doing here?!" we both exclaimed.

Sitting up on one elbow, she softly replied, "Well, I didn't want to ruin any work that David was doing on my teeth."

One Saturday afternoon, we had been out with our children visiting Dover Castle, when a patient phoned to say she

Chapter 34

was in absolute agony. I explained where we were and that I could see her later on that day. She was a regular patient, whom I'd known from my Teddington days.

As we swung into our driveway on our return, she was standing in the doorway, hopping from one leg to the other and clutching her face.

Jane took the children into our house and I quickly opened up the surgery, next door, to let the patient in.

She could hardly talk, could not sit still, and had taken umpteen painkillers, all to no effect.

Locating the culprit, I quickly injected a strong, local anaesthetic next to the tooth. She hopped about, holding on to her jaw for a minute and then collapsed, unconscious, to the floor.

Just like a sack of potatoes.

I was horrified.

I quickly checked for a pulse, breathing, etc., and got her into the recovery position.

My professional life flashed before me. This was disaster. No nurse; alone with a female patient, who was unconscious.

I wouldn't have a legal leg to stand on.

I prayed for help.

Gradually, she came to, and I carefully sat her up and gave her a sugary drink.

It transpired that she hadn't eaten for two days, and had been munching painkillers and drinking gin. I'm glad to say that she was so happy to be out of pain, she sent me a huge bouquet of flowers a day or two later.

Over our forty years of doing dentistry, we have shared moments of joy, sorrow, triumph and failure. People have burst into tears, or hugged us with gratitude. Others, I am sure, have gone elsewhere. It is hard to please everyone. You can only try your best.

Working with my wife and our team of staff was exhilarating, exhausting, stressful and joyful. Having the privilege to open our doors each day to our local community and to endeavour to meet their dental needs took a lot of energy and patience.

The staff we had over the years were wonderful in their commitment and professionalism. Sandra, Julie, Sharon, Claire, Sue, Louise, Helen, Rita and Monique, to name only a few, turned up regularly, worked hard and became known to all the patients who flowed through the practice doors.

The irony is that, just as you are getting really quite good - it's time to stop and retire.

Chapter 35

Lawas Sarawak Dental Outreach, 2019

Up to 2019, Jane and I had managed to avoid using our dental skills in Lawas, wanting to focus more on a Gospel outreach than doing dentistry.

That might, at first glance, appear a bit selfish or uncharitable. But there was a reason behind the thinking in that, as you will see in the following account. Arranging, setting up, and doing the dentistry in a different part of the world is tiring and time-consuming, and leaves little time and energy for the Gospel proclamation, which involves visiting homes, doing Bible studies and preaching at various events.

Every time we had visited, we had been asked if we could help people with their tooth problems, since dental care was very difficult to get in Lawas.

So, at last, we relented and set about planning a dental visit.

We went there to set up and run a dental clinic for a week, wanting it to be a Christian outreach to the Lun Bawang people living within travelling distance of the town. The church there, linked to The Borneo Evangelical Mission, distributed leaflets offering free dental treatment.

Jane and I checked in our 98kg of luggage (a personal best for us: seven bags; mainly dental kit) at Terminal 4 Heathrow, on Friday, 25th October, a drizzly, damp, cold, autumn day.

Fourteen and a half hours later, we landed in Brunei: 32°C, 95% humidity, exhaustingly hot. When the British Army sent troops out there, they allowed them three months to acclimatise before starting jungle training. We had a couple of days to adjust to the time difference, heat, etc., before heading up across the border to the Equatorial East Malaysian town of Lawas.

Jane was always brilliant in the heat, whereas I was more like a floppy lettuce leaf, so I was hoping we could find somewhere to set up our stall (dental treatment room) with some air-conditioning.

There were about sixteen thousand Lun Bawang people in northern Sarawak.

Chapter 35

They had a long and fiercely independent tradition of self-reliance. Many lived in longhouses, where a community of around forty-five men, women and children shared one extended house, usually on stilts, and always set in the jungle.

However, we had been told that dental help for them was in very short supply.

We started with a major problem; on arrival, we ascertained that we had not been given official permission to carry out dentistry in Sarawak. A recent law, passed in late 2018, made this crime punishable by imprisonment.

It seemed, therefore, that our best course of action was to fly down to Kuching (four hundred and fifty miles away) and ask the public health department how to obtain official permission to provide a charitable dental mission.

It was only a forty-minute flight to the capital of Sarawak, and we quickly got through the arrivals section. To keep communications going, I needed to buy a local sim card for my phone.

A kind young man at the kiosk suggested we use GRAB (like Uber) to take us to the public health buildings we were heading for to obtain the permit. When the taxi arrived, the Hakka Chinese driver, called Derek, wanted to know why we wanted to visit the Ministry of Health. On the way there, we told him about our dental mission and, amazingly enough, his neighbour and good friend happened to be one of the medical directors at the Ministry of Health.

He gave her a call and she kindly spoke to Jane and, subsequently, we had our case reviewed a day later at 8am, in person, by the Sarawak Director of Health, Dr Jamilah, who was a good friend of hers! Reaching the head of any civil service department is impossible to do. But, with God....

The public health department in Sarawak employed over eight hundred doctors, dentists, nurses, administrators, etc., so we felt it was only with God's help that we got admission to the top person.

We supplied all our qualification documents, etc.

God is amazing, how He sent people to us to do His will. We prayed that the Director of Public Health would look favourably upon this dental outreach.

Well, it took three days.

The director arranged for us to see the head of the dental public health, Dr Zairina. Our meeting involved seven hours of form-filling. She was incredibly patient and helpful, and we got there in the end. The paperwork there was, apparently, legendary. Simple tasks could take an hour or two; for example, they required a registration fee of $100 Malaysian each, but the health department only accepted a postal order or a bank draft.

Derek, our GRAB driver, who stayed with us the whole three days, drove us back into town and located the post office, only to find it had been out of action for the past two weeks, due to computer failure. We headed on to bank no 1, to be told that we had to have an account for a bank order. On to bank 2 and bank 3; we were able to process the money orders, but there was a huge form to fill in first, and only by the account-holder (a bit *Catch 22*-ish - we obviously did not have an account, so Derek did it from his own bank account).

We drove back through the busy traffic to the public health building; time taken: two hours. Then on to a section for passport photos. Meanwhile, the Malaysian Dental Council, which is based In Kuala Lumpur, contacted the Health Department, saying that they liked three months to prepare a temporary working authorisation.

This was for a dental licence that lasted two weeks!

Also, we both had to get a letter of good standing from the UK General Dental Council.

But they were all asleep, because of the time difference.

Jane was up between 1 and 3am, getting forms e-mailed to us from UK and then persuading the hotel desk to print them out for her from her phone. Then filling and returning them to London. I had been suffering from a severe viral throat infection and was beginning to lose the plot by then.

But my wife kept at it.

All documents were then couriered to Kuala Lumpur and we prayed for approval of the application.

So we flew back from Kuching to Brunei, having said our farewells to Derek, who kindly dropped us off at 6am, wishing us God's Blessing.

We drove, with all our dental kit in the new church van, to Lawas.

There were around four hundred patients lined up to see us. We prayed that they would all get some dental care and, more importantly, hear a Gospel message.

Jane

Nigel preached about the three gardens mentioned in the Bible - Eden, Gethsemane and the garden mentioned in Revelation 22. After that, all the young dancers who had been performing as a celebration of our visit came forward to commit their lives to God. We stand in awe of God.

Nigel:

Dr Tan, a young dentist working in the Public Health Dental Service, came to our service. She was not saved, but allowed Jane to go through CrossCheck with her and was around, watching us, during the week we were there.

We prayed she would come to Christ. She told us their dental department had seen Margaret's church flyers advertising free dental treatment, and they had been preparing to inform the local police. Until, that was, they had heard from the director of the Sarawak health services to help us as much as possible.

We set up our dental clinic in the church sanctuary. It actually looked quite respectable. With three trips to the local hardware store for vital parts, we were pretty much set to go.

By all accounts, getting the permit was impossible in the given timeframe. So we praised God and gave thanks that a sense of compassion, safety, kindness and gentleness settled over the sanctuary, as we treated people who travelled in from the surrounding villages and Kampongs.

It was a tiring outreach. We were seeing fifty to seventy patients each day and doing all their treatments. A lot were farmers and their families. It was all a bit chaotic, with lots of chatter and questions, because it had never happened before. There was a curiosity about why we were doing it for free. So, there were Gospel opportunities. We'd had people praying for us from all over the world and those prayers made all the difference.

By day five of the outreach, our clinic was now a well-oiled machine, praise God. We prayed with many of our patients, some in tears, not because of having teeth done, but for being prayed with.

Lemsut, a man from Kampong Pengalih, turned up with his sister one morning. He had late-stage squamous cell cancer of his tongue and was scheduled to have some radiotherapy a month later, but his disease was very advanced.

We prayed as a group with him and with *CrossCheck* he asked Jesus into his life. Again in tears. For Lemsut alone, our mission had been worth it.

Jane:

We have had an amazing time. I was grateful that God planned for us to go to Lawas to do our dentistry. How He loves the Lun Bawang people and had heard their cry. He made it possible for us to get the permission from the Head of Public Health to serve them.

I treated a gentleman who was suffering from several abscesses in his mouth. He had been in agony and had not been able to get any help from the government clinics. I was able to remove only two of the worst teeth, and asked if we could pray for him. He just sobbed as Nigel, our nurses and I gathered round him and prayed over him. The opportunity to minister with Christ's love was such a privilege on this outreach. Praise God for making it possible for us to show His love.

We treated around three hundred patients; our team of helpers from the church did amazingly well - no needle stick injuries, no accidents, no faintings or collapses. People were prayed with; *CrossCheck* was used on many occasions, and the church members all felt they had been an important part of the week's event. None of them had done any dental assistant work before, so it was an eye-opener for them, seeing the quantity of treatments we could accomplish.

Both of us caught had chest infections on the flight over to Brunei, so we had been really low for the first few days but, by God's Grace, all went well.

Proverbs Ch 3 v 5-6: *"Trust in the Lord with all your heart; do not depend on your own understanding. Seek his will in all you do, and he will show you which path to take."*

Chapter 35

Dr Zairina, head of dental health, Sarawak

Jane going through *CrossCheck* with Dr Tan

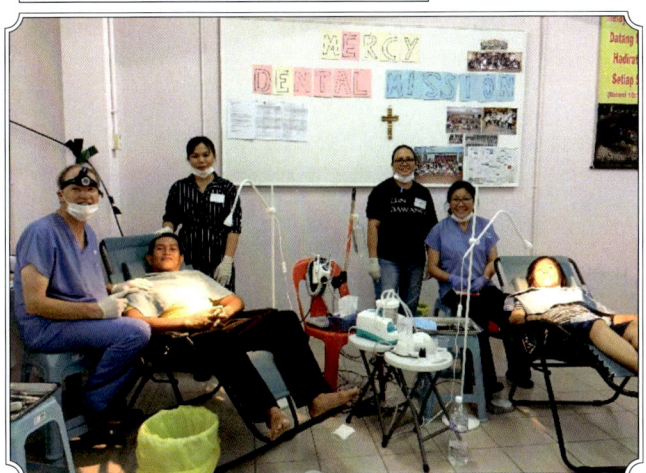

Lawas dental clinic

Our full dental team in Lawas

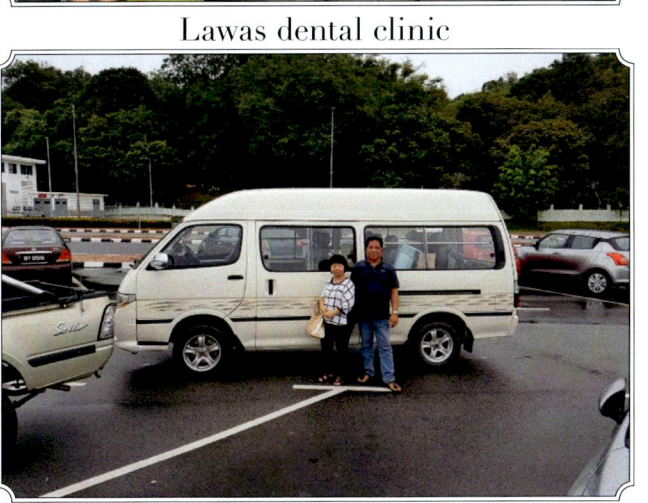

David and Margaret's new van

Lawas Town

257

Chapter 36

Well done if you have stuck with the story so far - you are nearly there.

I have talked a lot about God and Jesus in this book. You might well be thinking that this is all a bit religious and over the top, perhaps?

It took me until the age of thirty-five for the penny to drop, for my eyes to see who Jesus really is. If you, too, have doubts, you might like to work out for yourself the answers to these $64,000 questions:

Is Jesus who He really claims to be?

Is He the Son of God?

Is He our Saviour?

Was He crucified?

And did He rise from the dead after three days?

All these are good questions and need to be fact-checked and verified, something I and tens of thousands of others have done. You see, if it's not true, we have all been wasting our time.

So, at the end of this chapter, I have provided a list of books I have read over the years that have been transformational in my understanding of Jesus, plus one or two that have helped me with life skills. So, do take a look at some when you have a chance.

This book was written during the three year Covid 19 pandemic. International travel had virtually stopped, so our trips ceased also. We shall have to see where the Lord takes us in the years to come.

Lawas 2019 was the last mission trip that we went on to date, so lockdown 2020 has provided a good opportunity to take stock and to record the travels. We very much hope to continue, whilst we have the energy and strength.

Our dental registration, which is required for us to work anywhere in the world, has to be renewed each year with the General Dental Council, and we have to record our CPD (Continuous Professional Development) and keep our medical practice insurance up to date. All this costs time and money, so the dental part to our trips may well cease within a few years.

I have included our life story so that you can, hopefully, piece together how God has been working in our lives and see the difference He has made.

Chapter 36

We are far from perfect; I have many, many faults. But, with God's grace and mercy, I trust these failings can be washed away.

God has been there throughout our lifetime, from the very beginning, just as He has with you, the reader. It's a question of recognising Him, and trusting and involving Him in all that we do and say. That takes a bit of time, for most of us. It's a journey of discovery.

Hopefully, that comes out a little in our story.

We also tried very hard to give to Jesus all the credit for our trips.

This, sometimes, is actually quite hard to do.

When they hear about our travels, people like to say, "Well done; your charity work sounds very interesting. It must feel good to give something back."

We'd say thank you and, perhaps, try to test the water to see if they were actually interested, or just offering a few pleasantries to pass the time.

So, a little elaboration might take place, and a few anecdotes get told.

All would go well until our statement:

"Yes, we did the whole thing to glorify Jesus. Without Him, nothing would have worked or succeeded."

This would often be followed by a long silence; there would be a looking at a wristwatch or mobile phone, and then a sudden statement:

"Oh gosh, is that the time? I'm afraid I must dash."

But, occasionally, someone would pause, think and engage with more questions. It was then that our trips could be used for a Gospel outreach.

Also, when Jane and I gave talks to church groups, Rotary, Probus, etc., opportunities would present themselves to proclaim the Gospel.

So, what have we seen and learnt from all these assorted journeys?

It is difficult to quantify, but we discovered how transportable dentistry could be, and what a huge difference we could make to people's lives in areas where there was no dental care available.

Sometimes, we would meet people who had been in pain, or had suffered a continuous swelling and infection for years. One lady, in Benin, complained that she had been praying for fifteen years to get her bad tooth removed; she was distraught at the misery and discomfort she had been in for so long, and why hadn't God heard her prayers?

We could only apologise to her, saying how sorry we were to be so slow in answering God's call to us, to travel out and help His people.

We learnt a lot about ourselves and each other on these trips. Usually, we travelled to different and remote areas. Mostly, we were out of our comfort zone and, often, we were well and truly in a discomfort zone.

Mini-crises would take place - loss of passports or vital luggage, tummy upsets and full-blown diarrhoea, insect bites, allergies and weird rashes, security issues, travel problems, equipment and material failures, people's expectations not being met, or sudden requests for a Bible message, tutorial or sermon. Sometimes we'd get late night phone calls about events back in the UK.

On one memorable occasion, whilst we were away, some people had been staying in our house in the UK and the central heating had failed. It was winter, and -7°C outside. We had left them our contact details, and they phoned. The number they called was Thura, Dr Ko's son in Yangon (the only phone we could guarantee would work). He had to get a message to Homalin, north-west Burma; but there were no mobile phones at that time, so a man was despatched on motorbike to travel the five hundred miles by road.

This he heroically did, in eighteen hours. He gave the message to Dr Ko, who relayed it on to us.

Our answer was: "Just call the plumber and get it fixed."

This was relayed back by motorcycle and then by landline phone to the UK.

Total transmission time: three days.

We learnt a valuable lesson - make sure, when travelling, to leave someone at home with the authority to make decisions.

With all this going on, you could envisage a constant state of tension or worry and I'd like to state, at this point, that I am an inveterate worrier. I can worry for England, given the right circumstances. I can always think of things going wrong, or reasons we might be late (my family always complain that we arrive everywhere with hours to spare).

But on all these trips, having dedicated the time and the Journey to God, a sense of peace and calm descended over us and also those travelling with us. We slept well, problems came, problems went, but, in everything, we felt secure. The sense of peace was palpable. I think it was one of the main reasons we kept setting off on trips again and again.

We would also receive feedback via e-mails, *Messenger*, *WhatsApp*, or text, from those we met whilst journeying. We were still in contact with them in 2022 as I write these pages. As a means of Christian encouragement, it has been very rewarding.

Chapter 36

So, the big questions to ask after following all these short-term mission trips might be:

What difference have they made?

If I am being totally honest, the biggest difference we have made is probably to ourselves. The trips themselves have changed us. They have altered our priorities, our mindsets and our confidence in relying on our living God. In the Book of James, Chapter two, verses 14 to 24, we read about what is the point of having Faith if there are no deeds that we do to demonstrate that faith. It's a powerful challenge to us all.

How have these trips promoted God's Kingdom?

Just being out there on the mission field, you make a difference. If you carry the banner of Christ before you, it is possible to encourage, teach, help, console, counsel, support and walk alongside fellow-Christians, and evangelise to non-Christians. If you are not out there, how do you have a chance to form relationships and walk alongside others?

How could they have been improved?

The answer is, probably, by staying in each area for longer periods of time. That is probably the biggest weakness of short-term visits. Just as things were beginning to really happen, we would be heading home.

Enabling longer-term mission visits would require a significant adjustment back home in the UK.

Freeing up ties to family, church, friends, work, one's own home and any other commitments, takes good planning and understanding.

Many have done it, many still do. But, having said all that, I am so grateful for the trips we have managed, and would recommend any Christian to try it for themselves.

Our pennyworth of work on God's behalf, and their results, will be known only when we stand before Jesus on Judgement Day.

I am just thankful it is not by works, but by Grace and Faith in Jesus, that we are saved.

Food for Thought

OUR ACQUIRED, PERSONAL SKILL-SET will be very different from yours, but God can use each and every one of us. Could you, the reader, envisage going on a short-term mission or, perhaps, a long-term mission? Do you sometimes feel that God has been calling you to go somewhere?

What might you change in your own life, having seen these trips of ours?

We always find adjusting our lives difficult; we resist alterations to our tried and trusted routines and habits. Our heels dig in and we justify our reluctance with 101 statements.

You only have to think of Moses, standing by the burning bush, arguing with God and giving reasons why he was unsuitable to go and rescue the Israelites from Egypt.

We fellow humans haven't changed. But let me give you some excuses and justifications we have heard as to why people could not give a week or two to serve God.

"My work wouldn't allow it."

"I cannot speak a foreign language."

"We obviously couldn't leave the children."

"I'm not a good traveller." (Having just come back from a Spanish holiday).

"How could we get the funding?"

"My mum, (dad, aunt, brother-in-law, cousin, daughter, wife, husband) could not manage without me around."

"Well, If I had a dental or medical skill, I would definitely do it."

You get the picture. All quite legitimate reasons.

However, none are insurmountable.

Let me list a few skills we have actually seen people using for God on our travels:

Counselling, teaching, farming, building, plumbing, Health & Safety, church encouragement, Bible teaching, water-pump installation, accounting, CCTV security and safety, IT and computing, advertising.

And some occupations:

Chefs and cooks, hairdressers, cleaners, engineers, deck hands, nurses, midwives, doctors, dentists, hygienists, paramedics, pharmacists, vets, dieticians, electricians, plumbers, firefighters, fishermen, town planners, photographers, film-makers, actors, youth workers, prison workers, journalists.

Do you feel you could possibly allocate some time for God's work? Could you find two to three weeks a year or, perhaps, six weeks every two or three years?

Even better, take a sabbatical and arrange three or six months off work.

Many people do that nowadays.

What, if anything, might be helpful in your own walk with Jesus?

What might you pick up and use? Could you do some training?

A Cornhill Bible Course, perhaps, to sharpen your sword, which is the Word of God.

A Counselling Course at Waverley College.

A first aid and CPR course.

Here are some organisations that you might like to investigate:

Mercy Ships

https://www.mercyships.org

Since 1978...

Mercy Ships began its mission to provide hope and healing to those in need in 1978. Each year it sends hospital ships filled with volunteer professionals, who selflessly provide life-changing surgeries for children and adults who otherwise would go without. Together, they are saving and changing lives.

OSCAR

An Introduction to OSCAR - OSCAR

https://oscar.org.uk

OSCAR is an acronym for "One Stop Centre for Advice and Resources." If you're involved or interested in Christian or mission work, in the UK or overseas, OSCAR is your gateway to useful related opportunities, information, advice and resources.

Who uses OSCAR?

OSCAR is mostly, but not exclusively, aimed at UK Christians, whether they are based in the UK or around the world. More specifically, OSCAR is useful for:

- Christian and mission workers on the frontline.
- Christians open to the possibility of serving God in mission or ministry.
- Christian and mission workers recently returned from their place of work.
- Supporters of Christian and mission workers and mission in general.
- Non-UK Christians coming to the UK as Christian workers.
- Anyone responsible for 'resourcing' any of the above.

If your work or interest falls into one or more of these categories, OSCAR is designed to take the 'legwork' out of finding related information. It helps you locate the organisations, services and resources you need, and puts you in complete control of managing your own situation, whether you're a frontline worker, supporter or enquirer. This unique 'portal' is designed to empower you and save you much time, energy and money!

Operation Mobilisation

https://www.uk.om.org/Pages/Category/About

SERVE & GO

You were made for Him; to know His love and share His love.

There are billions of people around the world who have never heard the good news of God's love in Jesus. Join us. Take His love to those who don't know it.

You were made for this.

Global Connections

https://www.globalconnections.org.uk

Global Connections is a growing network of over 300 UK churches and agencies with a passion for mission. Their members include organisations of all sizes working in countries all over the world. Drawing on this wealth of experience, together they seek to address the key challenges in mission today.

Crosslinks

https://www.crosslinks.org/what-we-do/

Crosslinks enables everyone to take part in God's mission. We send people out to help make Christ known, and support Christians back home as they play their part.

In five continents and over 30 countries, Crosslinks has long-term mission partners, short-term volunteers and gospel-based projects. All Crosslinks people and projects are involved in frontline evangelism, or training pastor teachers.

CrossCheck

Throughout this book you will have probably noticed many references to the booklet called *CrossCheck* which we used, with great effect, everywhere we travelled.

It is a simple and short explanation of the Gospel of Christ, using five drawings and a narrative alongside, coupled with an Accept, Believe, Consider & Do action pathway to follow. It has been translated into many languages and is a great resource for Evangelism.

You can see it being read on this YouTube link:

https://youtube/F5BhiKVaC-Q

It is published by

BeaconLight
biblical training to share

Website : https://beaconlight.co.uk

Chapter 36

When The Storm Rolls.

When the storm rolls

When the storm rolls

When the storm rolls all around…. Hey!   (repeat)

I am weak, but God is Strong,

He will help, when things go wrong

When the storm rolls

When the storm rolls

When the storm rolls all around…. Hey!

Sing one round with actions

Stop the song and explain that some difficulties or problems are small, like loosing one's mobile phone, having a hole in a shoe etc

So, sing with tiny, high voice just using fingers for actions.

After the second time Stop the song again and explain some problems are serious such as cancer, our house burning down etc.

so you need big arm actions and plenty of noise.

https://youtu.be/sZbp2oh_5iA

When the Storm Rolls sung by Nigel and Jane

Thanks for this song should go to our friend Peter Empson

A Step or Two of Faith

A brief summary of CrossCheck

Reproduced by kind permission of Dr Paul Adams.

Box 1: God is the ruler and creator
Genesis Ch.1 v 26-27

Box 2: The big "I" in Sin separates us from God. Isaiah Ch.59 v 1-2.
Hebrews Ch.9 v.27

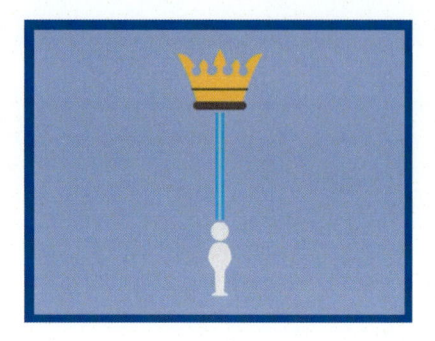

Box 3: God loves all that he has made. So he sent us Jesus, to pay for our Sin. John Ch3 V.16.   1 Peter Ch.2 v24

Box 4: Jesus rose from the dead leaving the way open for us to approach God
2 Corinthians Ch.5 v15 Acts 17 v30-31

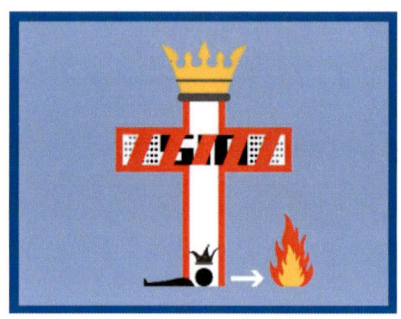

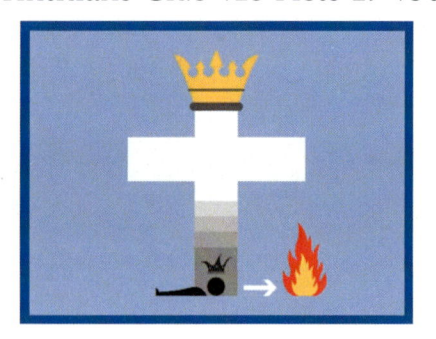

Box 5: God wants everyone to have his new life. At the foot of the cross is the doorway. Revelation Ch3 v20
John Ch.1 v12 Matthew Ch.28 v20

Box 5 (cont.) Jesus is standing outside our heart's door, and is knocking to come in. He will come into our lives. He will make his home with us.

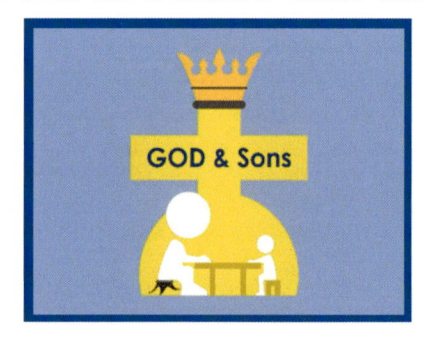

CrossCheck

Chapter 36

Nigel's Book recommendations

1 *The Case for Christ* by Lee Strobel.

This book is written by an investigative journalist. He originally set out to prove that the Christian faith was a load of superstition and fable. After conducting many interviews and researching all the information he could find, he became a Christian, because the evidence was so overwhelming.

2 *The Case for a Creator* by Lee Strobel.

Lee Strobel investigates the scientific evidence that points towards God. He interviews top professors and experts in their field, who state that there must be a Creator.

3 The Bible.

This should really come first! It's important to read a version that has a language and syntax that you can understand. I would recommend either *The Living Bible* or the *New International Version Bible* UK edition.

4 *Who Moved the Stone?* by Frank Morison.

A must-read book. The author began to write this book with the aim of trying to prove that Jesus didn't rise from the dead. But Frank found so much evidence, that he ended up believing that he did rise. It shows all the facts, plus some Bible stories.

5 *Unlocking the Bible* by David Pawson.

A really good reference book that goes through every book in The Bible, explaining why and when it was written.

David uses really straightforward English to explain sometimes quite tricky parts of The Bible. It sits by my bedside and I have given away over a hundred copies to people over the years.

6 *A Commentary on the Gospel of John* by David Pawson.

This is a most amazing book, opening up John's Gospel and relating it to other sections in The Bible.

7 *Before You Say "I Don't Believe"* by Roger Carswell.

It has become fashionable to believe that Christians are deluded, naïve, following myths, and that science has debunked the need for God in society today. But Christian faith is not a leap in the dark. It is founded on so much evidence that the non-believer is the one who has questions to answer. In *Before You Say "I Don't Believe"*, Roger Carswell asks thirty-four questions of those who don't believe. They are not the questions usually aired in the media; they are posed, not to cause an argument, but to bring readers to the point where they put their trust in Jesus. Be warned: it will take courage to read this book openly but, if you do, it could change your views on Jesus. Roger is an amazing speaker for Christ and has spent his life travelling around the UK explaining the Gospel.

8 *The Road Less Travelled* by M. Scott Peck.

This is a classic and essential reading. It moves us away from feeling life is unfair and "I don't want problems", to an understanding that we can make choices in our lives.

Not a Christian book as such, but very helpful.

9 *I'm OK, You're OK* by Thomas Harris.

This is an old one, but gives the reader an understanding of Transactional Analysis. That means how we are made up in three parts, adult, child and parent, and how each of the three can determine our character and thoughts. It should be noted that although this book concludes that we need to reach a state of being OK in ourselves. As a Christian we can only get there by accepting Jesus into our lives. Without him we'll never be fully Ok.

10 *The sixty minute Father*, *The sixty minute Mother* and *The sixty minute Marriage*

This series of books by Rob Parsons are packed with wisdom.

Jane and I attended a one day conference held by Rob Parsons early on in our Marriage in 1989. His honesty, foresight and advice transformed our own relationship and markedly improved our parenting skills. These three books, plus many others published by Care for the Family are excellent.

11 *Truth Unlocked* by Paul Adams and John Phillips
(published by Beaconlight)

This is a straightforward, easy to follow, workbook of 16 studies written to help new and established, Christians discover the essential truths revealed by God in the Bible. In two sections: Christian Belief and Christian Living.

All these books, except *Truth Unlocked*, are available from Amazon.co.uk.

Truth Unlocked can be obtained from https://beaconlight.co.uk